The God Virus

The God Virus

How Religion Infects
Our Lives and Culture

Darrel W. Ray, Ed.D.

IPC Press
Bonner Springs, Kansas

Editors: Deborah Shouse, Kirsten Mcbride

Publisher's Cataloging-in-Publication
(Provided by Quality Books, Inc.)

 Ray, Darrel W.
  The God virus : how religion infects our lives and culture / by Darrel W. Ray.
  p. cm.
  Includes bibliographical references and index.
  LCCN 2008939657
  ISBN-13: 978-0-9709505-1-2
  ISBN-10: 0-9709505-1-9

  1. Sociobiology--Religious aspects. 2. Psychology, Religious. 3. Religion and science. I. Title.

 BL261.R39 2009   215'.7
          QBI08-600322

Published by
IPC Press
15699 Kansas Avenue
Bonner Springs, Kansas 66012

Visit www.thegodvirus.net for additional information.

Published 2009

Printed in the United States of America

Dedicated to
Dan Dana

PREFACE AND ACKNOWLEDGEMENTS

The process of writing, interviewing and researching gave me the opportunity to hear the stories of many who have escaped religion. Most of their stories reflect the following four themes:

1. Events that opened their eyes to religious manipulation in their life or family;
2. Long hidden or suppressed doubts about the teachings;
3. Their ultimate act or declaration of liberation from organized religion; and
4. The double-edged sword of living without the crutch of a supernatural friend and learning to accept full responsibility for life.

Many of them recounted both the terror and the relief they felt after leaving religion behind. Terror at realizing there was no longer an imaginary friend; relief that no one was looking over their shoulder any more. Several described the experience as similar to that of a child learning to go to sleep without a favorite teddy bear. Others described it as simply growing up or outgrowing the need for the imaginary friends of childhood.

I don't want to leave the impression that everybody who contributed and assisted with this book agrees with it completely. Each of us has our own journey. My hope is that the questions and tools this book offers will lead readers to critically examine the influence of religion in their life and culture.

It is a pleasure to acknowledge the friends and colleagues who helped me improve this book in many ways. My son, Aaron, was the initial inspiration. Our talks about religion and philosophy led me to believe there is much to share from my life and academic training. Dr. Dan Dana, my lifelong friend and colleague, provided encouragement and support at every step. Our monthly supper talks helped refine many ideas. It is a profound gift to have such a loyal friend.

Missy Andeel, Susan Henrie and Jaime Vogt provided remarkable feedback that demonstrated to me the power of the god virus metaphor. I am grateful for their efforts and willingness to share their experiences with me.

Susan Hart and Judy Roepke stayed close to the project, offering support and feedback at each stage. Our many talks and shared experiences resulted in new ideas and some changes.

Life is full of coincidences. On a plane to Europe, I met Ceil Wirth and struck up a conversation with her about this book. She subsequently asked to read the manuscript. Her questions and editing suggestions led to many instrumental changes. We do not agree on everything, but her ideas and encouragement were welcome.

Other readers provided valuable insights and shared their experiences. Chris Coope, Julie Price, Dave Carleski, Michele Lubbers, Janet Boehm and my wonderful colleague, Laura Northcutt, each unselfishly gave time and energy to this project.

I am grateful also to Kenny Nipp, Earl Doherty and Hemant Mehta, who saw the value of the manuscript and encouraged me to see it through to completion.

Thanks to Shayne Schuldt, who did a wonderful job in the design and graphics of the book, including the cover.

I am also indebted to my two editors, Kirsten McBride and Deborah Shouse, for their attention to detail and critical eye.

Although I cannot use their names here, I am grateful to the many religious people I interviewed as part of my research for the book. While some were open to discussing and critiquing my ideas, most did not wish to be acknowledged.

CONTENTS

INTRODUCTION

"The chains men bear they forged themselves. Strike off their chains and they will weep for their lost security."

-John Passmore, Australian philosopher

Every day religion affects us in ways we may not realize. It makes your Uncle Ned spend hours praying for you; it gives your Baptist neighbor a reason to reject her own child who married a Catholic; it teaches your Pentecostal sister to spank her children to keep them from going to hell; it requires a Catholic priest to deny his sex drive; it causes people to give enormous amounts of money to religious organizations; and causes you to avoid talking to your cousin Jennie for fear she may try to convert you to Jehovah's Witnesses. Religion has both obvious and subtle influences – on you and on society.

This book explores the impact of religion on you and your world. It draws open the curtain of mystery and offers ways to understand and make informed decisions about religion.

Have you ever wondered what makes religion so powerful? What makes people profess deep faith even as they act in ways that betray that faith? What makes people blind to the irrationalities of their own religion yet see clearly the problems of other religions? How does it weave its way into our political system? If these and similar questions interest you, this book will help you understand its power in you, your family and your culture.

For thousands of years, religion penetrated societies, largely unexplained and unchallenged. It simply existed. Those who attempted to question or expose religion were often persecuted, books burned, excommunicated, or even executed. From Galileo to Darwin, Salman Rushdie to Theo van Gogh,[1] it could be hazardous to critique or explain that which the church, priest or imam said was unexplainable.

Before the germ, viral and parasite theory of disease, physicians had no tools to understand disease and its propagation. Priests told people disease was a result of sin, Satan and evil spirits. With the discovery of microbes, scientists gained new tools to understand disease. They could study infection strategies, immunity, epidemiology, and much more. Suddenly the terrible diseases of the past were understandable. The plagues of Europe, yellow fever, small pox, pneumonia, tuberculosis, syphilis, etc., were now removed from the divine and placed squarely in the natural world.

---

1   Galileo was put under house arrest for the last year of his life; Darwin's work has been suppressed by many religions since it was first published in 1859; Salman Rushdie has had a death threat over him since writing his novel *Satanic Verses* (Macmillan, 2000) and Theo van Gogh was murdered for producing a short film critical of Islam.

Various philosophers – from Spinoza to Voltaire, Feuerbach to Marx – blazed a path toward understanding religion and its role in society, but it was not until Richard Dawkins' idea of "viruses of the mind"[2] that we gained a ready-made way to examine religion as closely as we look at the epidemiology of the flu virus. This book will show how religions of all kinds fit in the natural world, how they function in our minds and culture and how similar they are to the germs, parasites and viruses that inhabit our bodies.

This book owes a great deal to Richard Dawkins and Daniel Dennett,[3] but it seeks to go a step further by showing how their revolutionary ideas work in everyday life. The paradigm that they pioneered can explain the fundamentalism of your Uncle Ned, the sexual behavior of a fallen mega-church minister, the child-rearing practices of your Pentecostal neighbor, why 19 men flew planes into the World Trade Center or why women blow themselves up in the crowded markets of Baghdad.

As a member of Western culture, you are affected by religious indoctrination. No matter what your own upbringing is, you live in a religious sea and cannot help but imbibe some of the waters. This book will help you look at areas you may have overlooked in your journey. Religious dogma, habit, beliefs or guilt may affect you in ways you may not recognize.

In recent years I have become alarmed at the role religion increasingly plays in society. Religion seems to inject itself into schools, courts, legislatures, presidential politics and local school boards, detracting from rational conversation about real-world problems like science education, economic development, disaster relief and war.[4] Outside the United States, the violence and intolerance expressed by fundamentalists and cults throughout the world bring an urgency to the task of understanding religion and its power. Some very scary people are preaching hatred and intolerance. Their words sound similar to the language of ethnic cleansing.

2   Richard Dawkins, *Viruses of the Mind* [essay on-line] (1991, accessed 20 November 2008); available from http://cscs.umich.edu/~crshalizi/Dawkins/viruses-of-the-mind.html; Internet.

3   Richard Dawkins, *The Selfish Gene* (Oxford University Press, 1976); Richard Dawkins, *The God Delusion* (Houghton Mifflin, 2006) and Daniel Dennett, *Breaking the Spell: Religion as a Natural Phenomenon* (Viking Adult, 2006).

4   The religious counterparts to these are the push for in-school alternatives to evolution, creationism, stem cell research opposition, religious leaders declaring various hurricanes god's wrath on certain cities like Orlando or New Orleans and George W. Bush calling the war in Iraq a Crusade.

Here are quotes from some well-known leaders:

I hope I live to see the day when, as in the early days of our country, we won't have any public schools. The churches will have taken them over again and Christians will be running them. What a happy day that will be!
-Jerry Falwell[5]

There will never be world peace until God's house and God's people are given their rightful place of leadership at the top of the world.
-Pat Robertson[6]

The long-term goal of Christians in politics should be to gain exclusive control over the franchise. Those who refuse to submit publicly to the eternal sanctions of God by submitting to His Church's public marks of the covenant - baptism and holy communion - must be denied citizenship, just as they were in ancient Israel.
-Gary North[7]

I want you to just let a wave of intolerance wash over you. I want you to let a wave of hatred wash over you. Yes, hate is good ... Our goal is a Christian nation. We have a biblical duty, we are called on by God to conquer this country. We don't want equal time. We don't want pluralism.
-Randall Terry[8]

5   Rev Jerry Falwell, *America Can Be Saved* (Sword of the Lord Publishers, 1979), 52-53, from Albert J Menendez and Edd Doerr, *The Great Quotations on Religious Freedom* (Prometheus Books, 2002).

6   Pat Robertson, *The New World Order*, New Ed ed. (Thomas Nelson, March 1992).

7   Gary North, *Political Polytheism: the Myth of Pluralism* (Institute for Christian Economics, 1989). Darling of Christian Reconstructionists, North predicted catastrophe in an a war with the Soviet Union in 1985 and predicted that Y2K would result in global catastrophe. He believes in ultimate Christian rule. He is a member of the Presbyterian Church in America.

8   Reported by *The News Sentinel* (Fort Wayne, IN), 16 August 1993. Randall Terry, founder of Operation Rescue. Terry, a Catholic, after several extramarital affairs, divorced in 2000 and is now remarried with three children. The long list of Terry's transgressions against his own beliefs is remarkable, if not unique, among those who are most bombastic in defense of their religion.

We - with God's help - call on every Muslim who believes in God and wishes to be rewarded to comply with God's order to kill the Americans and plunder their money wherever and whenever they find it. We also call on Muslim ulema, leaders, youths, and soldiers to launch the raid on Satan's U.S. troops and the devil's supporters allying with them, and to displace those who are behind them so that they may learn a lesson.

-Osama Bin Laden edict[9]

In each of these quotes hate, intolerance, supremacy and exclusivity are central concepts. An important goal of this book is to explain the power of religion to drive this kind of thinking and behavior.

The Australian philosopher John Passmore once said, "*The chains men bear they forged themselves. Strike off their chains and they will weep for their lost security.*" This book is about breaking hidden chains, discovering how religion subtly works in our culture and minds and learning how to live without the chains.

About the Author

I am a psychologist and a student of religion and society. Raised in a fundamentalist Church of Christ environment, I went to a small Quaker college as an undergraduate, later completed a master's degree in religion at a Methodist Seminary and a doctorate in Counseling Psychology at George Peabody College of Vanderbilt University. I was an agnostic by my early 30s and an Atheist by the time I was 40. While my journey informs this work, it is not biographical. It creates a framework through which you will be able to see and analyze religious beliefs and behavior, including your own.

A Note on Terminology

I use the term "non-theist" to refer to you, the reader. I wish to be inclusive of all who might fit this category: agnostics, deists, Atheists, freethinkers, spiritual people, etc. You might even be an Episcopalian, Unitarian, Quaker or non-religious, spiritual person. I refer to those who are highly religious, fundamentalists, superstitious or cult members as religionists. It matters not what you call yourself. I will explore with you the power of religion

---

9   The American Muslim, *Bin Laden's Fatwa: A Call to Harabah* [article on-line] (11 February 2003, accessed 21 November 2008); available from http://www.theamericanmuslim.org/fam.php/features/articles/bin_ladens_fatwa_a_call_to_harabah/; Internet.

on our lives and bring about a new paradigm for understanding religious behavior in our world.

Finally, I will only capitalize the names of specific gods such as Allah, Jehovah, Zeus and Jesus. The word "god" will be lower case unless it is included in a direct quote.

The Structure of the Book

Beginning with a "big picture" we move down to the social, the psychological and finally the personal. Chapters 1 and 2 take a broad view and state the case for religion's similarities to the biological world. Chapters 3 through 7 explore the social, political and psychological aspects of religion, including such topics as hypnotic techniques of evangelical preachers, the role of sex, guilt, and morality in propagating religion, and personality and intelligence. Chapters 8 through 10 examine religious influence in your life and family. You may find some new tools for understanding your religious history or upbringing. Finally, Chapters 11 and 12 are devoted to science and the future of religion.

CHAPTER 1:

RELIGION AS A VIRUS

"We despise all reverences and all objects of reverence which are outside the pale of our list of sacred things and yet, with strange inconsistency, we are shocked when other people despise and defile the things which are holy for us."

-Mark Twain

Overview

In this chapter, we will examine the remarkable parallels between the propagation methods of some biological systems and the strategies of religion.

A Thought Experiment

Imagine this scenario: You have a serious conversation with a deeply Christian friend. Your friend is intelligent, well educated and knowledgeable. You agree to record the session. The topic is Islam. During the session, you discuss that Mohammed was a self-appointed prophet and that he claimed he talked to Allah and angels. He wrote a book that he claimed is infallible, and he flew from Jerusalem to heaven on a horse.

During the conversation, you agree that Mohammed was probably delusional to think he could talk to god. You agree that the Koran was clearly written by Mohammed and not by Allah. It is ludicrous for him to claim that he is the last prophet and that all others are false. Neither you nor your friend can believe that he flew to heaven, let alone on a horse. It all sounds too crazy, and you both agree it is difficult to see how someone could believe such a religion. At the end of the conversation, you say that Muslims did not choose their religion; they were born into it. Anyone who was exposed to both Christianity and Islam would see that Christianity is the true religion.

Over the next few days, you transcribe the recording onto paper. Then you change all references to Mohammed and make them Jesus. Now the document reads something like this:

> During the conversation, you both agree that Jesus was probably delusional to think he could talk to Jehovah. The Bible was clearly written by men and not by Jehovah. You both agree it is ludicrous for Jesus to claim that he is the last prophet and that all later ones are false. Neither of you can believe that he rose from the dead, nor flew to heaven. It all sounds too crazy, and it is difficult to see how someone could believe such a religion. At the end of the conversation, you both agree that Christians did not choose their religion; they were born into it. Anyone who was exposed to both Christianity and Islam would see that Islam is the true religion.

Now, tell your friend, "I made a transcript of our conversation about Islam and would like to go over it with you." As you read it, watch her reaction. How does she respond to each statement? How soon does she get defensive? How quickly does she start making elaborate arguments that have no more factual basis than the first conversation? If you persist in this line of parallel reasoning, how long before she gets angry or breaks off the conversation? Could this conversation damage your friendship?

You can do the same experiment with other prophetic religions. For example, substitute Joseph Smith for Mormonism or Moses for Judaism. This experiment illustrates the god virus at work. It infects the brain and alters critical thinking skills. It leaves the skill intact for other religions but disables critical thinking about one's own religion. Keep this thought experiment in mind as we explore the virus-like behavior of religion in individuals and in society.

Religious Conversion Syndrome

Have you ever observed somebody go through a religious conversion? The person seems perfectly reasonable to you and has no particular concern for religion. Then a parent, friend or child dies or he gets a serious illness or is involved in a car accident. In just a matter of weeks, he seeks out and finds the answers to all of life's questions and starts studying and spouting all sorts of doctrine. During such a window of vulnerability, religion can commandeer a person's brain. In many cases, the person will join some kind of fundamentalist or charismatic group.

An associate of mine recently lost his father to cancer. Before this family trauma, he was a non-religious person. After his father's death, he got a severe case of religion that changed his personality dramatically. An evening spent over a good meal in a restaurant became an ordeal in Jesus references. There was no way to have a conversation with him on any subject without religion creeping in. It became very tiresome. Soon I stopped seeing him altogether.

Religious visions and conversions have been reported for centuries. They bear remarkable similarities regardless of religion or culture. William James noticed the similarities over a century ago in his book, *The Varieties of Religious Experience* (1902). What would make an Islamic conversion look and sound like a Christian one? Why would a Hindu epiphany bear a close resemblance to a native American vision quest?

Neurological science has shown that such experiences can be created with brain stimulation. Thus, simple neurological stimulation can evoke mystical experiences. Native Americans using Peyote, or Dr. Timothy Leary using LSD, demonstrated this long ago. We know that experiences that appear mystical are very likely neurological responses to any number of naturally occurring things in the environment or the brain. The near-death experiences reported by people for centuries and across all cultures have remarkable similarities to those reported in neurological stimulation experiments.

Dr. Olaf Blanks, a neurologist at Ecole Polytechnique in Lausanne, Switzerland, concludes from his research on brain stimulation, "It may be tempting to invoke the supernatural when this body sense goes awry, the true explanation is a very natural one, the brain's attempt to make sense of conflicting information." [1]

What has been called "mystical" for centuries can now be reproduced in Dr. Blanks' laboratory with electrical probes of the brain.

Who Are You and What Did You Do With My Friend?

Some people who experience a religious conversion seem to undergo a personality change. They can be quite congenial and easygoing when talking about mundane things, but when they start talking about their "faith," their demeanor changes. Their tone of voice modifies, their smile becomes tense, and they become defensive when questioned about their evidence for belief. It becomes difficult to have a friendly conversation with them. It looks like a scene from the cult movie *Invasion of the Body Snatchers* (1978), where alien pods take over the brains and bodies of people and change them into emotionless automatons.

Once a person has converted to a religion, it is difficult to have a rational conversation about the irrational aspects of his religion. It is as though something invaded the person and took over a part of his personality. You can no longer talk to him directly. Instead, it seems as if communication is channeled through a religious being that lives inside of him. Well-rehearsed answers come out of his mouth. Things like, "It is a mystery and we are not meant to understand it." Or "God expects us to follow his commands

1   Sandra Blakeslee, "Out-of-Body Experience: Your Brain Is to Blame," *The New York Times*, 3 October 2006 and Shahar Arzy, et al, "Induction of an illusory shadow person," *Nature*, 443 (21 September 2006): 287.

without question." "Jesus spoke to me and I know he is in my heart." It is quickly evident that rational analysis of these statements is not permitted.

Religious Infection

Richard Dawkins and others have noted the similarities of religions to parasitic behavioral control of certain animals. For example, Daniel Dennett writes about religion as a parasite in *Breaking the Spell*. I don't intend to replicate their work but to build on the idea of the parasitic nature of religion in a way that gives us guidance on how to live in a religious world.

For the balance of this chapter, we are going on a tour of religion using the metaphor of viruses. I make no claim that this metaphor works in every way, but it has remarkable power to explain much about individual and group religious behavior and gives religious skeptics a framework by which to understand the subtle influences of religion. Those familiar with Richard Dawkins' revolutionary idea of *memes* will quickly see the viral metaphor as another way to talk about a religious meme. I chose to use the "virus" concept instead of "meme" because viruses are well known to most people, and the biology of viruses creates a useful parallel for our discussion. In either case, I owe a great deal to Dr. Dawkins and his pioneering work, especially in his groundbreaking books, *The Selfish Gene* and *The God Delusion*.[2]

Parasitic Programming

Science fiction is full of examples of aliens taking over the minds and bodies of humans to further their own ends, but where did science fiction get the idea? Fact can be stranger than fiction.[3] There are many examples in biology of parasites, pathogens and viruses infecting the brain of a host and controlling the animal's behavior. To understand our model of viral religion, let us first look at some examples in biology:

- Grasshoppers infected with the hairworm (*Spinochordodes tellinii*) are more likely to jump into water where the hairworm

2   For a quick and enlightening read on the viral idea, I would encourage you to read Richard Dawkins' essay "Viruses of the Mind" at http://cscs.umich.edu/~crshalizi/Dawkins/viruses-of-the-mind.html; Internet. This notion is foundational for much of what we will examine in this book.

3   See the novel by Robert Heinlein, *The Puppet Masters* (Doubleday, 1951) or the movie by the same title directed by Stuart Orme starring Donald Southerland (1994). Invader parasites take over humans to rule the world. This was perhaps the first of the alien parasite books and it spawned many more.

reproduces. Thus, the parasite makes its host suicidal to further its own reproduction.

- The rabies virus infects very specific neurons in the brain of the mammal host to create aggressive behavior. This induces the host to attack and bite animals it might otherwise avoid or ignore. The virus takes over the brain of the host for its own purposes without regard for the well-being of the host, who usually dies.

- The lancet fluke (*Dicrocoelium*) infects the brain of ants by taking control and driving them to climb to the top of a blade of grass where they can be eaten by a cow. The ingested fluke then lays eggs in the cow gut. Eventually, the eggs exit the cow, and hungry snails eat the dung (and fluke eggs). The fluke enters the snail's digestive gland and gets excreted in sticky slime full of a seething mass of flukes to be drunk by ants as a source of moisture.

In these and many more examples, we see that parasites, viruses and many other pathogens literally take over parts of the brain and "control" the host. They reprogram the organism in the best interest of the parasite, to the detriment of the host.

A particularly interesting example is the parasitic protozoa *Toxiplasma gondii*. This protozoa causes infected rodents to lose their inborn aversion to cat smells. This behavior is beneficial to *toxiplasma*, because it reproduces in cats that have eaten infected mice and rats. Infected cats in turn spread toxiplasma through their droppings. Robert Sapolsky, writing in the March 2003 edition of *Scientific American,* says: "The infected rodents can still distinguish between all other kinds of smells but selectively lose their fear of cat pheromones, making them much easier for the cat to catch."

Sapolsky goes on to say,

> This is akin to someone getting infected with a brain parasite that has no effect whatsoever on the person's thoughts, emotions, SAT scores or television preferences but, to complete its life cycle, generates an irresistible urge to go to the zoo, scale a

fence and try to French-kiss the pissiest-looking polar bear. A parasite-induced fatal attraction...[4]

Taking this well-established strategy in biology, we can apply the viral concept to religion. While the parasite takes over the perceptions of the ant, religion similarly seems to take over the perceptions of those it infects.

Imagine that a religion is a virus[5] with its own unique mix of properties. Just as the HIV virus is different than a cold virus, both infect and take over the mechanisms of the body in ways that allow them to reproduce. Religions have five useful properties that are present in different degrees, including the ability to

1. Infect people.
2. Create antibodies or defenses against other viruses.
3. Take over certain mental AND physical functions and hide itself within the individual in such a way that it is not detectable by the individual.
4. Use specific methods for spreading the virus.
5. Program the host to replicate the virus.

Every religion is more or less effective in each of these areas. Let us take a closer look at each of these properties.

Infecting People

Virtually all religions rely upon early childhood indoctrination as the prime infection strategy. Other infection strategies include proselytizing, offering help and financial aid with strings attached, providing educational opportunities at religious institutions and many other approaches which we encounter frequently in the media and in daily exposure to religion.

Creating Defenses Against Other Religions

When a religion infects a person (a "host" in biological terms), it immediately begins creating antibodies against competing viruses. For example, newly minted Baptists will get Bible study that is full of verses and justifications for the rightness of their religion and a host of arguments against other

---

4   An essay by Robert Sapolsky, "Bugs in the Brain," *Scientific American* (March, 2003): 94.

5   For purposes of our discussion, I will use the term "virus" although parasite might be more appropriate in some cases. I want to avoid the totally negative connotations of the word "parasite." Most people realize that viruses can be benign, even beneficial, in some cases. That is not the general understanding of a parasite.

interpretations. In the early stages, it is a race to get as many antibodies as possible into the new convert so the host will have defenses against the rest of the world, and especially competing religions. Once a person is infected with Catholicism, he is rarely tempted to become a Muslim. Once a person is infected as a Baptist, she rarely becomes a Buddhist. Generally speaking, when children are infected with a specific god virus, they stay reasonably close to that religion for the rest of their lives. A Baptist may become a Lutheran or Presbyterian, but rarely Catholic, Muslim or pagan.

Religious immunity is a powerful program designed to ensure that the children are protected from outside influence. In a pluralistic society, this is important. The virus cannot control contact with other religions in the environment, so it takes prophylactic measures to keep people blind or unreceptive to other religions. This is especially important for children whose immunity is not yet complete.

Childhood religious infection is so strong that it seems to have the power to create a permanent imprint in most people. Imprinting was first identified by Konrad Lorenz and Niko Tinbergen, who won the 1973 Nobel Prize for Physiology and Medicine.[6] In their work with birds and other animals, they showed that many animals learn to identify their parents remarkably fast after birth. In a famous experiment with geese, they demonstrated that substituting a parent figure like a human led to imprinting on the substitute. After imprinting was complete with the substitute, they reintroduced the real parent goose. To their surprise, the goslings could not be reprogrammed to follow the true parent; instead, they followed the substitute figure.

This powerful and rapid learning is strong in many animals and appears to be non-reversible most of the time. Perhaps religious infection is similar. Once a person has imprinted to a given religion, he does not easily change religions. The rituals, songs, ceremony, etc., have a way of sticking with some people so that they do not feel complete unless they are in that particular ritual environment.

Taking Over Certain Mental and Physical Functions and Hiding Within the Individual

Even an adult host who is not overtly religious can act as if the virus is alive and well in his brain. Inquire about religious beliefs, and the host will

---

6   Nobelprize.org, *The Nobel Prize in Physiology or Medicine 1973* [article on-line] (accessed 20 November 2008); available at http://nobelprize.org/nobel_prizes/medicine/laureates/1973/index. html; Internet.

recite many of the doctrines he learned at age 5 or 10. Just as the chicken pox virus continues to live quietly in the body after the disease is gone, the god virus may live quietly in the host until something evokes it.

Stress can activate the chicken pox virus in adults, leading to the condition known as shingles. Similarly, stress tends to activate the god virus in many people. If they have a traumatic experience, they may reactivate their childhood religion. They start attending church, receiving more "antibodies" to help them stay on the straight and narrow. The virus takes over their mental functions, as illustrated by the display of new guilt-based behavior.

The god virus also has the ability to take over physical functions. For example, many religions attempt to take over sexuality, as with celibacy or abstinence vows. We will discuss this in detail in Chapter 5. To a lesser degree, the virus may change eating and dietary functions, requiring fasts or dietary restrictions.

Finally, the god virus has the ability to hide from internal detection. Once infected, the individual cannot detect major contradictions in his beliefs and behavior. Belief systems become self-evident to him, and no amount of logical discourse will move him from his belief. If a Mormon and Catholic were to debate the merits of their respective religions, neither could see his own inconsistencies and logical fallacies, but would see the other's quite clearly.

Using Specific and Efficient Vehicles to Spread the Virus – The Vector

In biology the organism that spreads disease is called a vector. A mosquito is a vector for malaria, and a tick is a vector for Lyme disease. In malaria, the mosquito bites a person with malaria and ingests the plasmodium parasite. The plasmodium then moves through the mosquito by creating a perforation in the mosquito's gut and passing to the salivary glands. When the mosquito bites the next person, she (only females bite) injects the plasmodium into the new person.

Vectors are critical in the life cycle of many parasites. The vector may or may not be harmed in the process of transferring the parasite. Bats seem less affected by rabies than raccoons, but both can be vectors. The flea that carries the *Yersinia pestis* bacteria for the infamous bubonic plague will die in its effort to infect the next rat or human. The bacteria literally block the flea's digestive tract to force it to regurgitate the *Y pestis* bacteria into its victim. It renders the flea incapable of digesting what it eats.

In a similar fashion, god viruses also need vectors: People can be programmed, even reengineered, to be effective carriers of the virus. We call these people priests, ministers, imams, rabbis, popes, televangelists, shamans, apostles, nuns, Bible professors and, to a lesser degree, elders, deacons or Sunday school teachers. The virus may reengineer these vectors significantly. Reengineering may include years of study in a seminary and learning massive amounts of sometimes obscure and far-fetched ideas as well as many tricks for passing the virus along. It may also include training in how to be celibate and **not** pass one's genes along to be less encumbered with reproductive overhead (spouse and children) and, therefore, more efficient as a vector for the virus. Delusion is employed in the sense of priests and nuns believing that they are married to an invisible god or to the church.

Programming the Host to Replicate the Virus

Finally, the god virus must activate a program for replication in any host. Certain behaviors are programmed to ensure that the virus is passed on to others, especially the host's children. These may include guilt-inducing ideas that create a sense of security in rituals. Examples include first communion, baptism, Bar Mitzvah, confirmation, daily prayer or Bible reading and confession.

Religious Immunities

In 1796, Edward Jenner demonstrated that infecting a person with the cow pox virus effectively immunized the person from the dreaded small pox virus. In other words, one virus immunizes against another.

Religions function in a similar manner. An infected Baptist is generally immunized against Catholicism or Islam. The religion creates a series of defenses within a host to prevent him from seriously considering any other religion. For example, a Baptist would rarely think of studying the Koran as diligently as the Bible. Many Catholics would not spend time studying the writings of John Wesley. A Shiite Muslim would not think to study St. Paul. A Sunni Muslim may find Buddhism unfathomable.[7] The god virus builds a wall so formidable that many people can't conceive of another religion, let alone understand it.

---

7   Evidence is seen in the Taliban destruction of the Buddhas of Bamyan, one of the cultural treasures of the world. In 2001, with the help of Saudi and Pakistani engineers, these giant sixth century statues were blown up.

From an outside observer's view, the behavior of members of the various religions looks and sounds remarkably similar. Listen to the preaching of Osama bin Laden and Pat Robertson, for example. Both say natural disasters are a god's judgment for some evil. Both denigrate the role of women in their respective religions. Both see Satan at work in the world. From a high-level view, all the major religions look and sound alike in many ways. With a few word changes, a Pat Robertson sermon could easily be turned into something bin Ladin might preach.

I use examples of well-known religious leaders, but the analyses could be taken from local churches or mosques just as easily. From years of listening to fundamentalist ministers, I can attest to the incredible statements they make from the pulpit with not a whisper of objection from an otherwise intelligent and reasonable congregation.

Both bin Laden and Robertson have fully functioning brains with all the capabilities for logic, reason, study, learning and critical thinking, but the god virus has disabled some of these functions as effectively as *Toxiplasma gondii* disables the rat's fear of cat pheromones. Nothing else needs to be changed! Simply disabling specific critical thinking skills is all that is necessary for the god virus.

Inhibitions and Prohibitions

An important part of viral control may be found in inhibitions and prohibitions, which keep the believer focused on rituals and actions that reinforce the religion on a daily, even hourly basis. These are often seen in sexual prohibitions: no sex before marriage, no sex during menstruation, no homosexuality, etc. Many religions also have food prohibitions and rules: Fish on Friday, no pork, fasting during certain holidays. Each religion takes a different approach, but all share the same objective: Keep the infected focused on their own religion and protect the unit of propagation – the family. Muslims accomplish this by severely prohibiting female freedoms and expanding male power to control the female and the family. Catholics accomplish it by requiring parents to raise their children as Catholic and mandating sex as strictly a procreative activity with all extramarital sex prohibited.

The prohibition is seen most dramatically in the celibacy of Catholic priests and nuns. Here the virus self-propagates by forcing the host to forgo procreation in service of passing the virus along to as many other people as possible. Just as the rabies virus takes over the brain of the raccoon and reprograms it to bite other animals – even at the cost of its own life – the Catholic virus directs the priest to spend all his discretionary energies propagating the virus. This is genetic suicide for the priest's genes, but gives the Catholic Church a powerful tool for propagation.

Vector Infection Techniques

Religious vectors use sophisticated methods of preparing and opening potential hosts of the religion. Religious vectors learn preaching techniques that emotionally open up the potential host. (We will discuss this in detail in Chapter 7.) Vectors are expensive for the virus to produce, so they are protected and supported, often to an extreme degree as seen in the protection of priests and preachers in the many recent sex abuse scandals.

Vectors can actually be more efficient as vectors when dead. Examples of efficient dead vectors include Jesus, Paul, Ali (son-in-law of Mohammed), V. I. Lenin (founder of the Soviet Union), Che Guevara (Latin American revolutionary) and Joseph Smith (founder of Mormonism). In the case of Joseph Smith, his death was a fortunate event for the whole movement. His usefulness to the virus had probably run its course, and he was less and less successful as a leader. But once dead, he became a martyr around whom the charismatic and brilliant leader Brigham Young could rally the faithful and establish Paradise in Utah.

Charity Only for the Virus

The god virus programs the host in very specific ways. All god viruses program charity into its followers, but it is a carefully defined charity. I learned this the hard way one Christmas when I was 19 years old. I was a poor college student who paid my own tuition at a private university and worked hard for every dollar I earned. My mom and dad were proud when I budgeted 20 hard-earned dollars for charity that Christmas. I didn't mention what charity I had chosen, but they assumed it was our church or some church-related charity. Weeks after Christmas my mom

"Ministers say that they teach charity. That is natural. They live on alms. All beggars teach that others should give."
-Robert Ingersoll, 1833-1899

was dying of curiosity and finally asked, "Where did you give your $20?" I told her I gave it to the ACLU defense fund for draft resisters.

I quickly learned that the ACLU is not a charity, and that god would not count that gift. I learned that you always give to the church or a religious charity or it didn't count. Until then, I didn't realize that there was an accounting department in heaven. From reading the Bible, I thought I had learned that you weren't supposed to advertise your giving like the Pharisees (Matthew 6:1-4).[8] I figured any giving I did was between god and me. If god didn't like it, he would let me know. I was feeling pretty good about my choice until then.

Charity and giving are clearly defined by the god virus. Since the survival of the virus depends on regular feeding, it does little good for the virus if you give resources to a non-viral entity, which is therefore not acceptable.

Infected individuals are also programmed to feel guilt if they do not give, or if they give to a charity that does not support the god virus. Catholics generally don't give to the Baptist college fund. Baptists don't give to Catholic Charities. No Nazarene gives to the mosque-building fund. No Islamic philanthropist writes a fat check to Jerry Falwell's Liberty University. In short, if you and your money are not in service to the virus, it doesn't count and may even count against you

A Good Vector Is Hard to Find

When I was growing up, in the course of 10 years, three ministers in our church were caught having sexual affairs with members. In two other churches of our denomination, five other ministers were caught in affairs, all within one tiny denomination in the Bible belt city of Wichita, Kansas.

It is especially interesting when vectors engage in prohibited behavior since they probably have the highest dose of the virus. Even more interesting are the excuses others make for that behavior. All too often, the behavior is excused with "he just made a mistake" or "he is only human." When the senior minister of my church was caught in an affair, he was allowed to keep his position! He repeated the "mistake" three times over a 10-year period before he was finally fired. I have seen this occur many times within churches.

8   "...that your alms be in secret; and your Father who sees in secret will repay you" (Matthew 6:4).

Why were these folks allowed to stay? Because good vectors are hard to find and expensive to develop. As long as a vector can efficiently feed the virus with money and hosts, the vector will generally remain. Scandal is a small price to pay for a highly effective vector.

Catholic priests are among the most expensive of all vectors. When the Catholic Church learns that a priest is sexually misbehaving, molesting children, having affairs with women or other men, the investment is threatened. That is largely why the church protects the priest-vector rather than the parishioners. It is easier to deal with parishioners than to find and develop a new vector.

The Catholic problem with pedophile priests is a major case in point. I would venture to guess that the Protestant religions have an equally large problem of clergy sexual violations. But because Protestants are more decentralized than the Catholic Church, violations are more easily hidden or violators transferred to another church.

Mutating Religions

Just as in biological systems, religions mutate frequently. Mutations occur constantly, but most never develop into new religions. The Baptists deal with mutations by simply letting the mutation form a new Baptist movement. It is an easy way to keep the main DNA of the movement close without losing it altogether.

Catholics deal with mutations by eliminating them. The Catholic strategy is to keep the DNA as pure as possible and minimize mutations. Thus, threat of excommunication is a primary method of cleansing, and burning at the stake was once popular.[9] The strategies of both Baptists and Catholics work reasonably well.

In biology, occasionally, mutations are so powerful they overwhelm

---

9   While many in the United States are familiar with the Salem Witch trials of 1692, there was a much bigger witch and heresy hunt going on in Europe in the 16ᵗʰ and 17th centuries. Historians estimate that 200,000 people were burned at the stake for various heresies during this time. Mary Tudor (Bloody Mary in England) was responsible for 274 executions by burning over her five-year reign, including the Archbishop of Canterbury in 1556. Burning was particularly favored by the Spanish Inquisition because it did not involve shedding the victim's blood, which was disallowed under the prevailing Roman Catholic doctrine, and because it ensured that the condemned had no body to take into the next life (which was believed to be a very severe punishment in itself). It was also thought at that time that burning cleansed the soul, which was considered important for those convicted of witchcraft and heresy. Capital Punishment U.K., *Burning at the Stake* (accessed 20 November 2008); available from http://www.capitalpunishmentuk.org/burning.html; Internet.

even the strongest defenses and infect entirely new populations. This can happen when the virus encounters a susceptible population. The same goes for religion – in the 1500s, Martin Luther's god virus swept through the largely uneducated and ignorant populations of northern Germany.

Luther's god virus was so powerful that it swept through the European population far faster than the original Catholic virus had done a thousand years before. Once let loose, the Protestant virus mutated rapidly. The Calvinist virus was a direct mutation from the Lutheran. The Anabaptist movement blossomed (Mennonites, Hutterites, Church of the Brethren) along with the French Huguenots, Quakers, German Baptists and many more.

A population that is isolated from other religions and largely uneducated is susceptible to the right kind of mutation or a totally new god virus. Buddhism, a mutation of Hinduism, swept through India from 480 BCE to 180 BCE and became the largest god virus in the world at the time. Islam accomplished a similar feat in the Middle East in only 200 years, from 600-800 CE.

Revive Us Again

If you are familiar with fundamentalist church services, you probably know that old hymn, "Revive Us Again." It is a clear call by the infected that they need a booster shot. Revivals are largely aimed at those who already have the virus. When I was a kid, our church had a revival every year. A guest preacher would preach rejuvenation and recommitment. Most of the people who "got saved" were already related to the church in some way. Rarely did someone come off the streets and get saved.

The revival phenomenon is an adaptive method for keeping the local beliefs strong and preventing outside forces from invading or getting a foothold. It could be seen as mutation prevention. It helps keep people on the straight and narrow. My years growing up in a fundamentalist tradition gave me many opportunities to witness revivalism at work. The focus is much more emotional than the regular church services. A charismatic guest preacher generally leads the revival. The best preachers create an emotional high in the congregation that results in more dedication to the god virus and more money to the church. While sacrifice and giving are most often the themes of a revival, the preacher also spends a lot of time preaching against various "temptations" in the world and against the latest things that might lead the flock astray, like popular television shows, movies or books. One could see the whole exercise as a "keeping the virus pure" process.

Other religious groups have their own methods of viral purification. Catholics tend to use retreats and marriage renewal as well as a tight bureaucracy that keeps close track of the flock. Mormons and Jehovah's Witnesses have well-organized hierarchies that keep all in line while sanctioning or expelling those who go astray.

Freethinkers, A Mutation out of Control

Sometimes a mutation can get out of control. The Protestant emphasis on reading the Bible allowed people to draw their own conclusions without priestly interpretation or central ecclesiastical control. As a result, dozens of mutations sprang up in Europe after Lutheranism began. When people were able to read for themselves, inevitably some of them concluded that the whole enterprise was a house of cards. Most kept their mouths shut to avoid losing their heads, but others made the leap to openly criticize religion and its role in society. These early critics of religion were the forebears of today's freethinkers and the freethinking movement.[10]

Freethinkers are interested in examining the world without the blinders of religious infection. They generally are non-religious or less religious. Some are spiritual or hold to some kind of spirituality. In many ways, freethinkers have reduced or eliminated their god virus infection.

Summary

Biological virus strategies bear a remarkable resemblance to methods of religious propagation. Religious conversion seems to affect personality. In the viral paradigm, the god virus infects and takes over the critical thinking capacity of the individual with respect to his or her own religion, much as rabies affects specific parts of the central nervous system. A simple thought experiment reveals how the god virus works to dull critical thinking. The god virus infects an individual and then inoculates against other viruses. Vectors in biology carry a parasite, virus or pathogen from one reservoir to another. Religious vectors act in similar ways. Priests, imams, ministers, etc.,

---

10   Giordano Bruno is often cited as one of the earliest proponents of freethinking. He lived from 1548 until he was burned at the stake by the Inquisition in 1600. Over the centuries, he was followed by many who questioned the suppositions of religion at their peril, including Galileo, Voltaire, Molyneux and Diderot.

carry the virus and infect new people. The virus carefully directs resources toward it and creates taboos against giving to competing viruses. Sometimes vectors fail. The expense of developing a vector makes it imperative to protect it even in failure as in the case of priest pedophilia. Mutations are constantly produced. Occasionally one breaks out, as in the case of Martin Luther, to infect vulnerable people and cultures.

CHAPTER 2:

HOW RELIGIONS SURVIVE AND DOMINATE

"The word god is for me nothing more than the expression and product of human weaknesses, the Bible a collection of honourable, but still primitive legends which are nevertheless pretty childish. No interpretation no matter how subtle can (for me) change this. For me the Jewish religion like all others is an incarnation of the most childish superstitions."
                    -Albert Einstein, letter to Gutkind, Jan. 3, 1954

Overview

In this chapter we will build a historical foundation for understanding religion in society. We will examine strategies religions use to propagate and perpetuate themselves. We will also look at parasitic and symbiotic propagation and compare some non-theistic religions to more traditional ones.

Survival Strategies

A religion always functions to ensure its own survival. While it may espouse various ideas about brotherhood, love and community, these are always secondary to religious survival. No religion dissolves itself because another religion is suddenly seen as "more true." The Baptists don't close their doors because they realize the Mormons are the true church. Muslims don't convert the mosque to a cathedral in recognition of Jesus as the true messiah. Religions simply do not give up. They modify and mutate. They do whatever it takes to keep the virus alive and viable in a changing environment.

In some cases, individuals are sacrificed in the service of the survival of a religion. This is exemplified by the extreme case of suicide bombers in the Middle East. Suicide in the service of the virus is also seen in the Tamil Tigers of Sri Lanka and in the Japanese Kamikaze in WWII. The host is deeply indoctrinated to believe there will be an individual reward in the next life for the ultimate sacrifice on earth and, therefore, complies.

Self-sacrifice also occurs in the celibacy of priests and nuns who commit genetic suicide to be efficient vectors of the Catholic virus. While this is a less violent approach, it serves the same function for the virus. The respective societies support both types of vectors. The suicide bombers' families often receive support and payments, and the non-procreating priests and nuns receive support from the church as they go about the business of infecting new hosts.

In both of these cases, the behavior of individuals is controlled by the virus in the service of survival. Just as surely as the *Toxiplasma gondii* takes over control of the rat brain, the god virus takes control of the suicide bomber, priest, preacher or nun and directs behavior to ensure survival or advancement of the religion.

Stamping out Heresy

A religion must protect itself from internal mutations and external threats. To accomplish this, it creates antibodies for every known competing god virus on the outside and possible mutations on the inside. Heresy is an internal mutation that threatens to weaken the religion from within by splitting off large groups. The Gnostic, Arian and Nestorian Christian heresies of the second and third centuries were major challenges to Catholicism.[1] The Catholic response was to create a written creed – the Apostle's Creed against Gnosticism (early 2nd century) and later the Nicene Creed against Arianism and other heresies (325 CE). The creeds were designed as an antibody to weed out those who adhered to heresy, to excommunicate and, if political powers were available, execute them. Just as your body uses antibodies to identify and kill foreign invaders, a religious creed can be administered to determine if someone is a heretic and eliminate them.

In 381 CE the emperor Theodosius published an edict that all his subjects should profess the faith of the bishops of Rome and Alexandria (i.e., take the Nicene creed) or be handed over for punishment. Even though large numbers of bishops opposed the Nicene Creed at the time, Catholicism was able to use the political structure to gain supremacy over these growing heresies. Many people were excommunicated or otherwise isolated – or even executed – in the effort to purify and control the flock.

> "When one person suffers from a delusion, it is called insanity. When many people suffer from a delusion it is called religion."
> -Robert M. Pirsig, *Zen and the Art of Motorcycle Maintenance*

A great deal of religious literature is a response to heresy. Most religions claim their literature was handed down by a god, but the god seems to be very concerned with all the heresies of the particular day and time when the scriptures were written. Reading the religious literature of any period in history is a study in the religious protection strategy of the day. Much of the

---

1   Arianism is most commonly used to refer to the theological positions made famous by the theologian Arius (c. 250–336 CE), who lived and taught in Alexandria, Egypt, in the early fourth century. The most controversial of Arius' teachings dealt with the relationship between God the Father and the person of Jesus and conflicted with trinitarian christological positions. For a time, Arianism rivaled all other forms of Christianity in popularity, especially in the east. Nestorianism is the doctrine that Jesus exists as two persons, the man Jesus and the divine Son of God, or Logos, rather than as a unified person. This doctrine is identified with Nestorius (c. 386–451 CE), Patriarch of Constantinople. This view of Christ was condemned at the Council of Ephesus in 431, and the conflict over this view led to the Nestorian schism, separating the Assyrian Church of the East from the Byzantine Church.

literature, after a canon[2] has been established, is concerned with the heresies that crop up. Paul and others showed great concern for heresy which shows how common heresy was even in the earliest church.

I am amazed that you are so quickly deserting Him who called you by the grace of Christ, for a different gospel; which is really not another; only there are some who are disturbing you, and want to distort the gospel of Christ.

-NSV Galatians 1:6-7

But false prophets arose among the people, just as there will also be false teachers among you, who will secretly introduce destructive heresies, even denying the Master who bought them, bringing swift destruction upon themselves.

-NSV 2 Peter 2:1

By 180 CE, Irenaeus of Lyons had written five books against several different heresies. Many more books were to follow over the next three centuries. The Catholic god virus had many mutations to stamp out.

Threats From External Viruses

Any god virus is susceptible to new, radically different viruses. Persian Zoroastrianism and Hinduism were not prepared for the highly parasitic Islam that swept out of the Arabian desert in the eighth and ninth centuries CE. The result was rapid Islamic conquest and conversion of large populations. Rulers like Xerxes and Alexander the Great had conquered many of these same communities in earlier centuries, but they generally left the local religion intact. The new Muslim virus was so powerful that it easily swept local gods and even ancient religions like Zoroastrianism and Hinduism aside.

Stemming the Tide With Fundamentalism

As a virus spreads, its growth eventually slows, which gives time for other god viruses to create antibodies against it. For example, the Islamic

---

2   A canon is the accepted and authorized religious literature of a given religion. The canon of Christianity was officially established in 393 at the Synod of Hippo under the authority of St. Augustine but for practical purposes was probably well established a hundred years earlier. The Mormon canon was completed with the death of Joseph Smith. The Jewish canon was probably established by 200 BCE, and the Islamic Canon was established within 100 years of Mohammed's death.

tide was eventually stemmed in India with Hindu antibodies that gave rise to Hindu fundamentalism. Indeed, fundamentalism in most of its forms is the active creation of antibodies to some threatening virus. As long as threatening religions or mutations are present, fundamentalism will churn out antibodies to keep the population under control and prevent mutations from getting out of hand.

Fundamentalism Defined

Fundamentalism is a set of prescribed thinking patterns and behaviors based on strict and legalistic interpretations of holy texts. In viral terms, it means that people are so deeply infected that they are immune to influence and generally ignore any evidence that contradicts their beliefs. Fundamentalism is exclusive in nature; individuals and groups see themselves as the only true believers or at least more righteous and accurate in behavior and beliefs. Fundamentalism is often parasitic in seeking to impose its beliefs through means of force, coercion, ostracism or political power, even at the expense of lost or ruined individual lives.

> *"Protestantism was the triumph of Paul over Peter, fundamentalism is the triumph of Paul over Christ."*
>
> *-Will Durant*

In some cases, a religion undergoes a permanent fundamentalist mutation. The Jesuits were such an adaptation for the Catholics. Faced with the heresies of Martin Luther and others, the Jesuit Order (Society of Jesus, est. 1540) quickly learned how to create strong antibodies through its sophisticated religious education and indoctrination of youth.[3] Their members have been called Soldiers of Christ and Foot Soldiers of the Pope since their founding. Through their efforts, the Protestants were stopped in Poland and Southern Germany.

The Inquisition was another such institution, also known as Supreme Sacred Congregation of the Roman and Universal Inquisition.[4] For centuries, its purpose has been to root out heresy, confront and eliminate it.

---

3   As illustrated by the famous quote by the Jesuit Francis Xavier, "Give me the children until they are seven and anyone may have them afterwards."

4   In 1908 the name was changed to "The Sacred Congregation of the Holy Office" and changed again in 1965 to "Congregation for the Doctrine of the Faith," an office once headed by the current pope, Benedict XVI.

How Minor Religions Survive

When a religion is clearly at a disadvantage, it often mutates into a form that is not threatening to the dominant religion. Just as a foreign virus in your body may cause a strong immune response, a foreign religion can evoke a strong fundamentalist response that can be fatal to the weaker religion. By mutating into something that is benign or perceived as non-threatening, the weaker religions may be able to survive. Judaism survived in Europe for centuries through such an adaptation. Since the Catholic Church prohibited usury or the collection of interest, the Jewish community provided this service to Christians. Mormonism stepped back from its virulent form in most parts of the United States after experiencing a series of strong, even violent reactions from other religions in New York, Illinois and Missouri. After most retreated to Utah, the Mormon groups that stayed behind became much less vociferous and violent.

No matter how benign a minor religion may seem, the potential for violence against the weaker religion is always present. The pogroms throughout the Middle Ages against the Jews, the Inquisition and expulsion of Jews from Spain in 1492, to the Holocaust, to the current threat to the Jews in the Middle East, are continuing examples of this phenomenon. Another example is the genocidal persecution of the French Huguenots, including the famous St. Bartholomew's Day Massacre in 1572 where 110,000 Huguenots were murdered. The persecution by the king and the Catholic Church continued for over 30 years despite edicts of tolerance and appeals to peaceful coexistence from both sides.

Viral Balance: Religion and Power

In a biological system, organisms may exist that are somewhat beneficial to their host in cooperation with other biota but become pathogenic when not balanced or held in check. In adults, taking antibiotics can seriously disrupt the biotic balance in the gut, giving opportunity for fungus and pathogenic bacteria to take hold. The same is true of the vagina where biotic balance keeps many pathogens at bay. Writing about this balance, Adrianus Nicolaas of the University of Groningen, The Netherlands, says this:

> The intestinal tract harbors a dynamic, complex bacterial ecosystem. The presence and composition of gut flora is known to be of great importance for resistance to pathogenic microbes (e.g. via competition for space and nutritional elements). The

composition of the gut flora influences the development of the mucosal immune system.... [5]

In other words, a well-balanced gut contributes to a strong immune system. If one or more gut microbes gets out of control, it can contribute to damage and disease.

Religions can also keep one another in check. In a pluralistic society, religions have difficulty usurping political power and legislating their beliefs. In the United States, the Mormon virus had total control of the political apparatus in Utah until around 1890, to such a degree that non-Mormons were murdered and driven out of this Mormon enclave. The Mountain Meadows Massacre of 1857 is one of the most famous examples, but is not unique in Mormon history.[6] The current level of Mormon control can be seen by simply driving though any part of Utah. Beside almost every Mormon Church stands a public school. Local school boards, controlled by Mormons, try to place schools close to the church so that the children can leave school for an hour each day to receive religious instruction. Clearly, the state is in the service of the virus with respect to education.

"It is a truism that almost any sect, cult, or religion will legislate its creed into law if it acquires the political power to do so."

-Sir Arthur C. Clark

In less pluralistic societies one religion may dominate. Some Islamic countries, for example, have strong control over the political power systems. Islam has been extremely effective because it is one of the first religions to successfully combine religious and political controls. Indeed, it is constitu-

5   World Intellectual Property Organization, *Modulation of a Balance Between the Gut Mucosal Immune System and the Intestinal Microflora* [article on-line] (2002, accessed 20 November 2008); available from http://www.wipo.int/pctdb/en/wo.jsp?wo=2002072142; Internet.

6   In 1857, one hundred twenty non-Mormons were crossing Mormon territory on their way to California. Fifty Mormons taking orders from local ecclesiastical leaders went out and under a white flag of truce tricked the travelers into giving up their arms. They then massacred all but 17 children under the age of six. Brigham Young himself had stated only a few months earlier, "If any miserable scoundrels come here, cut their throats." He never accepted any responsibility for the massacre but played a big part in an attempted cover up by blaming it on local Native Americans. Only in 1998 did the Mormon Church accept any responsibility and placed a monument at the site. Richard Abanes, *One Nation Under Gods: A History of the Mormon Church* (New York: Four Walls Eight Windows Press, 2003), 245-51. Also see ReligiousTolerance.org, *The 1857 Mountain Meadows Massacre* [article on-line] (accessed 20 November 2008); available from http://www.religioustolerance.org/lds_mass.htm; Internet.

tionally incapable of separating religion and politics. From Mohammed's initial conquests, his was a political religion. The notion of separation of church and state is inconceivable. The Islamic virus was well crafted by its founders to defend against all other god viruses. Islam may well be the best-defended god virus of the major religions.

Its excellent defenses come from the fact that Mohammed was exposed to a wide range of god viruses in his formative period. While somewhat isolated on the Arabian Peninsula, the nascent Islamic religion was close to the center of trade of goods and ideas between east and west. Most of the Islamic antibodies were designed before Islam was a hundred years old. They were effective against every religion they encountered. Islam's strong defenses were written into the Koran and subsequent writings and were based on what was learned from the Jewish, Christian and polytheists of Arabia and, somewhat later, the Zoroastrians of Persia.

Both Judaism and Islam began as political/military movements. Their roots from Moses and Mohammed were militaristic and political. Christianity was born as a non-militaristic religion under the domination of the Roman Empire. Only later did it form its militaristic face. Christianity inherited strong defenses from Judaism. St. Paul invented others, but they were designed to survive as a minority religion in a large and powerful empire. Its antibodies were more focused on the ability to survive in a hostile religious and political environment. Indeed, the writings of Paul are some of the best defenses ever developed for Christianity, focusing on fighting other god viruses and surviving in hostile territory rather than on infecting a political nervous system.

From early on, Christian writers created justifications for taking over political structures but were held in check or slowed down for three centuries by competing religious and political systems. Ultimately, they succeeded, but the initial weakness of Christianity gave it less expertise in the political arena than Islam and much less experience or justification for military methods of infection. As a result, its writings are rather poor guidance on how to infect the instruments of state. On the other hand, from the beginning, Islam's writings were well-designed guides. Paul, Jesus and Moses gave Mohammed great material on which to build.

The Christian virus depends heavily upon the Jewish virus for guidance. Christian preachers refer incessantly to Old Testament political schemas because there are none in the New Testament. The prophets, patriarchs and rulers of ancient Israel like Isaiah, Jeremiah, David, Solomon and Moses all saw the religion as inseparable from the political. To this day, this is the struggle of a secular Israel, where the Jewish religion is constantly putting pressure on the state to infect the political central nervous system. Because Israel's very existence depends on support and protection from the pluralistic Western world, it cannot afford to let Jewish fundamentalism take over. Nevertheless, there are many Jewish groups in Parliament with exactly that agenda.

Advanced God Viruses

Islam has some of the best defenses against other god viruses and has the potential to be more parasitically aggressive when consolidating political power with a society. More recent religions have had the misfortune of coming into a religious biota that was already crowded and somewhat balanced. For example, Mormonism began in an already crowded viral environment, and while its novelty and new defenses created an astounding opportunity for growth, it was nothing like the spread of Islam. Yet, Mormonism from its inception was designed to infect the political nervous system – Joseph Smith even ran for president in 1844. At each stage Mormons sought to take control of local political structure from its founding in New York state, to the move to Nauvoo, Illinois, then to Northwestern Missouri. However, because there were other strong religions present, they were not able to succeed until they migrated to the religious vacuum of Utah.

> "Religion does three things quite effectively: divides people, controls people, deludes people."
> -Carlespie Mary Alice McKinney

Islam developed in a fragmented society where polytheistic viruses were weak, Judaism was not parasitic, and Christian sects were fragmented. The Islamic virus was so well designed that Islam even avoided direct confrontation with other "people of the book."[7] As a result, Jews and many Christian communities were simply bypassed as long as they did not politically or militarily resist Islam. This allowed Islam to spread without

---

7   Mohammed held Jews and Christians above other religions because they followed the Bible. While he felt they believed their religions were corrupted, he still respected them and showed tolerance whereas he had none for other religions.

expending energy fighting well-established and older monotheistic or quasi-monotheistic religions.

Islam attacked Christianity as a false monotheistic religion. With its Holy Trinity – which makes it look suspiciously like a three-god religion – Mohammed claimed that Christianity was a corruption of Allah's word and was not truly monotheistic. Islam's clear monotheism gave it an advantage in converting even many Christians. Islam's creed, "There is no god but Allah and Mohammed is his prophet," is a powerful argument against the confusing and conflicting theories about the Trinity.

So as not to oversimplify, we should acknowledge that Islam had its own mutations that threatened it from within – Shii'a and Sunni being the most prominent split. Nevertheless, Islam had sufficient power to overcome other religions in its expanding domain and continues to grow today with remarkable efficiency.

Scientology is another advanced virus, but it too has had the misfortune of coming into an already crowded religious biota. Had Scientology or Mormonism been born in a less crowded or virally weakened environment, either might have swept the globe.

Fundamentalism – the Virulent Form of God Virus

Biological viruses walk a fine line between being too lethal and too weak. A highly virulent virus like the Ebola may kill its host so quickly that it has no chance to infect another host. Conversely, a weakened virus, like the smallpox vaccine, may be so compromised that it cannot reproduce.

God viruses face the same problem. Fundamentalism is the more virulent form of a religion. It generally must be kept in check lest it damage, cripple, divide or even kill its host society. Fundamentalism is most commonly "let loose" when the god virus is under attack or is in expansion mode. Thus, it can defend a religion from dangerous attackers, or it can create the energy to expand and defeat other religions. Fundamentalism can also turn on its own religion and cause havoc. The Iranian Revolution of 1978 was brought about by fundamentalists in Shii'a Islam to overthrow the Shah of Iran. Once this was accomplished, it continued to feed on the society and the lives of those who opposed it.

When fundamentalism gains ascendancy, rigid behavior is enforced and deviation receives quick sanction. Iran finally got the fundamentalist genie back in the bottle in the early 1990s, but it continues to flare out of control on occasion.

Fundamentalism can be seen as an inflammation. Human immune systems use inflammation as a tool for fighting infection. Unfortunately, inflammation can continue in some cases long after the threat has subsided. Unchecked inflammation can cause hay fever, atherosclerosis and rheumatoid arthritis in the human body. Religious fundamentalism may protect the parent religion for a time, but it can continue long after its usefulness has passed, causing collateral damage to institutions, families and the social fabric.

A society cannot survive for long with rampant fundamentalism. It must be brought back under control once the emergency has passed or the expansion is complete. Uncontrolled, fundamentalism feeds on society itself. Examples of this can be seen in the rigid and deadly rule of the Taliban in Afghanistan after the Soviet withdrawal. Similarly, China's experience with communist fundamentalism in the so-called Cultural Revolution probably led to the deaths of 30 million peasants or more. Many were denounced and taken to reeducation camps or executed for failing to follow the fundamentalist beliefs of the party.

Saudi Arabia has harbored a strongly fundamentalist virus since 1744 when the dynasty of bin Saud formed an alliance with the cleric Abd-al-Wahhab to establish the desert kingdom. Wahibism began as a very conservative reform movement in reaction to certain corruptions that were creeping into Sunni Islam in the 18th century. It was established to purify Sunni Islam and drive out practices like veneration of popular saints, tomb visitation and idolatry. Abd-al-Wahhab perceived a moral decline in Islam and sought to establish strict behavior standards for believers. Wahibism has been carefully followed and kept under control by the ruling class for two centuries.

> "You are never dedicated to do something you have complete confidence in. No one is fanatically shouting that the sun is going to rise tomorrow. They know it's going to rise tomorrow. When people are fanatically dedicated to political or religious faiths or any other kind of dogmas or goals, it's always because these dogmas or goals are in doubt."
>
> -Robert M. Pirsig

A compromise of sorts was struck decades ago that let this virulent virus focus its energy outside Saudi Arabia, as long as it did not challenge the ruling elite inside. Thus, Saudi authorities have been hesitant to confront the virus directly because the political central nervous system is itself highly infected. For example, Osama bin Laden was a close follower of Wahibism and from a prominent Saudi family.

Al Qaeda is even more fundamentalist than Wahibism but is a direct mutation from Wahibism. As long as Wahibism and Al Qaeda kept their focus on Afghanistan or other places, it was tolerated. But Al Qaeda has become a direct threat to the Saudi ruling class, which now faces the delicate task of weeding out Al Qaeda without fanning the flames of Wahibism.

By supporting Wahibism and its missionary efforts in other countries, the fundamentalist virus infected the weakened societies of post-communist Afghanistan and Pakistan. It has now become endemic to these areas.

Reservoirs of Biological Viruses

In nature, there are places where a virus can hide or stay for long periods and then break out in an epidemic. Bats are a reservoir for rabies virus, for example. From the bat reservoir, rabies can break out into other animals. The bacteria associated with the plague of the Middle Ages, *Y pestis*, is believed to have started from a reservoir of rats in east central Africa. From time to time the plague seemed to come out of that area and work its way north into the Middle East and Europe.[8] Somewhere in West Africa, the Ebola virus stays hidden and occasionally breaks out, generally through apes into human populations.

In biology, it is often unclear why a specific pathogen breaks out into the general population. Why do we get one type of flu one year and a different one another year? It appears to be related to the wide number of flu viruses in many different reservoirs. Each virus is held in check due to isolation, lack of efficient vectors or general immunity to the specific strain.

A virus can stay quiescent for years, during which time it may mutate and change many times until one variant finds the key to breaking out. Thus, the outbreaks of plague during the Middle Ages may have been a

---

8   Robert S. Gottfried, *The Black Death: Natural & Human Disaster in Medieval Europe* (The Free Press 1983).

succession of mutated pathogens from an East African reservoir. Each was different enough to overwhelm the defenses of those in its path.

Religious Viral Reservoirs

God viruses also have reservoirs. Afghanistan was the reservoir for two fundamentalist variants, the Taliban and Al Qaeda. The Taliban was a local variant of strict Islam that began as a reaction to perceived corruption in Afghan society. Al Qaeda, as noted earlier, was an offshoot of Wahibism in Saudi Arabia. Both sought to impose Shari'a law on society, which severely restricted women's rights and sought to eliminate western influence by outlawing television, photography, kite-flying, chess and other things.

While the two movements had different origins, they were both fundamentalist responses to perceived corruption and sought to purify the society and believers. After growing and developing inside the Afghanistan reservoir, these highly parasitic and aggressive viruses broke out in the 1990s to infect a wide geographic area. Once out of the reservoir, they had the power to gain a foothold in many countries by infecting young and even well-educated Muslims. Al Qaeda is particularly effective at infecting younger people. For example, it is rare for an Al Qaeda suicide bomber to be over 30 years old.

In centuries past, god viruses spread much like biological ones, following trade routes and armies. Today, religion can spread via the Internet and other forms of high-speed global communication. With this new electronic nervous system, fundamentalism can crop up anywhere and at unprecedented rates. It no longer needs traditional trade routes or conquering armies. Global infections can happen from remote reservoirs that are untouchable by western or any other armies.

Forms of Islamic fundamentalism have spread widely from England to Indonesia. The immune system for this type of infection has not yet been developed, and as a result, governments and other religious groups are struggling to contain it. Military response is not likely to succeed and has probably strengthened the Islamic fundamentalists. Interestingly, the development of Islamic fundamentalism has provoked Christian fundamentalism, which is now seen in strong measure throughout the U.S. military – discussed more in the next chapter. When President Bush referred to "a crusade" to combat Islamic terrorism, it resonated positively with many Christian fundamentalists and negatively with many Islamic fundamentalists. The two viruses can and do feed off one another.

In the United States, reservoirs of particularly parasitic viruses reside in places like Jerry Falwell's Liberty University or Pat Robertson's Regent University. For the greater part of the last 50 years, Southern Baptists seem to be the largest reservoir of fundamentalism, although it exists among Pentecostals and Nazarenes as well.

While these seem to be the obvious reservoirs, it is difficult to predict which reservoir will produce the most effective god virus. Who would have guessed in 1820 that Joseph Smith, a talented, charismatic fabricator of fantastic tales, would spawn the highly infectious Mormon virus? Who would have predicted that a small movement started in Wittenberg, Germany, in 1517 by Martin Luther would upend the twelve-hundred-year-old Catholic monopoly in Europe?

When the dominant religion is weak, as Catholicism was in 1517, new religions have a chance to break out. Many new mutations tried to break out in the century before Luther but were not strong enough or did not have a leader politically powerful enough to succeed. For example, John Huss created a competing virus around 1400 and founded the Moravian movement. This movement simmered for over a hundred years and had a strong influence on Martin Luther, but it never broke out into the mainstream.[9] To illustrate, when Luther visited the parishes of Saxony to determine the state of religious education he wrote in the preface to his book *The Small Catechism* (1528): "Mercy! Good God! what manifold misery I beheld! The common people, especially in the villages, have no knowledge whatever of Christian doctrine, and, alas! many pastors are altogether incapable and incompetent to teach." [10] The entire countryside was ripe for the picking. His new virus easily swept much of Northern Germany.

Marxism is another powerful god virus that smoldered for years in many small pockets of Europe and eventually broke out in Russia in 1917, because of the weakness of the Russian political structure and Orthodox Church.

9   John Huss (c. 1369-1415). Advocated the elimination of indulgences, use of the local language, and independence from Rome and pacifism. His teachings were declared heretical in 1411; he was burned at the stake in 1415. His followers went underground but maintained the movement until it was formally organized in 1457.

10   Martin Luther, *The Small Catechism* [book preface on-line] (accessed 20 November 2008); available from http://www.bookofconcord.com/smallcatechism.html#preface; Internet.

Its tenets are as faith-based as any pronouncement by Jesus or Jerry Falwell. Marxism has no more empirical evidence for its validity than Mormonism. The Marxist historical imperative was as close to a faith statement as the doctrine of the Trinity. Marxism had a particularly effective vector in Vladimir Lenin. As in many cases, once the virus was well on its way to dominance, its principal vector, Lenin, was more valuable dead than alive. Stalin, familiar with the methods of religious manipulation from his own seminary training, built the cult of Lenin after his death. The peasant culture, deprived of its traditional religious outlet in Orthodox Christianity, flocked to see the entombed Lenin. Lenin became the deity of Marxism and was displayed for all to see. No Pharaoh or Caesar was more deified after his death.

"Faith is believing what you know ain't so."
-Mark Twain

Fundamentalism Versus Fundamentalism

Fundamentalism always has a reservoir quietly hidden and capable of erupting. If it not held in check by the dominant virus or other viruses, it can take over a society, with the worst of consequences.

As observers of fundamentalism, we can see these developments and help educate people about what may be happening. We can point out that when two competing fundamentalist viruses collide, rational discussion disappears. Fundamentalism is incapable of compromise. Fundamentalist movements believe that theirs is the only way and that all others are corrupt and doomed. With such deep infection, productive dialogue is unlikely. Further, the presence of fundamentalism evokes fundamentalist responses from others. Mormonism evoked strong responses in Illinois and Missouri in the 1830-1850s. A similar response happened during the Crusades of the 11th to 13th centuries, where Catholic fundamentalism evoked an Islamic fundamentalist response leading to the conquest and reconquest of the Holy Land by each. This went back and forth until the Catholic side exhausted itself and withdrew altogether from Palestine.

Today we see Islamic and Christian fundamentalism vilifying one another from their respective pulpits. It is probably no coincidence that there has been a huge increase in fundamentalist activity in the U.S. military even as the military is in the Islamic world to battle Islamic fundamentalists. Fundamentalist groups like Christian Embassy have infiltrated the very top of the U.S. military and gained positions of influence in the Pentagon. From the U.S. Air Force Academy evangelical scandal, to Campus Crusade for Christ attempting to send thousands of conversion packets to soldiers in Iraq, evangelicals have worked hard to use the military for religious purposes. Scott Blom of Campus Crusade for Christ says in a promotional video: "Our purpose for Campus Crusade for Christ at the Air Force Academy is to make Jesus Christ the issue at the Air Force Academy and around the world. They're government paid missionaries when they leave here." [11]

> "Fundamentalism isn't about religion, it's about power."
> -Salman Rushdie

Fundamentalism always seeks to infect the institutions that make its propagation easiest. Whether the U.S. military or Islamists in the Pakistani army, the purpose is always to ensure efficient propagation using already established institutions.

Prevention of Fundamentalist Virus

With the advent of the scientific method, many of the manipulations of god viruses can be exposed. The Pope can no longer claim that the earth is the center of the universe. While many believe in prayer, they would rather trust their physician to heal their illness. Scientologists may claim that their E-meter tells all sorts of things about a person, but they dare not open it to the light of scientific inquiry.[12] Baptists may not like the idea that humans evolved from other creatures, but they have no way to put their creationist ideas to a test against say the Navaho or Hindu version of creation. These bastions of faith can be challenged through scientific inquiry.

Europe has not had a major fundamentalist outbreak since Hitler died, and Russia has avoided a major fundamentalist outbreak since the fall of the

---

11   Campus Crusade For Christ, *USAFA Promotional Video* [video on-line] (filmed Summer 2002, accessed 21 November 2008); available from http://www.militaryreligiousfreedom.org/press-releases/ccc_usafa.html; Internet.

12   The E-meter is a machine used by Scientology auditors to probe and make certain determinations about a person.

Soviet Union. These societies have strong science education and, so far, have avoided wholesale infection from the more virulent god viruses.

While we may never be fully safe from fundamentalism, the best prevention is solid education in the sciences. Right now, an experiment is going on in Asia and Russia. While the Marxist/communist religion has largely fallen out of favor, other religions have not been able to rush in and fill the void. This is not coincidental, as the governments of China and Russia have created and continue to develop a scientifically educated populace. They also monitor and interfere with outside religious efforts to infect their populations. In western countries where scientific education is strong, such as Germany, Sweden, Ireland, Hungary, The Netherlands, god viruses of all kinds have subsided in influence.[13]

Education is the key to perpetuation of the virus for the Taliban, Baptist or Catholic. If the virus cannot control public education, it will seek to divert resources from public coffers to fundamentalist school funding. From the madrassa schools of Pakistan to the Christian push for school vouchers in the United States, and the religious home school movement, religions seek to control education or to control the resources for education.

Non-Theistic Religions

Atheism as Religion?

Some claim that atheism is a religion. But that poses a problem of what you call people who do not believe in Zeus, Thor, Allah or even The Flying Spaghetti Monster![14] Atheism simply sees no evidence of any god.

"If Atheism is a religion, then health is a disease!"

-Clark Adams

Every religion we have mentioned has rituals, practices, holy writings or traditions, etc. Nothing like that has ever developed from Atheism. There

13   National Center for Education Statistics, *Mathematics and Science Achievement of Eighth-Graders between 1995 and 2003* (accessed 20 November 2008); available from http://nces.ed.gov/timss/results03_eighth95.asp; Internet.

14   If you are unfamiliar with the Flying Spaghetti Monster, see Church of the Flying Spaghetti Monster [web site on-line] (accessed 20 November 2008); available from http://www.venganza.org/; Internet. I think you will be quite amused.

are no holy men, holidays or holy books, and no agreed-upon canons of faith. In fact, the only thing you can get some Atheists to agree upon is that there is no god.

Communism and Other Non-Theistic Religions

While Atheism may not be a religion, some non-theistic religions have holy books and godlike figures. Just as Martin Luther created the Protestant virus, Karl Marx created a Marxist virus based on tenets of faith in an historical imperative. Marx had no more evidence for his historical imperative than Christians do for a second coming of Christ. Marxism infected many hosts, mutated in ways that helped it survive and replicated in the minds of thousands, then millions. It eventually evolved into the various practices of communism that in almost all cases led to a cult of personality such as found in Stalinism, Maoism and others in Korea, Cambodia, Cuba and Romania.

While these are not technically theistic, the head is god-like in the sense that Caesar or Pharaoh was a god. Communist cults even worship their dead gods! Thus, Lenin has an elaborate tomb that is still visited by thousands of people every year. Kim Il-sung, former dictator of North Korea, died in 1994 but he is officially the "President of North Korea eternal" to this day! He is as much a god to the North Koreans as a dead Pharaoh was to the ancient Egyptians. It seems bizarre to the western mind to venerate a dead dictator, but how is that different than a Christian worshipping a dead Jesus or Shii'a Muslims visiting the tomb of Fatima in hopes of getting a blessing? The behavior looks remarkably similar whether it is worship of a Pharaoh, a dictator or a messiah.

The virus maintains strength or revives itself as long as the godhead is alive or perpetuated in some fashion. When the godhead dies, the god virus dissipates, and other religions may gain strength. Protestant churches are frantically working to gain market share in the former Soviet Union to take the place of communism and the Russian Orthodox Church. For example, Jehovah's Witnesses have had so much success that they have been taken to court, sanctioned and banned from Moscow.[15] Pentecostal religions are growing and have caught the ire of the Orthodox Church and the Russian

15   ReligiousTolerance.org, *Jehovah's Witnesses Oppression in Moscow, Russia* [article on-line] (June 17, 2004, accessed 20 November 2008); available from http://www.religioustolerance.org/witness9.htm; Internet.

government as well. The Orthodox virus is weak, so it enlists the help of political authorities to stop other viruses from intruding.

Parasitic Religions

In biology, some hosts are more susceptible to a certain virus than others, and various mutations have differing effects on the population as a whole. That is why you might get a cold but your spouse does not.

It is similar for god viruses. While Jehovah's Witnesses are unlikely to become the dominant religion of Russia, their particular virus has the ability to infect a certain portion of the population, as do those of Scientology, Pentecostals and Baptists. These are aggressive viruses that propagate through proselytizing, a more parasitic religious approach. The parasitic approach uses a horizontal strategy whereby new people are infected by the virus by jumping across social and family lines. A symbiotic approach, on the other hand, is more vertical – passing the virus down from one generation to the next. Most religions use both types of propagation to some degree but emphasize one more than the other.

Highly parasitic viruses tend to pick out hosts who are most susceptible and then dramatically control them. Thus, parasitic viruses are likely to tear intact families apart in order to break the convert away from potential diluting influences. A good example is the Unification Church or Family Federation for World Peace and Unification founded by Sun Myung Moon, also known as the Moonies. The Unification Church requires sexual abstinence before marriage and insists that all marriages must be approved, if not arranged, by the church. Thus, Sun Myung Moon has selected for marriage hundreds if not thousands of people from different cultures in an effort to propagate his virus across traditional cultural boundaries.

Not surprisingly then, one of the main complaints against the Jehovah's Witnesses in Russia is its impact on families and society. According to an May 25, 2004 article[16] by the organization *Religious Tolerance*:

> Moscow courts have found the community guilty of forcing families to disintegrate, infringing the person, rights and freedoms of the citizen, encouraging suicide or the refusal on religious grounds of medical aid to the critically ill, and inciting

16 ReligiousTolerance.org, *Jehovah's Witnesses Oppression in Moscow, Russia* [article on-line] (June 17, 2004, accessed 20 November 2008); available from http://www.religioustolerance.org/witness9.htm; Internet.

citizens to refuse to fulfill their civil obligations established by law. Under Article 14 of the 1997 law, a religious organization may lose its legal status and have its activity banned on these grounds.

Parasitic religions demand a lot from their members and have strict behavioral or membership standards. Since they are constantly bringing in new members, the indoctrination and supervision must be rigorous. The hierarchy of the parasitic virus demands sacrifice of money and time from converts. Scientology, Jehovah's Witnesses, Hare Krishna and the Unification Church all behave in this way.

Symbiotic Religions

Many religions are less parasitic and more symbiotic. For example, the Druze religion of Lebanon, Syria and Israel is closed to outsiders. It has not accepted converts for over eight hundred years. This is a vertical strategy, propagating down generations largely within family and cultural boundaries. Other religions have similar strictures, such as the Yazidi of Iraq or the Amish in the United States. If you are not born into the community, you cannot become a member. If conversion is allowed, the requirements are such that it is practically impossible or very difficult.

This can be a successful strategy. The community keeps the virus strong and, in turn, the virus binds the community closely together. Symbiotic religions, like the Druze, Yazidi and Amish, have so completely infected their members that the strictures of the religion become totally integrated into daily life. Many Hindu sects might also be seen as symbiotic as might Hutterites.

It All Depends …

Many religions play both a parasitic and a symbiotic card depending on current circumstances. The Catholic virus tends to be somewhat symbiotic while at the same time having parasitic outbreaks. The Catholic virus was about as parasitic as possible during the conquests of Central and South America in the 16th century. The deaths of millions of native people were directly related to the practices of Catholic priests in facilitating the conquests. Despite the heroic efforts of a handful of priests like Bartolome de Las Casas[17], priests accompanying conquistadors and later settlers gave justification for the genocide and enslavement of whole peoples in the Americas. This is about as parasitic as a religion can be.

Of course, biological viruses and bacteria killed as many or more than the Catholic soldiers and priests, but the two acted in tandem – one facilitating the work of the other. Pope Benedict showed a surprising lack of awareness about the devastation his church caused when he made a major speech to the Bishops of Brazil in September 2007:

> ... what did the acceptance of the Christian faith mean for the nations of Latin America and the Caribbean? For them, it meant knowing and welcoming Christ, the unknown God whom their ancestors were seeking, without realizing it, in their rich religious traditions. Christ is the Saviour for whom they were silently longing. In effect, the proclamation of Jesus and of his Gospel did not at any point involve an alienation of the pre-Columbian cultures, nor was it the imposition of a foreign culture.[18]

Needless to say, his words evoked outrage among native groups and even many local priests. How can anyone be so blind unless he is completely infected with a god virus? Were people to say that the Jews were waiting for Hitler to show them the light, they would be called to task for such ignorance, but the Pope seems to get a free pass with such calloused statements.

Today the Catholic virus in Africa is going through a parasitic stage. By actively attacking condom use and birth control, the god virus facilitates the HIV virus. The result is conversion to Catholic sexual practices or death from HIV. Ironically, Catholicism has become extremely weak in its own home – Italy – where birth rates are among the lowest in the world. Somebody must be using condoms or birth control in Italy, or Italians have become remarkably celibate!

---

17   Bartolome de Las Casas (1484–1564) was a Dominican priest involved in some of the earliest voyages of conquest and settlement. He was largely responsible for starting a debate and protest in Spain over the conquistadors' treatment of Native Americans. He attempted to be the conscience of the King, Queen and Pope but largely lost the battle as priests accompanied by soldiers marched on in search of gold and slaves.

18   A Catholic Life, *Pope Benedict XVI's words on Native Americans to CELAM* [article on-line] (May 15, 2007, accessed 20 November 2008); available from http://acatholiclife.blogspot.com/2007/05/pope-benedict-xvis-words-on-native.html; Internet. Also found in the *LA Times*, 14 May 2007.

Summary

The god virus embodies strategies for survival and propagation. Advanced viruses have defenses that are more effective than others and, as a result, they have risen to dominance over the less developed. God viruses are always mutating, and new ones may break out of viral reservoirs at any time. The best prophylactic for god viruses, especially fundamentalist variants, is science education. The more science is taught or discussed, the fewer tools a god virus has to infect populations.

CHAPTER 3:
AMERICAN CIVIL RELIGION

"Religion is regarded by the common people as true, by the wise as false, and by the rulers as useful."

-Seneca the Younger (4 BCE-65 CE)

Overview

In this chapter, we will show that in modern society, religion and culture are not the same. We will introduce the concept of cultural coupling, which happens when a religion invades an established culture. We will look specifically at the evolution of the civil religion in the United States as a case study in religious coupling.

Religion and Culture

Culture and religion are different, though related, entities. Culture exists at a broader level than religion, especially in modern societies. Earlier societies, like the North American natives, aboriginals of Australia, Brazilian Amazonian tribes, and others, all had culture-specific religions. That is, the culture and religion were so closely tied together that they could not be separated. For example, it would be inconceivable to an Amazonian tribesman to convert to the Iroquois religion. Religion is a function of being a tribal member – the way the tribe lived and worshipped.

Thus, tribal religion is like a virus that can only live in one species. The virus may prosper in that single species, but if the species gains total immunity or goes extinct, the virus is eliminated. On the other hand, if a virus can mutate to a form that allows it to survive in other species, it can expand and survive in new ways. HIV is a virus that appears to have jumped from apes to humans several decades ago. The leap allowed the virus to go from a potential of a few hundred thousand apes to hundreds of millions of humans.

Uncoupling From Culture

A religious revolution occurred about 600-400 BCE with the mutation of non-culture-specific religion. Once religion was uncoupled from a given culture, it could spread to any culture. The revolution has occurred several times around the world with similar consequences. For example, Buddhism swept India and China in a short time, wiping out hundreds of local gods. Christianity swept Europe in the same way, eliminating much of Germanic and Celtic religion and culture. Islam swept the Middle East.

Zarathustra,[1] founder of Zoroastrianism, may have been the first to uncouple from culture around 600 BCE. Beginning in Persia, Zarathustra pioneered the concept of a universal battle between the forces of good, Ahura-Mazda, and evil, Angra Mainyu. Not surprisingly, the concept of Satan comes from this period. Zoroastrianism spread rapidly throughout what is now Iran and Iraq, eliminating many local gods and religions. Shortly after, the Jews were taken into the Babylonian captivity right in the heart of Zoroastrianism.

Judaism was a highly tribal religion until the Babylonian captivity exposed it to Zoroastrianism. After their captivity, the Jews returned to Judea with a fundamentally different understanding of their own religion. From 538 to 330 BCE, the Jews were also under Zoroastrian suzerainty. Zoroastrianism profoundly influenced Judaism. Jewish understanding of its god changed after the captivity and, with the addition of the concept of Satan, began taking on some of its modern trappings.

This set the stage for the complete uncoupling of Judaism and culture by St. Paul almost four hundred years later. If you are familiar with the Christian New Testament, you will recall the conflict between Paul and Peter over the status of gentiles in the new Christian sect. Much of the conflict between St. Paul and St. Peter (and other Apostles) was around the issue of whether Christianity could be uncoupled from Jewish culture. Peter and others believed new converts should be circumcised and perform other Jewish rituals and rites. Paul strongly disagreed, arguing that gentiles not be obligated to become Jews before joining the new sect. St. Paul won the argument.[2] The result was a dramatic uncoupling of Christianity from Jewish culture. This freed the Christian virus to go wherever it could penetrate without the trappings of Judaism to contend with.

Binding to the Culture

While cultural uncoupling allows a religion to spread, the religion seeks to take over a given culture to ensure its survival. The deeper the religious infection, the more secure the religion will be in a given culture. If the

---

1   The holy writings of Zoroastrianism recount the virgin birth of Zarathustra 600 years before Jesus accomplished the same thing. Zoroastrian sacred texts claims that Zoroaster existed with god and the angels 3,000 years before his birth – shades of the Gospel of John 1:1. There is little in the Jesus myth that was not done by some other deity, often centuries before.

2   Acts 15 and Galatians 2:11-14.

religion is able to infect the target culture sufficiently, it becomes such an integral part that it cannot be separated. Thus, Zoroastrianism became the state religion of Persia, supplanting hundreds of local gods and ensuring a secure place for itself for hundreds of years. One cannot imagine the Middle Ages without Catholicism. How could Saudi Arabia be separated from Islam? Each of these religions coupled strongly to the new culture.

In contrast, it is easy to see the conquests of Alexander the Great in political and military terms without recourse to Greek religion. The Greeks may have taken their religious ideas with them, but they did not impose them on the conquered people, as did Islam and Christianity. At the time of Alexander the Great, Greek religion had not completely uncoupled into a universal form.

Once a religion binds with a new culture, it has a tendency to latch on like a parasite and direct cultural development in ways that ensure security of the religion and propagation. Religion embeds in the culture as a rabies virus embeds in the brain of a dog or raccoon. Successful binding creates the illusion that culture and religion are one, and followers come to believe that the culture could not survive without the religion. Further, other religions cannot easily dislodge it since it is bound up in so much of everyday life. This is the status of Islam in most of the Middle East. For example, Egyptian civil law makes a change in religion a simple administrative procedure, if you are converting to Islam. If you are converting from Islam to anything else, it is legal, but is made practically impossible by the government.[3]

Many religious political groups in America see the United States and Christianity as inseparable. They believe the wrath of a god will come down if we don't adhere to their interpretation of religious texts – largely based on Old Testament ideas imposed upon current political movements. They see everything from hurricanes to the 9/11 terrorist attacks as god's judgment on the United States. As an example, in the words of Dinesh D'Souza, former policy adviser for Ronald Reagan,

> Muslim extremists are attacking America because not everyone in the U.S. follows a moral code given by an 'external being'

---

3   Human Rights Watch, *Egypt: Allow Citizens to List Actual Religion on ID Cards* [article on-line] (12 November 2007, accessed 20 November 2008); available from http://hrw.org/english/docs/2007/11/12/egypt17306.htm; Internet.

this new moral code leads to acts such as adultery and gay marriage.[4]

During the presidential campaign in 2008, Mike Huckabee, Republican presidential candidate, called for amending the Constitution to conform to god's law.

> [Some of my opponents] do not want to change the Constitution, but I believe it's a lot easier to change the Constitution than it would be to change the word of the living God, and that's what we need to do is to amend the Constitution so it's in God's standards rather than try to change God's standards.

Religionists like D'Souza and Huckabee seek to bind the United States to the Christian virus as surely as Islam is bound to Egypt. It is a goal that has eluded fundamentalist Christians since the founding fathers refused to mention any god in the U.S. Constitution.

The Enlightenment

The Western enlightenment was a new kind of uncoupling, in this case splitting religion totally from culture. Beginning with attacks by early humanists like Erasmus in the 15th century and later by competing Protestants in the 16th century, the Catholics lost their monopoly on European culture. This allowed thinkers, from Hobbes to Rousseau, Voltaire and others, the opportunity to open a crack between Christianity and western culture. This crack grew slowly and did not break open fully until the American Revolution and the subsequent French Revolution. All of western European history from the enlightenment to the end of WWII may be viewed as a colossal struggle to uncouple culture from the hold of embedded religions, be they protestant or Catholic.

The American Revolution and Culture

The appearance of a non-infected political structure is relatively new to history. No state had ever successfully prevented religious viral infection until the U.S. constitutional system was established on the foundations

> "The Government of the United States is in no sense founded on the Christian religion."
> -John Adams, 2nd U.S. President

---

4   Speech at Northwestern University, November 8, 2007.

of the enlightenment. Virtually every major state since the beginning of history had a state religion that played a role in legitimizing the ruler or the ruling class.[5]

The founding fathers of the United States knew that religion always tried to infect the central nervous system of the state. Due to the efforts of Madison and others, the Constitution makes no mention of a god, and church-state separations are enshrined in the First Amendment. The separation of church and state was one of the first attempts to isolate the political system from religious infection. This, along with the many competing religions in post-colonial America, effectively prevented any one religion from dominating or binding to the entire culture.

Political Infection

In biology, the rabies virus works its way quietly through the peripheral nervous system, using nerve pathways that are hidden from the immune system. Rabies weaves its way to the brain where it takes over the central nervous system in service of its own propagation.

> "Give the church a place in the Constitution, let her touch once more the sword of power, and the priceless fruit of all ages will turn to ashes on the lips of men."
> -Robert Ingersoll

God viruses work in the same way. They search for a pathway to the power centers of the state. Thus, regardless of statements to the contrary, religions tend to usurp the political system whenever they are dominant. Having the powers of state is by far the most efficient method of propagation and defense against competing religions.

It is wise to be skeptical of any religion that says it is not interested in political power. Given the right circumstances, most religions cannot resist the temptation. Every religion seeks political power as a means to bind tightly to the culture. It is in the very DNA of any religion.

In light of these ideas, let us look at the specific case of the American civil religion to see how religions attempt to bind with our own society.

---

5   It could be argued that Rome was relatively free of strong viral influence during the imperial period. The worship of the Emperor was a brilliant attempt to create a virus for political purposes, but was not particularly successful as a god virus.

Civil Religion and American Destiny

The American civil religion has been around since the first days of the republic. Robert Bellah (1967) described it in his ground–breaking work, *Civil Religion in America*:

What we have, from the earliest years of the republic, is a collection of beliefs, symbols and rituals with respect to sacred things and institutionalized in a collectivity ... American civil religion has its own prophets and its own martyrs, its own sacred events and sacred places, its own solemn rituals and symbols. It is concerned that America be a society as perfectly in accord with the will of God as men can make it, and a light to all the nations.[6]

The civil religion is a deeply embedded myth that has existed as a meta-religion since the nation's beginning. Not tied to any one doctrine, this nebulous belief system is loosely based on the Judeo-Christian tradition, with claims that a god has blessed this nation and is a guiding force in its destiny.

Manifest destiny was a central theme of the civil religion through the early 1800s and was used to justify the Mexican-American War (1846-1848) as well as the displacement of Native American tribes and expansion across the continent.

> *"What have been Christianity's fruits? More or less in all places, pride and indolence in the Clergy, ignorance and servility in the laity; in both, superstition, bigotry and persecution."*
>
> **-James Madison, 4th U.S. President**

John O'Sullivan's famous 1839 essay captured the concept for the whole nation at the time:

All this will be our future history, to establish on earth the moral dignity and salvation of man – the immutable truth and beneficence of God. For this blessed mission to the nations of the world, which are shut out from the life-giving light of truth, has America been chosen; and her high example shall smite unto death the tyranny of kings, hierarchs, and oligarchs, and carry the glad tidings of peace and good will where myriads

---

6   Robert Bellah, *Civil Religion in America*, Daedalus (1967), 96,1, pp. 1-21.

now endure an existence scarcely more enviable than that of beasts of the field. Who, then, can doubt that our country is destined to be the great nation of futurity?[7] Lincoln used the civil religion expertly to guide the nation through the Civil War, setting the standard for its use among politicians. In the 1960s, Martin Luther King, Jr., used it as a vehicle for the Civil Rights Movement, Governor George Wallace used it as justification for segregation in the South. While it may seem ironic that both men could use the civil religion for such opposing purposes, that is the nebulous nature of this myth. Wallace believed "states rights" were god-given, just as King felt racial equality was. Both ideas have held sway in the civil religion at various times.

The civil religion is as viral as any religion. Recall how any religion disables the critical thinking areas of the brain in its followers with respect to their own religion. They can see the irrationality of others' religious beliefs but are blind to their own. The civil religion has a similar ability to dull the critical thinking skills of entire groups so that criticism of the nation is tantamount to blasphemy. For example, those who criticized the Vietnam War were told, "America, love it or leave it" by some of the most religious people and leaders. More recently, many a minister preached a thinly veiled sermon in support of the invasion of Iraq in 2003. Others called those who dared to speak out against the invasion unpatriotic. War and religion usually go hand in hand into battle. Here are the words of Bob Jones, the fundamentalist President of Bob Jones University, on Larry King Live, March 11, 2003,

'The motto of the Confederacy was Deo Vindice, or "God on Our Side." Atlanta was burned to ashes by people who thought that the deity took the other view.'

-Christopher Hitchens

> And the war in Iraq will help to do a lot to address the source of a lot of this terrorism. And I don't see how anybody who loves peace could really be against this war and those who did destroy peace.

---

7   John O'Sullivan, "The Great Nation of Futurity," *The United States Democratic Review*, 6, 23, (1839): 426-430. Also see John O'Sullivan, *Manifest Destiny* [article on-line] (1839, accessed 20 November 2008); available from http://www.civics-online.org/library/formatted/texts/mani-fest_destiny.html; Internet.

The civil religion also imbues religious power to the president and expects certain religious acts from him (or her) in the name of the nation, like prayer breakfasts, regular references to god and conspicuous church attendance. As a result, the president is seen as the high priest of the civil religion by much of the nation. When disaster or national tragedy strikes, he is expected to call for prayer and attend services at high-profile churches like the National Cathedral in Washington, DC. The very existence of a church named "The National Cathedral" is a testament to the power of the civil religion. All recent presidents have attended services at the National Cathedral in times of national crisis or grief, even when they are members of some other church.

The civil religion is bound so strongly with American culture that many Americans cannot conceive of America without reference to this religion. George H. W. Bush illustrated this in an August 27, 1987 news conference: "No, I don't know that atheists should be considered as citizens, nor should they be considered patriots. This is one nation under God." Implicit in the statement is the idea that only those who believe in the god of the civil religion can be citizens. Those who have no god or those who worship something other than the Judeo-Christian god are not equal citizens.[8]

Another example of the expression of the civil religion happened in the U.S. Senate in 2007. It is the custom and privilege of each Senator to invite religious leaders from their home state to serve as guest chaplains and lead the Senate in prayer and meditation. On July 12, 2007, Rajan Zed of the Indian Association of Northern Nevada (Hindu), was invited by Senate Majority leader Harry Reid to lead the U.S. Senate in prayer. This did not go unnoticed; Christian fundamentalists were in the gallery ready to disrupt the prayer. Zed was interrupted twice, before the Senate gallery was finally cleared. As an expression of the civil religion, all chaplains have been Christian or Jewish since the tradition began in the 1790s, and none of them have ever been interrupted. The fact that the Hindu chaplain was invited was a milestone and a challenge to the civil virus and not surprisingly caused a reaction. In the following days, there was an outcry among many

---

8   Being from Texas, President Bush may have been influenced by the Texas Constitution, which states in Article I, Section 4; Religious Tests: *No religious test shall ever be required as a qualification to any office, or public trust, in this State; nor shall any one be excluded from holding office on account of his religious sentiments, provided he acknowledge the existence of a Supreme Being.* The author of this book could not hold public office in Texas. A Buddhist or polytheist might not meet the criteria either.

fundamentalists about the protesters being kicked out of the gallery.[9] To date, the American civil religion does not have room for full Hindu citizenship and less room for the Atheist. When will the Senate invite a Wiccan, Pagan or Atheist to lead the Senate in prayer or meditation?

The New Civil Religion

One could argue that the civil religion was a benign force before WWII. With the rise of the competing Marxist virus in Russia, American religion was transformed into a weapon of the cold war. The presence of a challenging virus often evokes fundamentalist movements. American civil religion rose up to confront the "godless communism" of the Soviet Union. Each virus fed off of the other – Christianity vs. Marxism. It is no coincidence that the Pledge of Allegiance was changed in 1954 to include "under God" and the motto on U.S. paper money came to incorporate "in God we trust" in 1957.

> "Prayer has no place in the public schools, just like facts have no place in organized religion."
>
> -School superintendent on The Simpsons, episode #1

The fifties were the height of the McCarthy era and the rise of an active civil religion where political witch hunts were used to persecute many who refused to toe the religious line. The United States saw a huge rise in interest in the civil religion and religion in general, while the largely non-religious European NATO countries saw continued decline in religious activity.[10] Today's rise in fundamentalism and active civil religion can be traced back to the perceived communist threat. With the disappearance of communism, the focus has shifted from godless communism to godless

9   "The chaplain of the Family Research Council says yesterday's historic Hindu prayer to open the U.S. Senate is 'just one more step away' from America's Christian heritage. The founders of the United States," says Pierre Bynum, "would never have wanted a pantheistic prayer to open that legislative body." See also Counterbias, *Dogmatists Seethe, Spirituality Betrayed* [article on-line] (23 August 2007, accessed 20 November 2008); available from http://www.counterbias.com/917.html; Internet.

10   See "Catholic Church withers in Europe," *Boston Globe*, 2 May 2005. General religious attendance in Europe fell from well over 50% after WW II to 20% or as little as 11% in some European countries.

secular humanism. Sermons against secular humanism have replaced those against communism.

Infiltration of the New Civil Religion

With the rise of sexual freedom, a dramatic increase in divorce, legalization of abortion and growing use of birth control, many of the more fundamentalist viruses in the United States felt threatened. The reproductive rights movement of the 1960s and 70s was a direct threat to god viruses of all kinds, including Baptist, Nazarene, Catholic and Mormon.

The Moral Majority was a mutation that allowed many disparate viruses to find common ground and create a strategy for infecting the political central nervous system. It was created in 1979 by Jerry Falwell, who recognized that if no single religious group could infect and dominate the political system, perhaps a coalition could. An important part of this strategy was to use the already developed civil religion to achieve the goals. Just as the lancet fluke infects the brain of an ant and drives the ant up the grass blade to be eaten by a cow, the Moral Majority infected the civil religion and drove it up the blade to feed politicians. Infected politicians now work to achieve the ends of the Moral Majority and other similar groups like the Christian Coalition. The civil religion is no longer a benign national religious expression, but a full–blown new civil religion that has strong fundamentalist tendencies.

> "The national anthem belongs to the eighteenth century. In it you find us ordering God about to do our political dirty work."
>
> **-George Bernard Shaw**

Falwell and others advocated the need for religion to bind to the culture and take control of the political system. Using the tactics of McCarthy and the language of the new civil religion, they were able to intimidate politicians and guide their candidates into office. As a result, today religion is a virtual test for high public office in many states. Candidates who do not meet the religious test face the prospect of being labeled anti-religious or worse.

As a sign of just how broad and diverse this coalition is, it is worth noting that Mormonism has been welcomed as a full partner. How is it that Mormonism has been able to join this coalition? In times past, Christian sects reviled Mormonism. Indeed, a brief read of the Book of Mormon shows that Mormonism is anything but Christian in nature, from sacred underwear to becoming gods of their own planets, to Native Americans as the Jewish Diaspora and to Joseph Smith as the last prophet – not Jesus.

The answer can be found in Jerry Falwell's umbrella strategy. Simply subscribing to the fundamentalist principles of the new civil religion is enough to gain entrance. Some of the principles include ideas like prayer in schools, Christianity as the official religion of the U.S., conservative judges in the courts, opposition to stem cell research, anti-gay marriage, placing evangelical chaplains in the military, anti-abortion and anti-sex education.

Infectious Results

The strategy has been somewhat successful. The result of the Moral Majority's infecting the federal system can be seen in small but effective acts:

- placing specific religious types of individuals on the Supreme Court,
- forcing all candidates for national office to display their religious credentials,
- placing fundamentalist chaplains in the Armed Forces,
- resisting non-Judeo-Christian military chaplains,
- promoting the more religious officers in the Armed Forces,
- restricting stem cell research,
- delaying approval of the Plan B drug for birth control,
- opening an embassy to the Vatican[11],
- restricting condom use and other birth control and prohibiting aid to organizations who might support abortion.

All these and more are recent developments that can be tied directly to the activity of this new civil religion.

---

11 United States politicians have always resisted the idea of recognizing the Vatican as a state and placing an embassy in the Vatican. It was an important concern when John Kennedy was elected. With the ascendancy of the new civil virus, Ronald Reagan saw an opportunity to gain advantage by doing something no American president had even thought appropriate, placing an embassy in the Vatican. Today, the United States recognizes the Vatican as a state with its own U.S. embassy. Had John Kennedy done this, he might have been impeached, certainly vilified, especially by the Republicans. This enormous change in attitude is an indicator of how much the civil virus has infected the United States political system.

This new civil religion is also active in opposing Islamic religious expression as well as creating an unfriendly or unwelcoming environment for other religions such as Hindu, Sikh, Pagan and Wicca. When Keith Ellison, Democratic representative from Minnesota, was elected as the first Islamic congressman, the new civil religion attacked him. Here is an example of its expression on CNN.

"Don't pray in my school, and I won't think in your church."

-Unknown

On the November 14, 2006, edition of his CNN Headline News program, Glenn Beck interviewed Rep.-elect Keith Ellison (D-MN), who became the first Muslim ever elected to Congress on November 7, asking Ellison if he could "have five minutes here where we're just politically incorrect and I play the cards up on the table." After Ellison agreed, Beck said:

> I have been nervous about this interview with you, because what I feel like saying is, 'Sir, prove to me that you are not working with our enemies.'" Beck added: "I'm not accusing you of being an enemy, but that's the way I feel, and I think a lot of Americans will feel that way.

Many others expressed similar sentiments about Ellison.[12] The new civil religion's purpose seems to be to ensure that the native religions remain dominant.

---

12   Media Matters for America, *CNN's Beck to first-ever Muslim congressman: "[W]hat I feel like saying is, 'Sir, prove to me that you are not working with our enemies'"* [article on-line] (15 November 2006, accessed 21 November 2008); available from http://mediamatters.org/items/200611150004; Internet.

Dennis Prager, a conservative, Jewish radio host, stated that Ellison should not be allowed to take his oath on the Koran since it "undermines American civilization." He didn't bother to note that there is no requirement in the Constitution to use any book – Bible or Book of Mormon, etc., – to take the oath of office. Townhall.com, *America, Not Keith Ellison, decides what book a congressman takes his oath on* [article on-line] (28 November 2006, accessed 21 November 2008); available from http://www.townhall.com/Columnists/DennisPrager/2006/11/28/america,_not_keith_ellison,_decides_what_book_a_congressman_takes_his_oath_on; Internet.

Rep. Bill Sali (R-ID) an Evangelical Christian, in an August 8, 2007, interview with the conservative Christian-based American Family News Network denounced the Senate leadership for allowing a Hindu to lead the opening prayer. He held that invoking a non-Christian god in the Senate threatened to endanger America by removing "the protective hand of God." He then went on to say, "We have not only a Hindu prayer being offered in the Senate, we have a Muslim member of the House of Representatives now, Keith Ellison from Minnesota. Those are changes and they are not what was envisioned by the Founding Fathers. The principles that this country was built on, that have made it great over these centuries, were Christian principles derived from Scripture."

While the new civil religion is not official policy of the United States, it functions in that way. Can you imagine a president today espousing the deistic beliefs of Jefferson or Lincoln? Can you imagine a president who would refuse to declare a day of Thanksgiving as Jefferson did? Can you imagine a president ignoring Billy Graham or his successor as the high priest of the civil religion? Can you imagine a president appointing an Atheist or even a Hindu, Muslim, Pagan or deist as attorney general?

Federal Infection

Since the 1980s this mutation of the civil religion has become very influential in the political world in this country. It has infected the highest levels of government. It has succeeded in putting a fully infected person in the White House with George W. Bush. Five infected justices now sit on the Supreme Court, all conservative Catholic. Many officers and officials of both federal and state government are now firmly in place and able to exercise the power of the virus over everything from stem cell research to sex education in the schools and the teaching of geology and evolutionary biology.

The civil religion virus does not care about creeds; it cares about growing and propagating. That is why it can bring some formerly despised groups together. For example, by drawing on Mormon power, it increases its ability to grow and infect the political central nervous system. Mormons are experts at this. They are the most successful of all American god viruses at infecting a political system. In Utah, it is almost impossible to achieve elected office or a position of any influence if you are not a Mormon (except in Salt Lake City). Mormonism is so strong that Mitt Romney was considered a serious candidate for president in 2007-2008 despite the Religious Right's traditional view that Mormonism is not a Christian religion.

> "I do not believe in the divinity of Christ, and there are many other of the postulates of the orthodox creed to which I cannot subscribe."
> -William Howard Taft, 27th U.S. President

The Civil Virus as Stealth Virus

In the Joseph McCarthy era, the most successful tactic was to label anyone who disagreed with him as a communist. This effectively froze the opposition. Even people as prominent as President Eisenhower were afraid of McCarthy.[13] McCarthy was an early vector of the new civil virus. He was skillful in attacking his opponents in such a way that they were immobilized for fear of being labeled communists and dragged before the Senate or investigated by J. Edgar Hoover and the FBI. An objective look at McCarthy quickly reveals that he was a poor example of the Christian values he espoused, but the virus is not concerned about such matters as long as the vector delivers.[14] By the time McCarthy died from acute hepatitis brought on by alcoholism in 1957, his usefulness to the civil virus was long past.

McCarthy's tactics are similar to a combination of tactics seen in chickenpox, herpes, rabies or HIV. Some of these viruses infect the nervous system of the organism where they can stay largely hidden from the immune system – a stealth virus. The nervous system itself becomes a reservoir for the virus to launch attacks as in the case of the chickenpox virus causing shingles in adulthood. Others, like HIV, attack the immune system itself. By disabling key components of the immune system, the virus can propagate unnoticed and unimpeded.

> "Question with boldness even the existence of a God; because, if there be one, he must more approve of the homage of reason than that of blindfolded fear."
>
> -Thomas Jefferson, 3rd U.S. President

The Taliban used these two tactics in Afghanistan. Lenin and Stalin used them in Russia. Hitler used them as well. The key is to freeze the opposition in such a way that any rational response can be labeled as the "enemy." Hitler labeled anyone who opposed him as communist; Stalin labeled opposition as capitalist or fascist and the Taliban labels opponents as ungodly, as does the new civil religion. The approach precludes rational discussion or logical examination of the facts. Because infected people cannot see the folly of their religious

---

13   To see the degree to which Eisenhower was connected to McCarthy, we can note that despite warnings and his own suspicions about McCarthy, he still greeted him at the Wisconsin border and invited him to ride with him through the state on his 1952 whistle stop campaign tour. Eisenhower significantly changed a major speech he gave in Green Bay so as not to offend McCarthy or his supporters. Tom Wicker, *Dwight D. Eisenhower: The American Presidents Series*. (Times Books, 2002), 15.

14   An alcoholic, McCarthy's lies, manipulations and deceit caused havoc in the country and hurt many careers. Ultimately, he was called to task by the Senate and censured. This was only the third time in Senate history that a Senator has been censured.

beliefs, a simple call to that part of their brain leaves them susceptible to non-rational arguments.

The new civil religion in this country has adopted these two tactics. First, the virus attacks the immune system. Second, it infects the political body. Anyone who questions this new civil religion is called ungodly, anti-Christian and unpatriotic. This freezes the immune response, renders the opposition helpless and eliminates rational debate based on science or reason. Ann Coulter, the ultra right wing talk show hostess, has used this tactic continuously. Her book, *Godless: The Church of Liberalism*, is a good example.

Michele Bachmann, Republican congresswoman from Minnesota, successfully won her congressional seat by continually referring to her opponent's lack of religious belief and patriotism, even as she hid her own fundamentalist beliefs and associations. She is an extremely conservative Christian who advocates promoting religious curriculum in public schools, religious home schooling at public expense, teaching creationism in the classroom and many other stealth efforts to assist the civil virus in taking over public monies for education. She denied connections with fundamentalist groups who supported her but gave speeches at their conferences. Her law degree is from Oral Roberts University, something she was reluctant to disclose and tried to keep under wraps during her early career. Religion drives her politics even as she denies it.[15] When asked about her religious beliefs mixing with her politics, Bachmann responded, "I believe in God. But that is not really relevant." Bachmann is just one example of many who gained their seat in Congress with stealth tactics and a clear religious agenda.

> "We did not get our freedom from the church. The great truth, that all men are by nature free, was never told on Sinai's barren crags, nor by the lonely shores of Galilee."
>
> **-Robert Ingersoll**

The Kansas Republican Party effectively used the same two tactics to get a slate of candidates elected to the State Board of Education twice.

---

15   City Pages, *Somebody Say Oh Lord!* [article on-line] (23 February 2005, accessed 21 November 2008); available from http://citypages.com/databank/26/1264/article12984.asp; Internet.

Once elected, these individuals proceeded to work hard to infect the entire educational system with the civil virus. Their antics included redefining science so intelligent design could be taught in the public schools.

In any society with a strong god virus, code words and phrases are often used to trigger behavioral responses. Communism, sex education, same-sex marriage and prayer in school have all been code words used to activate viral behavior in the infected. Once activated, the virus controls the discussion. During the 30-years war, 1618-1648, Catholics used "godless Protestantism" and Protestants used "papist" as code words to rally the infected. In Plymouth Bay colony in the late 1600s, Puritan settlers used the code words "papist," "witchcraft," "corruption of youth" and "wrath of god." In all these cases, the code words trigger unthinking behavioral responses in defense or advancement of the god virus.

The key is for the god virus to disable rational discussion and appeal to the primitive fears of those who are already programmed to respond strongly to viral threats. When large groups within the electorate are infected with more parasitic or aggressive viruses, it is easier to evoke strong responses. There is no doubt that Moral Majority, Focus on the Family or 700 Club[16] members are infected with an aggressive god virus. The leaders of these groups take the already programmed followers and train them to respond in more specific and politically focused ways.

> "I have examined all the known superstitions of the world, and I do not find in our particular superstition of Christianity one redeeming feature. They are all alike founded on fables and mythology."
>
> -Thomas Jefferson

At the individual level, the god virus disables the ability to think critically about one's own religion. At the civil level, the virus disables the ability to have reasonable and rational discussion of national issues. As we will see in Chapter 5, the primary focus of any major virus is to control biological reproduction, sex and marriage. This is true whether the religion is Islam, Hindu, Christian or any number of others. The new civil religion virus focuses on this as well. James Dobson's Focus on the Family is a good

---

16   James Dobson and Pat Robertson's respective national religious organizations. Both have an underlying political focus similar to the Moral Majority.

example. The focus is on the family as a vehicle for propagation of the new civil religion. It does not focus on all families, only on families that are best fit to perpetuate the virus.

To better understand how this works, let's look at the concept of viral load in biology.

Viral Load

Viral load refers to the concentration of virus found in the system; that is, the amount of virus the body is supporting and feeding. When viral load becomes heavy enough, symptoms appear and pathology becomes evident.

Most societies contain some religious viral load. Attacks on the U.S. immune system in recent decades have left it vulnerable to viral infection in ways not seen since the founding of the nation.

The power of the new civil religion is so strong that presidential candidates are required to wear their religious credentials on their sleeves. Do people today condemn deist Thomas Jefferson for his unabashed refusal to endorse a day of Thanksgiving and prayer? He was blatantly called an Atheist, which he did not deny, yet he served with distinction as the author of the Declaration of Independence, ambassador to France and secretary of state, and was elected twice to the presidency. Could that happen today? Do people condemn Lincoln's derision of most religion and refusal to join any religion? Did anyone care about Teddy Roosevelt's church attendance? Did anyone care if Woodrow Wilson or Franklin Roosevelt prayed every day? None of these past presidents would pass muster with the civil virus today. The viral load is heavy in the political nervous system. The infection is chronic and will affect the political discourse of the nation for decades to come.

The European Uncoupling

Cultural infection is not necessarily inevitable or permanent. European countries have much weaker if non-existent civil religions. Cultures can disinfect themselves to some degree. The following is a joke that circulates in the once devoutly Catholic areas of Belgium, "People go to church four times in their life, and they must be carried in two of them." The average person in Europe is a non-believer or a nominal believer.[17] As a result, religion does not play as big a part in European politics as it does in the United States. European culture effectively uncoupled from religion after WWII. Where religion was once a dividing line between people, it now is non-existent. Catholics, Protestants and Jews all intermarry, whereas they once fought interminable wars.

A 2005 lead story in *USA Today* was headlined "Religion takes a back seat in Western Europe."[18] Even in Ireland, the most religious country, church attendance has fallen from 85% to 60% since 1975. Other countries have seen even greater declines. A 2000 Swedish-based study of western European countries shows that 60% of the French say they "never" or "practically never" attend church. In Britain it was 55%, other countries ranged from 29% to 48%. In contrast, the United States shows only 16% saying they never or practically never attend church.

> "Send me money, send me green, Heaven you will meet, Make a contribution and you'll get a better seat ..."
>
> -Metallica

It took two world wars for the Europeans to realize that the prayers of millions of people were not answered. It doesn't take much intelligence to see that the god isn't working too well when 92 million people die in two world wars,[19] or to see the complicity and cooperation of the Pope, Lutheran clergy and Christians with Hitler during WWII.[20]

This dramatic uncoupling of religion from culture has reduced the influence of the Pope and various religious leaders. It has also left Europeans wondering what causes Americans to be so easily influenced and manipulated by such leaders. Many find it difficult to understand why U.S. presidents and politicians have to display their religious credentials to get elected.

---

17 This is changing in some areas with a high influx of Muslim immigrants. In this case, the Muslim virus is beginning to exert influence.

18 USA Today, *Religion takes a back seat in Western Europe* [article on-line] (11 August 2005, accessed 21 November 2008); available from http://www.usatoday.com/news/world/2005-08-10-europe-religion-cover_x.htm; Internet.

19 Estimates of the dead in WWI are 20 million and WWII, 72 million.

20 John Cornwell, *Hitler's Pope: The Secret History of Pius XII* (Viking, 1999). Daniel Goldhagen, *Hitler's Willing Executioners: Ordinary Germans and the Holocaust* (Vintage, 1997).

Today, Europe faces a new challenge with the influx of Muslim immigrants. From British Muslims demanding recognition of Shariah law, to veils being worn by government female employees, to demands that Islamic creationism be taught, Islam has started the process of infecting European culture. It looks remarkably like the demands American fundamentalists make in the U.S. political arena. Muslims are demanding recognition of their religious practices and beliefs in the public domain without respect for secular law or long-standing church-state separation principles.

Ironically, the U.S. creationist movement worked closely with the fundamentalist Islamists in Turkey to force the teaching of creationism in Turkish public schools.[21] This amazing alliance has now fostered a movement in Europe with Islamists demanding that creationism be taught in European schools. In the coming years, Europe will find itself in a new struggle with the Islamic god virus, a struggle similar to fundamentalist infection of the American political system.

Economics and Religion?

The Ayatollahs of Iran are not too concerned with Iran's economic prosperity. Fundamentalist Islam would take a culture back to the Stone Age if it allowed more successful propagation. This is something that well-educated, less virally infected individuals in the West do not understand. How can someone not be concerned with economic progress? Just read a few verses in the New Testament to get a clue:

> *Sell all that ye have, and give alms; provide yourselves bags which wax not old, a treasure in the heavens that faileth not, where no thief approacheth, neither moth corrupteth.*
>
> *-Luke 12:33*

> *It is easier for a camel to go through the eye of a needle, than for a rich man to enter into the kingdom of God.*
>
> *-Mark 10:25*

---

21   In the 1980s, Duane Gish and John Morris of the Institute for Creation Research traveled to Turkey to help Islamists develop a creationist curriculum for Turkish public schools. The curriculum was adopted in the early 1990s.

For the love of money is the root of all evil: which while some coveted after, they have erred from the faith, and pierced themselves through with many sorrows.

-1 Timothy 6:10

Look at the economic model of Mohammed! In Islam, usury[22] is a sin. The same was true in the Catholicism of the Middle Ages.[23] Indeed, it continued to be a sin until recent times. What kind of an economic model prohibits charging interest? Interest is a fundamental principle of capitalism. Religions generally have very primitive economic models. The virus is primarily interested in propagation economics. To illustrate this, let's look specifically at Christian church economics and budgets.

Church Economics, or the 5% Solution

When people give to their religious organization, they are frequently reminded of the good their money will do. If we examine the "good" objectively, we need to ask, Where does the money actually go? For our discussion I will define "good" as a result that gives more food, resources or functional information to a target needy group. Examples would be an African village that receives equipment and training to generate their own electricity or regenerate their farmland for better, more sustainable agriculture. It could also be functional schooling for children who would otherwise not gain an education. The term "functional schooling" refers to education that teaches real-world skills like math, languages, reading, writing, financial management or vocational skills – as opposed to memorization of the Koran or the Bible.

Using this definition, a Madrasah that spends 80% of its recourses teaching the Koran to children and 20% teaching them to read and do math would, at best, be providing 20% of a functional education. A Christian

---

22   The practice of charging interest on loans - not the modern definition of excessive interest, although that was a problem in the Middle Ages as well.

23   The 12th canon of the First Council of Carthage (345) and the 36th canon of the Council of Aix (789) have declared it to be reprehensible even for laymen to make money by lending at interest. As for the Jews, for a long time they could act with impunity in such matters. The Fourth Council of the Lateran (1215), c. 27, only forbids them to exact excessive interest. *The Catholic Encyclopedia,* 1912 Volume XV.

school that spends 30% of its resources teaching the Bible and religion is only 70% functional.

When I was in college, my church had a beautiful modern gymnasium with room for two basketball courts. It was rarely used. I noticed this and proposed to the church board an after-school recreation program for the neighborhood children. The immediate response was, "This is an older neighborhood, the children that come will be lower class and may tear up our beautiful facility."

After months of talk, writing and rewriting proposals, I finally got my church to pay me minimum wage for two hours each afternoon so I could open the facility to the neighborhood. The program was a success. We averaged 25 or more kids per day with no more wear and tear on the facility than would be expected from regular use. The program lasted until I could no longer manage it. I could find no one to take my place so it closed and the gym saw no other community use for the next 30 years.

How much was my church paying for these beautiful facilities? How much value did anyone receive from them? Only a tiny fraction of my church's money went to anything that could be defined as functional. This beautiful resource was largely wasted. The religion was clearly not interested in serving the larger community.

An article in the summer 2000 *Church Leadership Journal* discussed how churches should budget.[24] Here are its recommendations.

Church Budgets

- Staff compensation – 40-60% (60-65% must be strongly communicated as "Staffed to Grow")
- Facilities – 20%
- Debt retirement – 8%
- Utilities – 5%
- Maintenance – 5%
- Insurance – 6%
- Missions – 16% (50/50 between foreign & domestic)
- Programs – 10% (no salaries here)
- Administration – 6%
- Denominational fees – 5%

---

24   "Church Budgets & Pastor's Salary Packages," *Church Leadership Journal* XXI, no. 3 (Summer 2000): 88.

The numbers add up to more than 121% – these are their figures, not mine. A quick look at this budget recommendation shows a lot of money going to things that do not directly help anyone. Assuming my church and others like it follow a similar budget, let's look at how much "good" my church was doing. Subtracting all monies used in viral propagation, staff compensation is largely dedicated to religious instruction. Facilities and debt retirement are mostly related to religious work as are administration and denominational fees. My church had a Boy Scout troop that met in the building, but only Protestant Christian boys were allowed. Maybe the boys learned some functional skills, but as a member of that particular troop, I saw a lot of "God and country" type of instruction, including prayer and blatant Protestant propaganda.

Considering the tough time I had getting the board to let a few neighborhood kids use the gym, we can see that non-religious use of the facilities were uncommon. From these examples we can conclude that virtually all costs associated with facilities, utilities, maintenance and insurance were religious in nature. No one was using the facilities to teach children reading or to help elderly people find a cool place to go in the summer heat when they had no air conditioning.

That leaves programs and missions. Most of the programs involved teaching children religious ideas: Christmas and Easter programs, summer Bible school programs, church camps, adult and children's choir, etc., all were primarily viral focused. Were people better able to deal with real life, finances, disease, childcare or a host of other daily problems as a result? While my church claimed to teach these things, most of what passed for religious instruction in childcare, finances, disease control or prevention was heavily steeped in non-functional religious ideas and

> "Religion supports nobody. It has to be supported. It produces no wheat, no corn; it ploughs no land; it fells no forests. It is a perpetual mendicant. It lives on the labors of others, and then has the arrogance to pretend that it supports the giver."
>
> -Robert Ingersoll

downright superstition. Things like prayer vigils for cancer victims, abstinence classes for teens, Christian financial management, among a host of other activities, all focused on the virus. These activities healed no one from cancer. I saw no evidence of unwanted pregnancy prevention. Church members would have been better off taking a secular financial management class, where they would not have been pressured to give 10% to the church.

How about missions? Most mission money goes to those who are preaching a religion's specific message. My parents became missionaries after they retired, so I was able to get an inside picture of what other missionaries were doing with the money given them. By far the greatest amount of money went to paying missionary preachers and building churches. I saw very little of that money going to teach children to read, how to manage a small farm more effectively or how to build local infrastructure and conserve resources. Instead, thousands of Bibles and religious tracts were purchased and distributed, religious services were conducted, hundreds of people were baptized, hundreds of children memorized scripture verses, but at the end of the day, there was little done to bring people out of their poverty or provide them with the skills needed to live in a fast-moving modern world.

I heard returning missionaries give talks on the good they were doing. They did not talk about teaching people to run their own business or raising more educated children. They did not tell of higher-quality produce from farms and gardens or less disease and death. Instead, they proclaimed the glory of god in new churches built, numbers of people baptized, numbers of Bibles distributed, as well as men and women who graduated from the missionary Bible college.

Of the money given to a religious organization, something less (probably far less) than 5% provides something of functional value. Most money is directed to ensuring propagation of the religion. How does that compare to a non-religious charitable organization? The Better Business Bureau Wise Giving Alliance recommends that charitable organizations spend 65% of their budgets on program activities and 35% on fundraising and administration. In general, a dollar given to a religious organization will result in 5 cents going to some functional activity. A dollar given to the Red Cross, United Way, Habitat for Humanity, or many other non-religious organizations will result in a 65 cent functional benefit if they follow the Better Business Bureau guidelines. By comparison, church giving is a 95% investment in the virus and 5% in people.

Taking this analysis to other religious organizations like the 700 Club, the Moral Majority or Focus on the Family, hundreds of millions of dollars are given to these organizations with little or no accountability. The money offers almost no functional good. It is channeled into activities that include a good deal of political activity in the service of the new civil religion. James Dobson's Focus on the Family spends vast amounts getting a thinly veiled political message out to legislators and politicians. Dobson sent out an email to his entire flock in August 2008 asking them to pray for rain over Invesco Field to force Barack Obama to cancel his Democratic Party acceptance speech. His prayers were not answered, but it was a clear use of his organization as a political entity in promotion of the virus. Ironically, the next week hurricane Gustav disrupted the Republican Convention. Dobson did not seem to see his god's hand in that.

Church financial scandals over the years have also shown how easily money can be misused. Headlines like these seem to populate the news media on a regular basis:

- Money Scandal in Florida Diocese Adds to Church Woes
- Church Corruption, Questionable Gifts Live On, Long After Bakker Scandal
- Raising Financial Integrity Amid Money Scandals[25]

With no financial accountability or oversight, many churches and ministries are free of any real constraints unlike non-religious charitable organizations.

The civil religion has developed very successful ways to fund its propagation through these organizations. Most have loose or no affiliation with long-established denominations. Neither Dobson's Focus on the Family, Falwell's Moral Majority, Pat Robertson's 700 Club or the Christian Coalition have effective financial oversight and seem exempt to tax law that disallows religious organizations to engage in political activity. These groups are the treasury of the new civil religion.

Summary

Uncoupling from tribal religion allows religion the ability to infect any culture. Once the culture is infected, the viral religion seeks to bind the religion to it. The American civil religion has been taken over by a more

---

25   "Raising Financial Integrity Amid Money Scandals," *NY Times*, 9 October 2000 and "Raising Financial Integrity Amid Money Scandals," *Christian Post Reporter*, 3 January 2008 and Associated Baptist Press, *Church corruption, questionable gifts live on, long after Bakker scandal* [article online] (24 July 2007, accessed 22 November 2008); available from http://www.abpnews.com/index. php?option=com_content&task=view&id=2789&Itemid=120; Internet.

virulent god virus and used to gain influence and control over the political system and, ultimately, to bind with the culture. The political immune system is greatly weakened by the high viral load it bears, to the degree that religion is now a test for public office. The tactics of this virulent virus are designed to freeze rational discussion and weaken immune responses, thus paving the way for permanent infection of both the political structure and culture. The god virus infects a culture like it infects individuals. While not an economic entity or a political entity, it can and will use economic or political avenues for propagation. The god virus is not interested in economics. Politics and economics are merely tools for the virus.

CHAPTER 4:

GOD LOVES YOU – THE GUILT THAT BINDS

"You are digging for the answers, Until your fingers bleed, To satisfy the hunger, To satiate the need. They feed you on the guilt, To keep you humble and low, Some man and myth they made up, A thousand years ago."
-**Melissa Etheridge, "Silent Legacy" song on the *Yes, I Am* album**

Overview

Now that we have looked at the social and political aspects of the god virus, we can examine the more personal and psychological components. We will start with the role guilt plays in propagation of many religions. How does it drive behavior? How is it used to bind people to the god virus?

Father Joseph

When I was in private clinical practice, a 48-year-old Catholic priest came to me for counseling (I'll call him Father Joseph although that was not his real name). He was very concerned that things be kept quiet and confidential. He was concerned that he masturbated and used pornography. He had enormous guilt over this but could not stop himself. He showed signs of depression. After several sessions, he admitted that he had self-destructive thoughts. *"I think it would be better if I were dead than to have these terrible thoughts and urges. I have them even as I am saying Mass or counseling a couple."*

He felt there was no one in the Church to talk to, so he sought me out. As I listened to him, he sounded like a normal human male. A male with no approved sexual outlet. All his training and education had taught him that masturbation and pornography were deadly sins. It pained me to listen to his anxiety and guilt. The best I could do was let him know that all he told me sounded quite normal, that the human male sex drive is extremely powerful and that it is not natural to suppress it in this manner.

Through many tough therapy sessions, we worked on the huge conflict between his training and his natural drives. I am not sure he resolved the issue but about six months later, another priest called for counseling, having been referred by Father Joseph. A similar scenario unfolded.

Both of these very dedicated and caring men were distraught over something that is perfectly normal. Their conflicts, guilt and anxiety led them to depression – and worse. The religious virus had so taken over their minds and programmed them sexually that both of these men could see no way out. I don't know what happened to either of them once our sessions were finished. Despite a life of dedication, they could never be good enough. Acting on normal drives was enough to condemn them in their own eyes as well as the eyes of their god.

You Are Never Good Enough

Guilt has become one of the greatest tools of western religions. Of course, guilt existed long before Judaism, Christianity or Islam, but these religions have developed highly effective, guilt-inducing techniques. Individual guilt development harnesses energy for the god virus. That is, the more guilt you feel, the more you look to your religion to salve the guilt. When the priest or minister helps you through some of your guilt, the relief is huge. It binds you even closer to the religion, ready for the next time you feel guilt.

Guilt is a never-ending, circular road that maintains viral control and prevents you from expending energy in positive ways. The only way to truly eliminate religious guilt is to surrender to the virus. After you have surrendered, if you still feel guilty, that is proof that you have not truly surrendered. It is a self-reinforcing and imprisoning viral method. You are never good enough. Father Joseph was as dedicated as or more than most people in any religion, yet he still was not good enough.

> "Guilt: Punishing yourself before God doesn't."
> -Alan Cohen

From the time I was 11 years old through early adulthood, I prayed fervently for god to take away my urge to masturbate. Parents, church, Sunday School teachers, even gym teachers, implied that masturbation was sinful and that you would go to hell for doing it. As much as I prayed, I did it even more. Even at church camp! God surely would send me to hell, if not kill me outright for masturbating at church camp! What is more, I was masturbating to the thought of the sexy preacher's daughter at the camp. That had to be a deadly sin.

Not until I came across Masters and Johnson's *Human Sexual Response* (1966) and later Alex Comfort's *The Joy of Sex* (1972) did I realize that my religion was totally wrong about masturbation. As I quickly lost my guilt, I soon began asking, "What else could be wrong in my religion?"

You may have had similar experiences with religious guilt if you were raised in a religious environment. Religious guilt is generally negative and something to be closely examined in your journey to break free of the god virus. The problem is that programming can be so deep you don't realize you are functioning out of religious guilt.

Double Messages in Religion

One of the challenges of adulthood is dealing constructively with past viral programming. Religious indoctrination is extremely confusing, with hundreds of mixed messages received throughout a lifetime. Many people carry the remnants of childhood programming in their day-to-day adult lives. Here are some of the beliefs people are exposed to in their early training.

- God loves you, but he will send you to hell if you don't do exactly as he says.
- God loves you and gave you an intelligent brain to see and understand his creation, but you will be condemned for asking prohibited questions.
- God loves you and gave you incredibly pleasurable sex, but you dare not use it except within strict limitations.
- God loves you and your children. If you do anything to lead them astray, he will punish you. (Mark 9:42)
- Allah loves you and created women as beautiful creatures that you are forbidden to enjoy, except in marriage and behind closed doors.
- Allah loves you, but you may not see heaven if you don't obey your husband and get along with his other wives.
- God loves you and wants you to prosper. If you are poor or hungry, you must be doing something wrong in his eyes.
- God loves you; he causes you pain, grief, disasters, floods, hurricanes, and much more so you will see his will, repent and do as you are commanded.
- God loves you, he created Satan to tempt and test you.
- God loves you. That is why he makes it so hard to resist temptation and stay on the straight and narrow.
- God loves you. He loves all Christians. He hates Muslims, Buddhists, Hindus, and all those who deny him.
- God loves you, so you should reject your parents, children, neighbors, relatives or anyone who is a hopeless non-believer.[1]
- God loves you, but if you get divorced, you are unclean. (Matt 5:31-32)

---

[1] "If any man come to me, and hate not his father, and mother, and wife, and children, and brethren, and sisters, yea, and his own life also, he cannot be my disciple" (Luke 14:26).

- God loves you. That is why he sent his son to die. Millions of other people have died in his name and you should be willing to as well.[2]
- God loves you, but you were born unclean and can never be clean without god.

These kinds of messages create a double bind. A feeling that you are never good enough and that it is your own fault no matter how hard you try. That is why you need Jesus, Allah, or some other god to lean on. "All have sinned and fallen short of the glory of god" (Rom. 3:23 NIV). This is a great god virus quote. It sets up every believer for ultimate failure. God made you imperfect and the only way to feel good about yourself is through him.

Listen to just a few minutes of preachers like Paul Washer, a popular youth preacher with dozens of YouTube™ videos. Virtually every minute of his videos is about guilt, damnation and apostasy. The only path that will save you is to follow exactly his prescription.[3]

The religious life is one of constant circles and backtracking. You were born a sinner and always are a sinner. You must seek forgiveness from the god that made you unclean from birth. Get forgiven. Be born again, but don't sin again.

When you sin, it starts all over. You must seek forgiveness. The virus implants a constant sense of guilt and unworthiness that cannot be eradicated. Much as Shakespeare's Lady Macbeth wandered the halls of Dunsinane Castle washing her hands and saying, "Out damned spot," religion creates an indelible emotional spot that cannot be washed away.

The Guilt Cycle

Many children are taught to feel guilt from parents, relatives or authority figures. Such childhood guilt is often more related to parental insecurity or emotional problems than any bad behavior on the part of the child. Consider a mother who makes her child feel guilty for not kissing her good night or a

---

2   "If anyone would come after me, he must deny himself and take up his cross and follow me. For whoever wants to save his life will lose it, but whoever loses his life for me and for the gospel will save it" (Mark 8:34-35 (NIV)).

3   Search for any Paul Washer video to get a similar message. You Tube™, *Shocking Youth Message Stuns Hearers* [video on-line] (accessed 21 November 2008); available from http://www.youtube.com/watch?v=IR-25FpnOko&feature=related; Internet.

grandparent who chides a child for not calling him every day. These kinds of behaviors can create guilt in a child that is carried into adulthood.

The drive to reduce or eliminate guilt is very strong. As a result, people may do any number of things. They may call their grandparent every day well into adulthood. They may never miss an opportunity to kiss their mother. They may find themselves going out of their way to get parental approval well into adulthood. Many an adult has discovered that some of the guilt they feel came from inappropriate childhood training. Any psychotherapist's practice is full of people learning to deal with childhood guilt. Guilt is a powerful psychological force, and the drive to reduce guilt can motivate behavior for years, if not an entire lifetime. Understanding the drive to reduce guilt will help us understand the power of religion.

The Religious Guilt Cycle

Martin Luther himself struggled with this guilt cycle. His solution, while creative, did little to assuage the guilt of the millions of Lutherans who have followed him over the centuries. Luther's solution was to see salvation through faith, not works. His was a response to the Catholic tendency to believe one could purchase indulgences or do good works to achieve salvation. Luther's focus on faith made things worse since faith is so difficult to assess. It is easy to keep a ledger of good works or to believe that some god has an accounting department. But what does faith mean? How do you know Christ has bestowed his grace upon you? Luther's doctrine of justification, while designed to assuage his own guilt and provide a pathway to god, was just as much an uncertain morass. His certainty in salvation allowed him to condemn the Jews and encourage their persecution and to suppress the peasants' rebellion of 1524-25. He seemed to feel no guilt about that. Unfortunately for his followers, Luther's solution provided only more uncertainty about salvation and the commensurate guilt at falling short.

For a contemporary example, we need look no further than Mother Theresa. While alive, she was held up as a standard for faith and religious piety. In death, her letters reveal a very uncertain woman, torn by guilt. If even a future saint is not free of guilt, where does that leave an ordinary follower?

Have you ever noticed that the addict, alcoholic, smoker and/or religious addict generally feels guilty over his or her behavior but then goes right on doing it? They might say:

- "I promised my kids I would stop smoking. Now I am smoking even more."
- "I told myself I wouldn't drink last night, then I closed the bar down."
- "I promised god I would spend more time with my kids; now I find myself working overtime every week."
- "When they passed the offering plate, I felt guilty when I only put $10 in."
- "I promised god I would not masturbate again, but then I did it twice this week."
- "I promised god I wouldn't have sex with my girlfriend until we were married, but she tempted me, and we did it last night."

Rather than change the behaviors that caused the guilt in the first place, guilt often drives people to do more of the same. The guiltier you feel, the more you seek to assuage your guilt with the very thing that induced it in the first place. This creates a perfect feedback loop from which you cannot escape without outside help. Much like a computer that gets into a loop and freezes, your brain gets caught in a guilt loop that only gets worse.

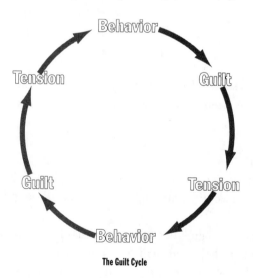

The Guilt Cycle

As you are bearing this emotional burden of guilt, along comes the priest, rabbi or minister with the promise of help. He or she accomplishes this by breaking the loop and running it through the religion and back to you. It goes like this:

> You can't conquer this by yourself. Give yourself to god and he will help you conquer it. You will overcome your weakness and get forgiven for your sins. You will no longer have to live with this burden of guilt.

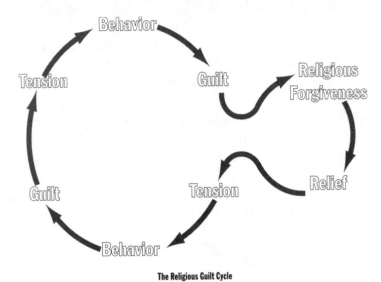

The Religious Guilt Cycle

The effect is some relief but at a high cost. Each guilt-forgiveness cycle imbeds the virus deeper and deeper, making it harder and harder to get relief.

Two Kinds of Guilt

It is difficult to see guilt as independent of religion. To better understand this, let's look at two different kinds of guilt: socialized guilt and religious guilt.

You feel socialized guilt because of socialization in a given culture. Many people feel guilty if they accidentally run a stop sign. My grandmother could feel guilty for days about forgetting to call someone on his or her birthday. I have felt great guilt over forgetting an important anniversary or event. This is the guilt we feel for violating a social norm – socialized guilt.

In many cases, socialized guilt is no better than religious guilt, but there are times when socialized guilt is good. Guilt is appropriate when you violate someone else. An example would be if you cheated or intentionally hurt someone. I would hope that you feel guilt. The inability to feel guilt in this situation is a sign of a sociopathic personality.

Lesser things may evoke appropriate guilt. Any act that hurts another person, such as malicious gossip, cheating or stealing from someone are all things that should create appropriate guilt and a desire to not do it again. I don't want to have a relationship with a person who does not feel guilty about that kind of behavior. It has nothing to do with religion but everything to do with good socialization in our culture.

Some things are only guilt-inducing in the context of religion; indeed of a certain religion. Thus, you wouldn't feel guilty if you weren't a believer or you might not feel guilty if you believed a different religion. Masturbation is a clear example of how religion uses a normal human behavior to induce guilt. Catholic doctrine condemns masturbation, and most fundamentalist Protestant groups subtly condemn it, as does Islam. On the other hand, if you were a Wiccan, Quaker or Unitarian, you would think nothing of it.

Masturbation is such a basic and universal activity that control of it cannot be the real objective. Even the fundamentalist James Dobson, founder of Focus on the Family, admits that 99% of adolescent boys masturbate. He admits it is a useless fight in adolescents, but claims masturbation has no place in marriage because it detracts from sex in the marriage.

What is the purpose of prohibiting something that cannot realistically be prohibited, something that cannot even be monitored? The purpose is to create religious guilt. Even though it cannot be stopped, it invokes the guilt cycle that bonds the person closer to the religion, as we just saw.

Family Values, Religious Guilt and Shame

In the political climate in the United States today, the term "family values" is thrown around a lot. Its meaning is a code for a strict or narrow interpretation of family and sexual behavior. Hence, family values do not include gay marriage. Family values means no to abortion. It means abstinence and not discussing birth control with teenagers and much more. Most religions espouse some kind of family values, but often not for the good of the family. Family values means, "The family has value for the virus." When the family does not have viral value, the virus may dissolve the family. The focus is on keeping the family as an intact, functional vector for the virus. Choosing a religion different from your family's may get you ostracized, if not worse. A Muslim woman who tries to convert to Hinduism may be the target of a so-called "honor killing." An adult Nazarene who converts to Buddhism will not be treated the same in his or her family as the sibling who becomes a Nazarene minister. A Nazarene child who expresses interest in becoming a Catholic might get a quick and unpleasant dose of "family values."

Family shame is a key part of this viral defense. A family member who acts against the virus shames the whole family. The virus hygienically deals with this by making the family feel intense shame, which in turn motivates the family to take action against the offending member.

In Luke 12:51-53 Jesus said,

> Do you suppose that I came to grant peace on earth: I tell you, no, but rather division: for from now on five members in one household will be divided, three against two, and two against three. They will be divided, father against son, and son against father; mother against daughter, and daughter against mother; mother-in-law against daughter-in-law, and daughter-in-law against mother-in-law.

Cutting people out of the family and social structure is an effective way to intimidate those who remain to keep in line, thereby eliminating potential contamination.

In the United States, strong fundamentalist families often disassociate themselves from wayward family members. A Mormon child who becomes a Catholic might not find a welcome place back at home. To choose another virus is to invite tension and rift within the family as the dominant religion fights to expel the invading one.

Imagine a strong Baptist family and a wayward adult child who is now a Pagan. At Thanksgiving dinner the Pagan adult child gathers the family around the table and says, "Let us all say a prayer to the goddess for the bounty she has bestowed upon us this past year." How would the family react to that prayer? What would happen next year? How might they treat him or her?

The virus is concerned with the value of the family for propagation; anything else gets a strong negative response. Families have a hard time staying together when there is a strong opposing viral infection in one or more key members.

Parenthood and the God Virus

Rational parents want to raise well-educated and well-balanced children with full logical and critical faculties. But once infected, no parent is rational. As a result, parents are unable to teach their children critical thinking skills with respect to religion, especially their particular religion.

As any parent knows, children have minds of their own. They are susceptible to whatever god viruses are present in the environment, especially fundamentalist and cult viruses. One of the many parental nightmares is to have an adolescent or young adult enticed into a cult and taken from the family. No wonder most religions spend a good deal of time and resources on giving the young defenses against other cults and religions. Many a youth sermon or Sunday School lesson carefully teaches the particulars of a given religion as opposed to others. In my denomination, it was baptism by immersion. Unless someone was baptized properly, she may not go to heaven. They also taught that baptizing a baby was immoral (à la Catholics) since a baby cannot make a decision for Christ. The Baptists taught that you had to be baptized by them or it didn't count.

Amish Rumspringa a Viral Inoculation

At age 16, Amish children go out to live in the world until they decide to be baptized. After some time of running around (called *rumspringa)*, the young adult must make a decision to be baptized or forever live outside of the Amish community, and largely out of contact with family.

The Amish practice of rumspringa is brilliant. Tom Shachtman, in his book *Rumspringa: To Be or Not to Be Amish*, writes:

> The Amish count on the rumspringa process to inoculate youth against the strong pull of the forbidden by dosing them with the vaccine of a little worldly experience. Their gamble is also based on the notion that there is no firmer adhesive bond to a faith and way of life than a bond freely chosen, in this case chosen after rumspringa and having sampled some of the available alternative ways of living.[4]

It is interesting to note that Shachtman uses the viral metaphor. The Amish recognize the need to inoculate their children and recognize that like

---

4   Tom Shachtman, *Rumspringa: To Be or Not to Be Amish* (Farrar, Straus and Giroux, LLC., 2006), 1.

some kinds of inoculation, it may not take, or it may backfire and cause the disease. Nevertheless, it is considered worth the risk of losing some.

For the Amish, the children who do not come back are best gone so as not to have a problem in their midst. Expulsion of a defective host keeps the virus healthy and strong. The fact that most Amish children are wholly unprepared for the modern world almost guarantees that they will come back. Thus 80-90% return to be baptized and stay the rest of their lives. Some would say that it is cruel to abandon those who don't come back. But this is not a relevant concern. The issue is not humane treatment of people, but purity of the Amish god virus. If that means some must be sacrificed, so be it. Religions have functioned in this way for centuries. Shunning, ostracism and excommunication are all versions of maintaining viral purity.

Parental Behavior, Guilt and Shame

Parents worry that they need to do the best in the eyes of other parents. This is more related to shame than guilt.[5] Heaven forbid that the minister would think I was not raising my child in the way of Christ! Is he in Sunday school every Sunday? Is she doing her Bible lessons each week? Am I reading the right religious books to him or her before bed? The virus feeds off anxiety, guilt and shame to ensure that every available resource is used to infect the child.

During childrearing years, parents can become virtual slaves of the virus. Their every move and action is examined by other church members, the minister, Sunday School teachers and other parents. The greatest fear of an infected parent is that he or she will fail in sufficiently infecting the child. What if my child grows up and leaves the church? What if my daughter disgraces the family by getting pregnant without being married? What if my son is gay? All of these thoughts evoke tremendous fear that is closely related to the shame of letting god down and failing in the eyes of others.

"It is impossible to convince some children that there is no Santa Claus. They do not fully grasp reality."

-R. Reboulet

---

5   For purposes of our discussion we will define guilt as something contained inside yourself. Shame, on the other hand, requires you to be concerned about what others think. You might feel guilty if you stole something, but you would feel shame if your mother, minister or neighbor found out.

Many parental anxieties center on sexual shame and guilt. However, rather than open discussions about sex and reproduction, often there is no discussion at all. The guilt associated with sexuality is so strong in many highly religious families that it prevents rational discussion between parent and child. The more guilt a parent feels, the less she can actually communicate with the child about sex. This is one of the by-products of sex-negative religion, which we will discuss in Chapter 5.

We must remember that the virus does not have a mind or will of its own; it strives only to propagate and uses whatever resources necessary to accomplish that goal, the same way that a biological virus or parasite works. The more infected the parents are, the more resources the virus can steal for propagation. Most god viruses thrive on guilt, although they claim otherwise. The greater the guilt, the more parents are willing to throw whatever resources they have into ensuring their children are completely infected. The ultimate resource allocation is home schooling or religious private schooling. Not that home schooling or private schooling is bad; they are one way guilt-driven parents ensure they do not fail the virus. God is always watching, so you'd better do all you can to ensure that other viruses or secularism don't influence your children.

Extended Family and Children

Raising children can be difficult, especially if you have parents, grandparents, aunts and uncles looking over your shoulder saying things like: "When will he be baptized?" "He is going to a Jewish school, isn't he?" "I'm sure she would do much better in the Christian preschool." "You aren't going to let your Catholic grandmother send him to parochial school are you? We have a much better Baptist school right here in town."

There isn't an easy way to deal with such interference except to let those around you know your views of religion and what is and is not acceptable with respect to their involvement with your children.

> "Religion is comparable to a childhood neurosis."
>
> -Sigmund Freud

A friend of mine had non-religious children who stayed with fundamentalist grandparents for the summer. During their visit, the children were subjected to all sorts of scare tactics, including such notions as, "When the curtains move at night, it is the devil trying to get in your room. Pray to god to keep him away." The children were upset for months afterwards. This type of behavior was quite common in my own upbringing and continues in many families and churches today. The purpose is to open the fear portal in children for more effective infection.

While most people respect parents' rights to raise their children the way they see fit, something brings out the worst in relatives when you say you are raising your children religion-free. It is almost a license for them to do all they can to undermine your goal and infect the child with their god virus. It is as if they see the child as fair game since you are not doing your viral job. Non-religious parents need to recognize this kind of viral behavior in family and friends and deal with it in a way that helps their children see the virus at work.

One particularly effective method is to expose children to a wide range of religions early and often. With wide exposure come opportunities for discussion about the effects of different religions on people and behavior. Children with such exposure see for themselves the wide variety of strange religious beliefs and behaviors. When my children were 10 and 14 years old, we took the Mormon tour in Salt Lake City. The subsequent discussion lasted for hours. I said very little as they talked back and forth about the experience. With little help from me, they concluded that Mormons have a lot of strange ideas like baptism of people after they are dead, holy underwear, becoming gods themselves and much more.

The task is not to protect the child completely from god viruses. It is to help the child observe and interpret religious behavior in many different religions. This may become an inoculation of sorts against many, if not all, religions.

As I reflect on my upbringing, I realize that my family did nearly everything possible to thoroughly infect me. We attended church three times a week, Bible study, prayer meetings, choir, youth group, Bible camp and much more. My aunt and uncle were Quakers with a very different worldview. They were suspect by the rest of the family because they went to a much more "liberal" church.

My aunt and uncle took a low-key approach, never discussing any religious views until I specifically asked them when I was in my late teens. They were open, understanding and quite informative. In talking with them I realized how much my parents and grandparents had not told me. There was a whole world of religious ideas that I had never heard of! I can thank these saintly people for opening my eyes. It wasn't what they told me. It was the accepting way they listened and discussed without getting fundamentalist and dogmatic. I had never experienced that with my family or anyone else. The result was a life-long openness to questioning religion, including writing this book.

Summary

Religion uses mixed messages as a tool to create a cycle of guilt. The natural drive of people to reduce guilt feelings allows religion to step in and promise an elimination of guilt. Since the ploy rarely works perfectly, people are soon back for another fix of guilt reduction. The net effect is to drive people closer to the virus.

Recognize the role guilt plays in religious infection and learn to deal with it proactively. Learn to eliminate residual religious guilt and put appropriate boundaries around socialized guilt. Regular exposure of children to many different religions may be the best inoculation against infection by many different types of god viruses. Openly discuss the beliefs and behavior of various religions and be aware of the guilt cycle in yourself.

CHAPTER 5:

SEX AND THE GOD VIRUS

"Life in Lubbock, Texas, taught me two things. One is that God loves you and you're going to burn in hell. The other is that sex is the most awful, dirty thing on the face of the earth and you should save it for someone you love."

-Butch Hancock

Overview

This chapter will explore the methods religions use to control sex and sexuality. The most successful religions have learned how to utilize this powerful human drive in the interest of religious propagation. We will look at the effects of sex-negative and sex-positive religions in terms of a spectrum of control. To understand this important topic, let's start by looking at the experience of a woman we will call Sara.

Sara's Story

I met Sara and her lesbian partner in a restaurant to talk about her experience in leaving the Jehovah's Witnesses. She had been a lifelong member of the church and had married her sweetheart from the church when they were 18 years old. In subsequent years they had three children. Over the years of marriage, Sara felt a huge hole in her life. She had a high sex drive, but she was not attracted to her husband and found herself always thinking about women. At the same time, her husband, more and more frustrated with her lack of responsiveness to him, became abusive physically and emotionally.

Sara was torn between her training as a good Jehovah's Witness wife and her deep desire for a woman's touch. Everyone told her it was her duty to satisfy and obey her husband; the Bible was clear that she was committing a sin against god by denying her husband.

Through years of soul searching, Sara finally made the decision to take her children and leave her husband. Years of church teaching had taught her to fear and mistrust the courts and the government, so she used none of the resources available to women in her situation. She saved up money, rented a place far from her husband and stole away one night with her children.

After only a few weeks, her husband and a group of elders from the church appeared at her doorstep and took the children. She appealed to her husband to let her keep her children, but she was informed that the church had conducted a trial and that she was now disfellowshipped from the church. No one could have contact with her, including her own children. Their father would have sole custody and would not allow any contact with her.

Sara went into a deep depression. Not trusting the courts, she made no legal claims for her children. And having been taught that psychologists were evil, she refused to talk with anyone who could help her with her depression.

Not until she met her partner was she able to begin climbing out of her depression and take some positive action for her life and children. She enrolled in college, went to court to get partial custody and began living with her partner. Her partner was supportive and understanding, but her deep programming made it all but impossible for Sara to see any options for herself or her children. It took several years before she was able to begin seeing alternative ways of thinking and behaving.

Her life is still difficult, especially with her children. The court order for visitation rights and custody is undermined and thwarted at every turn by church elders who tell her children they will be disfellowshipped if they talk to their mother. Only one child talks with her, secretly calling late at night after everyone is in bed. If Sara calls, no one answers or whoever answers the phone immediately hangs up.

Sexual Control

Many would chalk Sara's story up to the programming of a cult, but it is not so easily dismissed. This type of programming is present in most other religions. Many evangelical and fundamentalist groups have a deep distrust of psychologists and psychiatrists and believe homosexuality is a major sin. Catholics try to keep children in the Catholic fold by demanding they be raised Catholic, even in a mixed marriage. They prohibit same-sex relationships and masturbation and allow sex only within marriage with no artificial birth control. Priests and nuns are expected to deny natural and normal drives for very unnatural and decidedly not normal celibacy. Nazarenes shun anyone who is openly homosexual or in a same-sex relation-ship, distrust secular psychologists and preach sexual abstinence outside of marriage. Muslims may stone to death married men and women who have affairs and persecute homosexuals. A woman may not be seen with a man who is not her relative in most Muslim countries. Hindus place great shame on a woman who divorces or has sex before marriage. Public kissing is a crime in India.[1] All major religions and most minor ones sanction women who express their sexuality in ways proscribed by the religion. The difference

1   When actor Richard Gere kissed his cohost on an Indian charity show, the Associated Press reported April 26, 2007, "NEW DELHI – A court issued arrest warrants for Hollywood actor Richard Gere and Bollywood star Shilpa Shetty on Thursday, saying their kiss at a public function transgressed all limits of vulgarity." MSNBC, *Indian court issues warrant for Gere over kiss* [article on-line] (26 April 2007, accessed 20 November 2008); available from http://www.msnbc.msn.com/id/18328425/; Internet.

between Jehovah's Witnesses and other religions is only in degree. As we will see in this chapter, sexual control is a key religious strategy.

The Sex-Negative Environment

This graphic is not a scientific one, but it is an attempt to place the various god viruses on a spectrum from sex-negative to sex-positive. The primary factors in the rating are degree of control and severity of sanctions. Punishment by death, for sexual practices, is found in Islam, Hindu and the Old Testament.

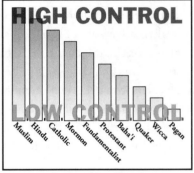

Spectrum of Sexual Control

Some current Christian fundamentalists would like more Old Testament-type sanctions in our society. Here are some verses that they cite.

And the man that committeth adultery with another man's wife, even he that committeth adultery with his neighbour's wife, the adulterer and the adulteress shall surely be put to death.

-Leviticus 20:10

If a man also lie with mankind, as he lieth with a woman, both of them have committed an abomination: they shall surely be put to death; their blood shall be upon them.

-Leviticus 20:13

Following these passages, we might find that a significant portion of the current U.S. population might be subject to the death penalty.

Catholicism thrives in a sex-negative environment. Protestants also create a sex-negative environment but can survive with something less. Islam is among the most sex-negative religions. Sex-negative religions seek to control all aspects of sexuality; from masturbation to the role of women; from conception to sexual pleasure. The measure of sex negativity is the degree of sanction for violation. For example, if a young girl in Saudi Arabia is seen with a non-related boy she is not married to, both may be stoned to death.

Death is an extreme sanction, but other sanctions are almost as effective. A recent news item from Iraq told of a young girl who had been raped by her cousin, thereby shaming her family. Her father drove her to the Syrian border and dropped her off, thus expelling her from the family. She subsequently was forced into prostitution in Syria. Shaming one's family leads to serious, if not lethal, sanctions in much of Islam.[2] Most major religions maintain restrictions on females such as prohibiting them from becoming clergy, stronger sanctions for sexual violations, enforcing stricter dress codes and requiring certain practices during menstruation and childbirth. Female guilt is assumed in many religions as illustrated by the biblical story of Eve tempting Adam in the Garden of Eden.

As we saw in the last chapter, Christianity uses guilt to ensure sexual and marriage fidelity as well as fidelity to the church. Guilt is an important cause of sexual dysfunction in males and females. Sex for pleasure, from the religion's point of view, is a waste of energy, especially if it detracts from propagation of the god virus. For that reason, sexual pleasure is seen as suspect in Catholicism.

The Catholic virus has put a huge number of its eggs in the sexual basket – celibacy, abstinence, no abortion, no contraceptives, Mary was a virgin, Jesus was not married and non-sexual, none of the Apostles was married (all were non-sexual).[3] St. Paul was obsessed with sexual control, as were most of the ante-Nicene fathers.[4]

Other forms of control can be seen in dress, especially that of women. It is interesting that the habit of Catholic nuns resembles the burka of Islam.

---

2   See the discussion of guilt and shame in Chapter 4. For a recent example, a 57-yr.-old father murdered his 16-yr.-old daughter for refusing to wear a hijab to school in Toronto, Canada, Dec. 11, 2007. If it is happening in Toronto, one can imagine that it is far more likely happening in deeply infected countries like Pakistan where it might not even be seen as newsworthy. ABC News, *Slain Over Hijab? Father Allegedly Strangles Daughter Over Head Scarf* [article on-line] (12 December 2007, accessed 21 November 2008); available from http://www.abcnews.go.com/GMA/story?id=3987812; Internet.

3   Most Christians cannot see the oddity of a non-married Jesus walking around Israel with 12 unmarried men following him. What would you think if you heard of an unmarried man wandering around town with 12 full grown, unmarried men following him and hanging on his every word. It is also amusing to ask Christians how Christ could be called rabbi when only married men could have that title in ancient Israel.

4   *Ante-Nicene Fathers* are a collection of non-Biblical Christian writings of early church fathers up to 325 CE when the Nicene Creed was adopted. Early Church Fathers, *Ante-Nicene Fathers* [book on-line] (accessed 21 November 2008); available from http://www.ccel.org/fathers.html; Internet.

Both are symbolic of sexual control and surrender to a male figure – husband, father, pope, Jesus, bishop, etc.

James Dobson's Focus on the Family can be analyzed using this model. It quickly becomes apparent that it is not *"Focus on the Family,"* but *"Focus on the Virus."* The family is the vehicle for the virus.

"Of all the sexual aberrations, chastity is the strangest."

-Anatole France

Guilt based on strict interpretations of sexuality in the Bible is the hallmark of James Dobson's viral efforts. A religion has no problem disbanding the family if it does not meet the religion's needs. Christianity as well as most other religions may support divorce if one parent falls away from the virus or converts to another. Better to have the parents divorce than risk infection of the children from another virus.

Gil Alexander-Moegerle was a founding member of Focus on the Family until he got divorced. In his book *James Dobson's War on America*[5], Alexander-Moegerle discusses his removal from Focus on the Family. James Dobson viewed Alexander-Moegerle's divorce as an affront– the Dobson virus could not allow him to remain and potentially pollute the organization.

Religion-Friendly Environment

Religions seek to create an environment that makes it easy to propagate. In most cases, religious propagation is closely tied to biological propagation. As the family goes, so goes the virus. The virus must make sure that it is passed on to the next generation. For this reason, it creates an environment where it can ensure the young will be infected as efficiently as possible.

The Family

First, the religion must try to ensure that the family consists only of virally infected parents. All major religions place some sanctions on marriage outside the faith. Hindus do not marry Muslims, Muslims are not allowed to marry Christians, and so forth. The sanction can be so strong as to invoke the death penalty if violated. In recent years, the news media

5   James Dobson, *War on America* (Prometheus Books, 1997).

have been full of examples of Islamic girls being killed by their families for merely wanting to marry a non-Muslim. Marriage between related sects may also be prohibited. Catholics are discouraged from marrying Protestants. Shii'a Muslims are discouraged from marrying Sunni. The Druze disown anyone who marries outside the religion. Mormons do all they can to ensure people marry within the faith.

In "mixed marriages," a demand is often made with respect to raising the children. For example, the Catholic Church insists on children being raised as Catholic in a Protestant-Catholic union. Couples may be refused a Catholic wedding or sacraments if they fail to make this commitment.

The Children

Second, the religion must ensure that the young are properly infected. This is a time-consuming and resource-intense requirement. For this reason the religion focuses on keeping the family unit intact so it can concentrate resources on infecting the next generation. Many mechanisms are brought to bear on this task, such as:

- Parental guilt, "Am I doing enough to teach my children about god?"
- Sexual fidelity, "Have I taught my children how important fidelity is to god?"
- Viral flooding, "Am I keeping my children busy with religious activities to ensure other religions or secularism can't influence them?"
- Viral isolation, "Am I doing all I can to keep my children heavily involved with other children at religious school, church camp, Sunday School, Wednesday prayer meeting, Thursday Bible study, youth choir, scripture memorization," etc.

In a pluralistic society, it is difficult to isolate children from other religions. Until complete infection is achieved, there is a constant danger of attack and infection by another religion, or worse, the idea of no religion. Infection is much more difficult in a pluralistic society than in a more monolithic culture like a village in Afghanistan. When a religion is completely bound to the culture, the culture is brought into the service of the virus with more powerful effect. Since there are no competing religions in the environment, isolation has already been achieved. This makes infection efficient. It also makes it easier to impose heavy sanctions on wayward children.

Control of Sexuality and Reproduction

Uncontrolled sexuality prevents efficient propagation and risks wasting viral resources. The primary way to control sexuality is to create an environment of prohibition and sanction. All of the major western religions and many of the eastern ones have learned to harness the power of the sex drive in service of the god. This is probably the single biggest factor in the evolutionary success of the major religions today: They learned how to harness the power of the sex drive for viral propagation through the use of guilt, suppression of women's sexuality, indoctrination of the youth in the virtues of having sex only inside of marriage and other techniques.

> "Of the delights of this world, man cares most for sexual intercourse, yet he has left it out of his heaven."
>
> -Mark Twain

Within this context, the religion takes over the mating and reproductive parts of the brain and directs specific behavior. This behavior is NOT what humans are inclined to do and may, in fact, be dramatically different. It may not even be in the best interest of the individual, but it is in the best interest of the god virus. Religion is not concerned with the pleasure aspect of sex. The concern is propagation. This leads to a sex-negative environment that is friendly to the virus.

Sexual Suicide

The power of the virus is so great that it can induce sexual suicide. For example, Catholic priests and nuns are required to stop all sexual activity, including masturbation. Normal, biological drives are redirected or eliminated to allow the vector to focus all its energy on viral reproduction. The process creates huge psychological and emotional issues for priests and nuns, leading many to pathological behaviors.

While Islam does not make such unnatural requirements as celibacy, young suicide bombers in Islam in fact commit sexual suicide by giving up their reproductive capacity in the service of the virus. Virtually all suicide bombers in recent years have been young and clearly of reproductive age.

Reproductive Control

Control of reproduction is a fundamental strategy of the virus. Where the strategy is undermined, the virus is weakened. For example, god viruses are weak in Europe where access to birth control and abortion is higher than in the rest of the world. Ironically, the abortion rate is far lower in Europe, as are teenage pregnancies. Many religions in the United States claim that they want to reduce abortions and teenage pregnancy, yet in areas where religion is strongest, the rates are far higher. Don't be fooled by the viral words; if reduction in abortion or teen pregnancy were the goal, it could be achieved in a few years. Look at the following statistics:[6]

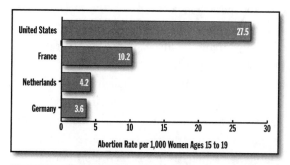

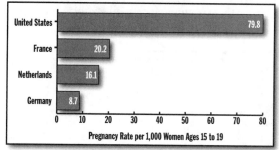

The god virus is not concerned with abortion or teen pregnancy; it is concerned with propagation.

God viruses are highly threatened by low birthrates. That is why many of the Christian viruses are so focused on the question of when life begins. Abortion and birth control limit the potential hosts. Availability of abortion and birth control tends to push the environment toward the more sex-positive.

---

6   Sue Alford and Ammie N. Feijoo, *Adolescent Sexual Health in Europe and the U.S.—Why the Difference?* 2nd ed.(Advocates for Youth, 2001).

None of the major god viruses does well in sex-positive environments. Without sexual control, they face a serious challenge to their existence. Can you imagine the Catholic virus as sex-positive? Could you imagine Pope Benedict XVI, Pat Robertson, James Dobson, Billy Graham, etc., carrying a sex-positive message of openness, sex as pleasure to be enjoyed to please yourself and your partner or partners as long as it is consensual and safe?

I don't think you will hear those sermons soon. As vectors of the virus, their job is to ensure sufficient sexual control to propagate the virus. Therefore, their sermons will be about abstinence, self-control, the terrors of abortion, the scandal of the Plan B drug and the horror of giving birth control pills or condoms to teenagers. Sexual control is the message, and it cannot be otherwise for a sex-negative virus.

Abstinence-only programs, advocated for by American fundamentalists, are a miserable failure according to most research. Nevertheless, these programs have the effect of creating sufficient guilt and fear in children to keep them bonded to the religion. The research shows these programs don't reduce pregnancies, sexually transmitted diseases, age of first sexual intercourse or the number of partners.[7] As can be seen by the accompanying graph from a large meta-analysis of abstinence programs, there is no difference between abstinence groups and control groups. The groups are virtually identical.

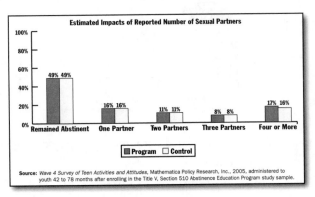

Estimated Impacts of Reported Number of Sexual Partners

Source: Wave 4 Survey of Teen Activities and Attitudes, Mathematica Policy Research, Inc., 2005, administered to youth 42 to 78 months after enrolling in the Title V, Section 510 Abstinence Education Program study sample.

7   Mathematica Policy Research funded by the U.S. Congress to evaluate abstinence-only programs found, "That youth in the four evaluated programs were no more likely than youth not in the programs to have abstained from sex in the four to six years after they began participating in the study. Youth in both groups who reported having had sex also had similar numbers of sexual partners and had initiated sex at the same average age." See Mathematica Policy Research, Inc., *Impacts of Four Abstinence Education Prgroams* [article on-line] (accessed 22 November 2008); available from http://www.mathematica-mpr.com/abstinencereport.asp; Internet.

If these programs are so clearly ineffective, why does the government keep funding them with millions of dollars? It gives the new civil virus and allied god viruses a direct line to children in the public school systems. Abstinence is not about sex, it is about exposure to the god virus with the assistance of public school money. If reduction of pregnancies and sexually transmitted diseases were the real goal, why not emulate non-religious European societies where all of these are far lower? Most of Europe has cheap birth control and appropriate sex education for the young. These ideas are anathema to the god virus because every hour of training in an abstinence-only program helps imbed the guilt cycle into young persons so they will become more infected. They then get relief from their guilt through the god virus.

The Special Case of the Clergy

The Catholic Church has only recently been brought to task over the priest sexual abuse scandal, but Protestant churches have a scandal of their own that is yet to be fully exposed. In a January 23, 2007, article about two North Texas Baptist pastors accused of molesting young girls, Joe Trull, professor at New Orleans Baptist Theological Seminary, had this to say:

> Possibly if you looked at the statistics, I think there would be a higher incidence in nondenominational and Baptist churches because of a lack of accountability. Pastors there have not been prepared by their denomination. There is still that attitude in seminaries and colleges that prepare these pastors that they're on their own. It's that CEO mentality. And the thing that grieves me is that there's absolutely no sense of how this misconduct affects other ministers and churches.

Trull goes on to say:

> In other denominations, [pastors] know that if charges are brought, truth will win out, Doctors and psychologists know if they are caught, they will lose their credentials and there will probably be a malpractice suit. Most Baptists and nondenominational ministers know that "If I get caught, I can move to California and start a new church." [8]

Oversight is extremely difficult in these independent churches, as their

---

8   Associated Baptist Press, *Baptist churches more vulnerable to clergy sex abuse, experts say* [article on-line] (23 January 2007, accessed 21 November 2008); available from http://www.abpnews.com/index.php?option=com_content&task=view&id=1753&Itemid=120; Internet.

governing structures are entirely dependent on the vector. While they have governing boards, the vector is largely responsible for their appointment and knows how to run someone off who asks too many questions.

Continuing from the article mentioned above, Trull writes:

> Christa Brown, an attorney from Austin, Texas, insists that Baptist leaders would not let autonomy delay action if they truly cared about protecting children from abuse. Brown works with the Survivors Network of those Abused by Priests, an organization of clergy sexual-abuse survivors. She maintains www.stopbaptistpredators.org and has asked the Baptist General Convention of Texas to hire independent experts to investigate sexual-abuse cases within the convention.

This is strong proof that the virus cares more about protecting the preacher than stopping abuse. It is unlikely that Baptists will take effective action in the near future. The independent model has been extremely effective. I have personally witnessed five different congregations torn apart by pastoral sexual affairs.[9] In each case, the pastor was able to overcome those who asked too many questions and eliminate them. After several incidents occurring over 10-15 years, in each case, the minister was finally forced out but only moved on to continue his predatory behavior at another church.

"When I get down on my knees, it is not to pray."

-Madonna

Those infected have great difficulty seeing inappropriate behavior in the vector. They are virtually hypnotized into believing he can do no major wrong.[10] Sex-negative religion sets everyone up for some kind of fall: whether divorce, sexual abuse, sexual dysfunction, pedophilia or adultery.

9   The congregations represented Presbyterian, Baptist and the Independent Christian Church.

10   How often do we see headlines like this: "Megachurch leader in mega-sized sex scandal"? It seems to happen quite often. This was the headline on *MSNBC*, Nov. 19, 2007, about an Atlanta mega church where sexual misconduct of the founding minister was ignored for 35 years despite many complaints by women, until DNA testing found that his "nephew" was really his son by his brother's wife. Sounds like something out of the Old Testament. MSNBC, *Megachurch leader in mega-sized scandal* [article on-line] (19 November 2007, accessed 21 November 2008); available from http://today.msnbc.msn.com/id/21888916; Internet.

As in the crime of rape, clergy sexual abuse is more about power than sex. Especially in mega churches,[11] charismatic vectors have a great deal of power and opportunity.[12]

From an anthropological perspective, ministers in mega churches clearly put themselves in an alpha male role within the social structure. In most cases, they have total control over who serves on the board and the budget. As the alpha male, the minister tends to attract a high proportion of females to males. The sex ratio in these churches is female dominated, as high as 60/40, and even higher in some. Within this context, the alpha male has groupies, like a rock band; females who work hard to get close to the alpha male by working on committees, volunteering, etc. The high-status male is sexually attractive to the females, which gives him the opportunity to choose the most desirable among his followers.

It may sound far-fetched, but it fits well within the structure of any polygamous society. In early Mormon culture, the high-status alpha males got the pick of the desirable females. In Middle Eastern Islamic culture alpha males, those who are tribal leaders or have huge resources clearly, have the pick of desirable females. A cursory study of many cults from Jim Jones' People's Temple to Warren Jeffs' Fundamentalist Church of Jesus Christ of Latter Day Saints reveals the same pattern. Mega churches produce a tribal group with similar hierarchies and some of the same sexual patterns. Power is the aphrodisiac, as Henry Kissinger once suggested.

Some religions are sex-positive, but they keep a low profile in the United States. These include Wiccan and Pagan groups.[13] Some of the less mainstream groups like Unitarians, Quakers and Baha'i are also more sex-positive, but they are still quite influenced by the larger sex-negative culture. They may not use the reproductive control strategy as much, if at all.

---

11   A mega church is generally defined as having 2,000 or more attendees, on average, each Sunday. A mega church might have tens of thousands of members.

12   Dee Ann Miller, *The Truth About Malarkey* (1stbooks.com, 2000) is a disturbing account of Protestant clergy abuse and the trials of the victims as they seek justice.

13   For an excellent article on a sex positive philosophy see Charlie Glickman, *Electronic Journal of Human Sexuality* Vol. 3 [journal on-line] (6 July 2000, accessed 21 November 2008); available from http://www.ejhs.org/volume3/sexpositive.htm; Internet.

Living in a Sex-Negative Environment

If you are a non-religious person you can no more avoid the influence of the sex-negative environment than a fish can avoid pollution in its stream. From access to the Plan B drug or abortion, to the fundamentalist pharmacist refusing to sell birth control, to public funding for abstinence programs, you are affected by religious control efforts all around you.

"The basic religious idea of all patriarchal religions is the negation of sexual need."
-Wilhelm Reich

As a psychologist, I see a good deal of sexual dysfunction directly related to religious guilt. When parents are afraid to have sex while the children are in the house, they are displaying specific viral behaviors. I have worked with many women who simply cannot enjoy sex if the children are anywhere near. The message is that children should not be exposed to their parents' sexual nature. Where did this come from?

Not many centuries ago in our culture and in many cultures still today, parents had sex in the same room where the children slept. How does a Hutu couple living in a one-room hut avoid sexual activity within sight or hearing of their children? How did nomadic Cheyenne or Shawnee Indians hide sexual activity from their children while living in a tent? How did Iroquois Indians living in an open lodge have sex? The answer is, they didn't worry a lot about it. Sex was seen as a normal, natural activity. These cultures don't make a display of sex, but they don't try and hide it from their children. Hiding implies guilt. Remember the story of Adam and Eve? They hid their nakedness from god.

Before the invasion of the hugely successful, sex-negative viruses of Christianity and Islam, many cultures were more sex-positive.[14] The rise of non-culturally based viral religions has led to sex-negative environments in many areas of the world that were once sex-positive. As a sex-negative religion invades a culture, it strongly influences the mores and taboos of that culture. Whether the old mores and taboos were more sex-positive or sex-negative, they inevitably move toward the sex-negative after the invasion.

14   See such studies as Margaret Mead, *Coming of Age in Samoa* (Harper Perennial, January 1, 1971) and Ruth Benedict, *Patterns of Culture* 1 edition (Mariner Books, January 26, 2006) for examples of both sex-positive and sex-negative cultures that largely predate western influences.

Christian missionaries for two thousand years have been invading native cultures and creating sex-negative environments. The process has been so complete that even cultures that have not converted to one of the main religions have felt the influence. Just as smallpox hit communities in the Americas that had never seen a white man, sex-negative ideas have passed to societies who never saw a missionary.

A look at the missionary influence on Hawaiian culture is a classic study. Marriage was loosely defined, and sexual contact was not particularly regulated. One author notes that before contact with westerners, Hawaiians put more control on eating than on sexual practices.[15] As an example of sex-positive culture, sexual ethnographer Milton Diamond wrote:

> As they slept in the family house, they observed their parents having coitus. Among the Mangaian Islanders, as it was described by Marshall (1971, p. 108), probably is similar to the 'privacy' that was found in Hawai'i and elsewhere in Polynesia: A Mangaian may copulate, at any age, in the single room of a hut that contains from five to fifteen family members of all ages — as have his ancestors before him. His daughter may receive and make love with each of her varied nightly suitors in the same room ... But under most conditions, all of this takes place without social notice: everyone seems to be looking in another direction.

Your Sexuality

If you were raised in the United States, you were raised in a sex-negative culture and probably have some sex-negative ideas and behaviors. Eliminating the virus from your life means taking a hard look at activities that may be outside your consciousness. Compare your attitudes to those of pre-contact Hawaiians. It does not appear that they experienced any guilt over sex. That would be one benchmark against which to measure our cultural and individual sex negativity.

You probably received feelings of guilt about sex from parents, priests, nuns, preachers and Sunday school teachers. How does a Pope give anyone advice on sex? A Pope, priest or nun teaching about sex or giving advice

---

15   Milton Diamond, Ph.D., *Sexual Behavior in Pre-Contact Hawai'i: A Sexological Ethnography* (University of Hawai'i at Manoa, 2004), 43.

on sexual matters seems rather odd. Almost as bad is an uptight, highly sex-negative fundamentalist preacher telling you about the joys of Christian sex! What kind of advice does Ted Haggard have that would enhance your marriage?[16]

Here are some questions to ask yourself as you try to diagnose the effects of the virus on you today:

- How does my sex-negative training affect my relationships?
- How does it affect my enjoyment of sex with others or with myself?
- Do I find myself fixated on things that were prohibited by my training?
- How much is my own sexual response affected by guilt or early viral training?
- What did my parents teach me about sex?
- Were my parents open and direct with me concerning sex as I was maturing, or were they secretive and nervous around sexual issues?
- Have I had sexual partners who were strongly affected by the virus? How did that affect my relationship and ability to enjoy them?
- Do I feel guilt about masturbation and pleasuring self?
- Am I self-conscious about my body in ways that may be related to the virus?

Evolution of the Sexual Culture

While our culture is largely sex-negative, there have been some sex-positive developments. It began slowly with the women's suffrage movement and Elizabeth Cady Stanton and Susan B. Anthony's efforts to teach and support family planning in the late 1800s. With birth control in 1960s, feminism in the 1970s, the gay movement of the 1990s, and the polyamory[17] movement in recent times, many pockets of sex-positive culture have developed.

---

16   For those who don't recall, Ted Haggard was the fundamentalist minister who was caught with a Denver male prostitute in 2007. He went through six weeks of counseling with other fundamentalist ministers who report that he is completely cured, an amazing feat only a fundamentalist could achieve.

17   Polyamory (from Greek [poly, meaning many or several] and Latin amor [literally "love"]) is the desire, practice or acceptance of having more than one loving, intimate relationship at a time with the full knowledge and consent of everyone involved.

Fundamentalism has tried to control sexual expression but has not been very effective. In fact, there seems to be a correlation between pornography and fundamentalism. When I was in graduate school in Nashville in the 1970s there was a church on every block, but far more porn shops than in northern cities with far fewer churches. The same was true than in Houston, Atlanta and other southern cities. Porn seems to follow fundamentalism. I guess the more they rant against something, the more people want it.

> "The more prohibitions you have, the less virtuous people will be."
>
> -Tao Te Ching

While the religious right rails against pornography, no reputable study has established a link between pornography and child or sexual abuse. At the same time, some interesting research shows a clear link between parental sexual abuse and religious orientation. According to research by Brown and Bohn:

> A disturbing fact continues to surface in sex abuse research. The first best predictor of abuse is alcohol or drug addiction in the father. But the second best predictor is conservative religiosity, accompanied by parental belief in traditional male-female roles. This means that if you want to know which children are most likely to be sexually abused by their father, the second most significant clue is whether or not the parents belong to a conservative religious group with traditional role beliefs and rigid sexual attitudes. [18]

The god virus is very active in trying to define what sexuality is permitted and what is not. From homosexuality to monogamy, religion continually tries to limit or eliminate normal human sexual expression. Question the training and assumptions you received from your family and culture and decide for yourself what is appropriate sexual expression, not what the god virus wants.

I have always been open-minded about sex, but one day when I was about 35 years old, a non-theist friend of mine challenged me on some homophobic

---

18   Carolyn Holderread Heggen, *Sexual Abuse in Christian Homes and Churches* (Herald Press, 1993), 73.

statements I made. I immediately denied that I was homophobic and got quite defensive. I started thinking about his observation and reflecting on some of my childhood training and experiences. I soon realized that I had some irrational ideas about homosexuality that had been hidden from my awareness.

As I go through life, I find these little surprises quite invigorating. Just when I think I have figured myself out, something comes along to upset the apple cart. This is the stuff of real life. Hard as it is sometimes, it is powerful and empowering, so embrace it when the opportunity presents itself.

Summary

Modern, highly evolved religions propagate best in a sex-negative environment to maximize viral control over the family unit and to guarantee efficient propagation. The alleged focus on the family is really focus on the god virus. Indeed, the virus will disband the family to preserve its ability to propagate. Do not be fooled by the words; look at the effects of a given behavior from opposition to birth control to guilt in the bedroom, the viral purpose is propagation – not the happiness of its victims. The virus is so powerful that it can literally shut down sexual drive and reproduction, as in nuns and priests or married couples that severely restrict their sexual practices. Sex-positive god viruses are rare and getting more so with the invasion of the powerful sex-negative western religions. Take a good look at yourself, and you may find a surprising amount of residual indoctrination in your behavior.

CHAPTER 6:
THE MYTH OF UNCHANGING MORALITY

"Human beings will find a balanced situation when they do good things not because God says it, but because they feel like doing them."
-Olof Palme, Swedish Prime Minister (1927-1986)

Overview

We will examine the constant changing and shifting of values within the god virus. Despite protestations, religious values change constantly and in dramatic forms at times. The myth of unchanging morality is useful in maintaining viral dominance while adjusting to the local culture.

Morality and Values

Where do you get your values and morals? You got much of what you believe from your family and those responsible for your upbringing. While you may have been told that these beliefs and morals came from some religious source, in reality, they came from your culture. A cursory look at religious values and morals over the last few centuries shows that religion changes with the culture. For example, what was once a terrible sin is now widely accepted – divorce. St. Paul said a woman should always have her head covered in church.[1] Who remembers when women had to cover their head in a Protestant or Catholic Church? It was still a requirement in Catholicism as recently as 1969.

No virus could survive if it did not adjust morality through time. For example, the Catholic Church would be far smaller if it kept its 1950s moral view of divorce. Annulments increased from a base of 368 in 1969 to an average exceeding 40,000 per year in the United States through the 1990s to present. Since the 1990s, the United States, with only 4% of all Catholics in the world, accounted for 75% of all annulments. It is clear that the Catholic Church is adjusting the morality of divorce, to compete in the U.S. culture. Without the annulments, those people and their financial resources might be lost to the church.[2]

Some Baptist churches would be empty if they maintained their 1900s prohibition on gambling and alcohol.[3] Better to have tithing Baptist gamblers than no church at all, I guess. Where would the Episcopal Church be if it maintained its 1900s view of women? How would Southern Baptists

---

1   But every woman who has her head uncovered while praying or prophesying, disgraces her head ...(1 Corinthians 11:5).

2   Clarence J. Hettinger, "The End of the Annulment Explosion," *Homiletic*, vol. 3 (2007): 96.

3   This is reminiscent of The Four Great Religious Truths: 1. Muslims do not recognize the Jews as God's chosen people. 2. Jews do not recognize Jesus as the Messiah. 3. Protestants do not recognize the pope as the leader of the Christian world. 4. Baptists do not recognize each other at Hooters and liquor stores.

fare if they had maintained their slavery views of 1850? Southern Baptists were founded as a proslavery church in the great schism over Northern anti-slavery activity.[4] They had dozens of biblical verses to back them up. A reading of the Bible shows no divine problem with slavery. Nowhere does the Bible say slavery is wrong, so the antislavery ideas could not have come from Christians, despite their claims. Instead, antislavery sentiment came from enlightenment ideas that were adopted by some religious groups and not by others. If morality is unchanging, why is there no proslavery church anymore? How could something so important suddenly lose its moral imperative? It is similar to the revelation of god to the Mormon president in 1890 that officially ended polygamy, allowing Utah to become a state. When the culture changes, the religion changes, or it loses influence and the ability to propagate. Huge moral issues seem to disappear in the face of cultural change.

As late as the 1960s, it was a scandal for women to wear pants, especially inside a church. Could a Nazarene church keep its doors open if women who wear pants were excluded from the rolls? Sex before marriage was unthinkable in most churches in the 1930s. I wonder how many U.S. Catholics have premarital sex now? Premarital sex does not get the attention and condemnation it once did in many religious groups. Dramatically declining birth rates among Catholics would indicate that birth control is no longer seen as a sin despite church doctrine. The Church does not appear to sanction anyone for using birth control.

Religious leaders who claim morality is unchanging have short memories. Groups like the Society of Christians for the Restoration of Old Testament Morality make broad claims about unchanging morality, yet few would propose a full enforcement of biblical passages that endorse slavery, stoning of adulterers or witches. Few would banish those who believe the Latin Vulgate Bible is of higher authority than the King James Version, etc. Even among so-called fundamentalists, the religion does whatever it needs in order to survive in the biota of surrounding god viruses and culture.

---

4   One of the primary reasons for the split in 1841 was the right of Baptist ministers to hold slaves. Slavery was not disavowed in the Southern Baptist Convention until June 20, 1995, in a formal "Declaration of Repentance". Christian Century, *SBC renounces racist past - Southern Baptist Convention* [article on-line] (5 July 1995, accessed 22 November 2008); available from http://findarticles.com/p/articles/mi_m1058/is_n21_v112/ai_17332136/pg_1; Internet.

The Myth of Moral Superiority

Study after study over the last 20 years has shown no correlation between morality and religiosity.[5,6] We will explore some of this research, but first let's set the stage.

Most people claim that they are more moral because of their religion. Yet most religious people I have observed seem no more moral than those who are not religious, despite their claims. Religious people seem to break the Ten Commandments just as much as those who never go to church, but we should put this to some kind of statistical test. For example, who gets divorced more? Who commits crimes or goes to prison more? These might be rough estimates of relative morality.

> "God is the immemorial refuge of the incompetent, the helpless, the miserable. They find not only sanctuary in His arms, but also a kind of superiority, soothing to their macerated egos; He will set them above their betters."
>
> -H. L. Mencken

If someone were to make the claim that religion makes him more moral, I would ask, "How would you prove that?" The answer is usually something along the lines of "religiosity equals morality." The more religious a person is, the more moral he is in his eyes and maybe in the eyes of other religious people of his faith. The standard is anything but objective. In fact, people are hard pressed to define the standard of morality. That is, the god virus makes a person feel more moral without regard to objective reality.

Baptists, Catholics, Nazarenes and Muslims all make claims that their religion makes them more moral. If this were true, we would expect to see some evidence of this in commonly available statistics on crime.

5   Bart Duriez and Bart Soenens, "Religiosity, moral attitudes and moral competence: A critical investigation of the religiosity-morality relation, Department of Psychology, Katholieke Universiteit Leuven, Belgium," *International Journal of Behavioral Development* Vol. 30, No. 1, (2006): 76-83.

6   B. Duriez, "Are religious people nicer people? Taking a closer look at the religion-empathy relationship," *Mental Health, Religion & Culture* 7, no.3 (2004): 249-254.

Crime and Religion

Many a Sunday morning sermon has derided the immorality of atheism or secular humanists. Yet self-identified Atheists are almost non-existent in the prison system. Self-identified Baptists, Evangelicals, Catholics and Muslims show prison rates roughly equal to the general population. There is no statistical evidence that religious affiliation has any positive effect on criminal behavior. Baptists seem to commit crimes roughly equal to their numbers in the general population. The same is true for Catholics, Methodists and most others.

The one group that seems to be underrepresented in the prison population is self-identified Atheists and Agnostics.[7] One study found Atheists are .5% of the federal prison population out of a possible 6-10% in the general population; that is, they are underrepresented by 70%. Some prison surveys find no Atheists at all.[8] Europe, with its much higher number of Atheists, doesn't have nearly the crime rate of the United States. Pagans and Wiccans, who are vilified by Christians as immoral because they don't worship the Christian god, don't make up a higher percentage of the prison population. If criminal behavior is a rough measure of morality, then many groups seem to have morality at least equal to that of Christians. To date there is no evidence that religion or religiosity has a positive impact on crime.

> "He that will not reason is a bigot; he that cannot reason is a fool; he that dares not reason is a slave."
>
> -William Drummond

7   Harris Interactive, *While Most Americans Believe in God, Only 36% Attend a Religious Service Once a Month or More Often* [article on-line] (15 October 2003, accessed 22 November 2008); available from http://www.harrisinteractive.com/harris_poll/index.asp?PID=408; Internet. This survey found that "79% of Americans believe there is a God and that 66% are absolutely certain this is true. Only 9% do not believe in God, while a further 12% are not sure."

8   Denise Golumbaski, Research Analyst, Federal Bureau of Prisons, *The results of the Christians vs atheists in prison investigation.* [article on-line] (5 March 1997, accessed 20 November 2008); available from http://www.holysmoke.org/icr-pri.htm; Internet.

Religion and Medical Service

A study published in the *Annals of Family Medicine* looked for differences between more religious and non-religious physicians serving the poor or underserved.[9] The conclusion was that **Physicians who are more religious do not appear to disproportionately care for the underserved.** In this sample, 31% of those scoring high on religiosity worked among the poor or underserved compared to 35% of those who described themselves as Atheist, agnostic or none. In his conclusion, study author Farr Curlin, M.D., wrote,

> This came as both a surprise and a disappointment. The Christian, Jewish, Muslim, Hindu and Buddhist scriptures all urge physicians to care for the poor, and the great majority of religious physicians describe their practice of medicine as a calling. Yet we found that religious physicians were not more likely to report practice among the underserved than their secular colleagues.

Divorce and Religion

Many evangelical groups see divorce as a sign of immorality and rail against it from the pulpit. We might expect to see religion having a positive effect in this area but we would be wrong. The highly Christian and religious state of Oklahoma has a higher divorce rate than the less religious citizens of Massachusetts. Throughout the United States, divorce rates are highest where evangelical religious practices are strongest, in the Bible Belt.[10]

A 1999 study of divorce by the Barna Research Group found that evangelicals and fundamentalists had divorce rates higher than more liberal religious groups, and much higher than Atheists.[11] The Southern Baptist Convention became quite incensed by these findings, causing a major debate in the denomination and some challenge to Dr. Barna. This reaction prompted George Barna, the lead researcher, to write a letter to defend his research. Standing by his data, even though it is upsetting, Dr. Barna

---

9   Farr A. Curlin, MD, Lydia S. Dugdale, MD, John D. Lantos, MD and Marshall H. Chin, MD, MPH, "Do Religious Physicians Disproportionately Care for the Underserved?," *Annals of Family Medicine, Inc.* 5 (2007): 353-360.

10   David Crary, "Bible Belt Leads U.S. in Divorces," *Associated Press* 12 November 1999.

11   See Chapter 10 of this book for the statistics from this study.

wrote, "We rarely find substantial differences between the moral behaviors of Christians and non-Christians. We would love to be able to report that Christians are living very distinct lives and impacting the community, but ... in the area of divorce rates they continue to be the same." [12]

A few years later, the Southern Baptist Convention admitted that the statistics were probably right and began developing a DivorceCare package for Baptist churches. As of 2002, almost half of all Southern Baptists churches had adopted the program.[13] No evidence has since been produced to show whether the program has had any effect on Baptists' divorce rates.

While these are not definitive studies of comparative morality, they do not bode well for religious claims of superior morality.

Immoral Lessons From My Church

I received a thorough fundamentalist education. I was forced to sit through countless sermons and Sunday School lessons about the unchanging morality of the Bible. So, what did my religion teach me?

As in most of life's lessons, the real learning comes not from the spoken word but from observed behavior. All religions of the Book[14] place a great deal of weight on the word but tend to overlook the simple notion, "What impact does the word have on behavior?" Do people who get more of the word behave better?

> *"Sunday School: A prison in which children do penance for the evil conscience of their parents."*
>
> *-H. L. Mencken*

My religion was full of contradictory and strange messages. Do any of the following sound familiar to you?

- Women should be honored and respected but they are inferior to men. (Colossians 3:18).

---

12   George Barna is an evangelical and long-time pastor. The mission statement on his website states, in part, "We seek to use our strengths in partnership with Christian ministries and individuals to be a catalyst in moral and spiritual transformation in the United States. We accomplish these outcomes by providing vision, information, strategy, evaluation and resources." Barna Group, *What is The Barna Group, Ltd.?* [article on-line] (accessed 22 November 2008); available from http://www.barna.org/FlexPage.aspx?Page=AboutBarna; Internet.

13   *The News and Observer*, by Yonat Shimron, July 12, 2001.

14   Religions of the Book include Judaism, Christianity, Islam.

- People who have a lot of education should be treated as suspect unless they graduated from a Bible College.
- Ministers are the examples for the church. Follow their words but not necessarily their deeds. They are human after all.
- God loves everyone but you don't need to; Blacks are welcome in the kingdom of god but not in our church, Whites don't marry Blacks, Christians don't marry members of other religions, Gays are going to hell.
- You have to believe to get into heaven. If you end up in hell, it is because you didn't believe enough.
- The Bible is the perfect word of god. If you read it and find some inconsistencies, it is because you are imperfect and can't read it right. God's word does not need interpreting. Just read it, it is in black and white, but the preacher will tell you how to interpret it if you get it wrong.
- God wants everyone to be saved but Catholics, Jehovah's Witnesses, Mormons are probably not going to be saved. Muslims and Buddhists certainly won't.
- So-called mainstream churches like Episcopalians and Presbyterians don't follow Jesus. They pervert the word of the God.
- Pornography will pollute your mind and make you incapable of controlling yourself. Most criminals do pornography.
- Sex is sinful, except in marriage and even there, it is suspect. Sex before marriage will make you get divorced later.
- God loves America; if you question America, you obviously don't love its god.
- Give to the poor, but only to the deserving poor.
- Only missionaries from our denomination, or closely aligned ones, are doing god's work.
- If someone does not believe in our religion, it is okay to let her know she is going to hell. In fact, it is your duty to inform her.
- Science is good as long as it doesn't question the Bible or teach evolution. Always be suspicious of scientists.
- Too much education can undermine your faith.
- Money will ruin you if you don't tithe to our particular church.

There were no actual Sunday School lessons or sermons on these topics, but they were taught loudly and clearly through behavior and attitudes of people like the church elders, minister, parents, youth leaders and Sunday School teachers. Many sermons and Sunday school lessons taught one thing verbally but church members sent subtle contradictory messages.

When I was a child my grandmother loved to sing me to sleep with this song:

Jesus loves the little children,
All the children of the world.
Red and Yellow, Black and White, they are precious in his sight.
Jesus loves the little children of the world.

But when the black children that god loved came to swim in the city swimming pool, grandma got upset, as did many other Christians in town. I guess the interpretation is that god can love them, but grandma didn't have to. It was a subtle, but effective, moral lesson about how I should behave and view people of other races.

Most of these lessons could not be questioned. Here are some of the discussions that came from asking too many questions:

Q: Can homosexuals go to heaven?

A: "Of course, not! Why would you even ask such a question?"

Q: Can America be wrong about the Vietnam War?

A: "No, and the very fact that you asked makes you un-American and un-Christian. Are you a communist or a liberal?"

And who would dare ask, "If the 40-year-old preacher with a wife and three kids can have an affair and be forgiven by the church, what is wrong with me having a little sex before I get married?"

If your religious training was like mine, chances are much of it was downright immoral. Immoral in the sense that the values that were taught were racist, sexist, insulting and cruel to other groups, and misleading if not downright wrong about human relationships, sexuality, science, education, other religions and many other things.

Situational Religious Morality

Every fundamentalist preacher talks about god's unchanging word and that god's morality never changes. The myth of unchanging morality allows the virus to control current behavior. If people have amnesia, it makes it easier for the priest or preacher to dictate what is acceptable behavior today. It is religious situational morality. An unchanging morality would mean there is a way to calibrate a given behavior against a moral measuring stick. In reality, the priest or preacher controls the measuring stick and adjusts it according to the best interests of the virus in the specific culture.

How many preachers rail against integration these days? Heard any sermons on the evils of casino gambling in your local church lately? Has your local priest preached a series on the evils of birth control in the last ten years or so?

> "It has been contended for many years that the Ten Commandments are the foundations of all ideas of justice and law ... Nothing can be more stupidly false than such assertions. Thousands of years before Moses was born, the Egyptians had a code of laws ...far better than the Mosaic"
>
> -Robert Ingersoll

We would think that murder is an unchanging moral absolute. "Thou shalt not kill" seems very clear. But this commandment also changes with the times. The Jews who wrote and followed the Ten Commandments didn't think it murder to stone adulterers to death or to kill all the women and children in a city during the war to liberate Palestine. The Catholic inquisition and Tomás de Torquemada didn't think torture unto death was murder. Would these be considered murder today?

Slave owners in Mississippi were within their rights to kill an errant slave. It was not prosecutable as murder. In 1850 it was not considered murder for a Christian mob to hang a black man who disrespected a white woman. Lynch mobs could hang blacks with impunity for almost 80 years after the Civil War, and no one was charged with murder. Was it murder or not?

For an Islamic man in Pakistan, it is not murder to kill his sister if she is found alone with a man not related to her. For a Christian prison guard, it is not murder to administer the death penalty to a duly convicted murderer. It was not considered murder to drop napalm bombs on Vietnamese villages in 1968. Murder is a remarkably fluid thing and does not seem to have any relationship to the Ten Commandments.

Morality is defined in terms of the current culture. The virus tends to follow along and intervene only when its survival is threatened. Since culture is constantly shifting, the god virus is always trying to position itself for survival within the culture. In a society that is not deeply infected – that is, coupled to the religion – the virus has to constantly mutate to stay viable. In cultures with strong coupling, such as Saudi Arabia, the moral yardstick is more stable over time.

The Secret Message of the God Virus

It is important to look behind the words of religious leaders to understand the real messages they are sending. We can apply the viral paradigm to show how apparently benign religious statements are really efforts to maintain position within the culture. Newspapers reported in September 2007 that Pope Benedict in a major speech, said, "Europe has become child poor, we want everything for ourselves and place little trust in the future."[15] His message was to produce more children and prohibit abortion. He claimed that Europe has become immoral and cannot distinguish right from wrong.

Let's apply the god virus paradigm to Pope Benedict XVI's statement to understand the hidden intentions. First, is he calling for more children in Europe? On the surface, this appears to be a benign request. To understand, we should ask if he would be satisfied with more Muslim children in Europe? Would he praise a Europe where Atheists started having twice as many children as they currently do?

I don't think this is his message. Neither would he exalt Lutherans if they began having large families. The Pope wants Catholics to have large families as they did in the past. It is a simple, yet cloaked call to ensure the Catholic virus gains strength in Europe.

Next, he decried immorality in Europe. What does he mean by immorality? Is the murder rate up? Has there been a large jump in armed robberies or rapes? Are there more hate crimes or persecution of minorities? The answer is that while all of these crimes continue in some measure, they have declined throughout Europe since WW II and remain far lower than on other continents.

> "With or without religion, you would have good people doing good things and evil people doing evil things. But for good people to do evil things, that takes religion."
> -Steven Weinberg

15   Vatican Radio, *Pope's Homily at Mariazell* [article on-line] (9 August 2007, accessed 22 November 2008); available from http://www.radiovaticana.org/en1/Articolo.asp?c=153806; Internet.

At the same time as the Pope delivered this speech, the Austrian Catholic Church was in the throws of a major priest sex scandal. Around the same time, in another speech, the Pope stated, "The Church wants to show 'repentance' for the murder of millions of Jews by the Nazis."[16] An interesting juxtaposition for the Pope to call for a return to morality even as he is admitting the Church's role in one of the most heinous crimes in world history and dealing with major sexual misconduct among his own priests.

When religious leaders decry immorality, what they generally mean is, "You are not following the dictates of the god virus." Morality is an entirely separate issue. The Pope is not concerned with immorality in the sense of crime rates. He is concerned with adherence to practices that will increase the influence of the Catholic Church. The key to understanding this is to ask, "If all the Pope desired could be achieved under a Muslim caliphate, Protestant theocracy or with a secular government, would the Pope rejoice?" Most likely not! Thus, what is cloaked as a simple call for a return to morality is nothing more than a blatant attempt to increase the power of the Catholicism over others.

We have focused here on the Catholic Pope, but the same analysis could be conducted on the religious pronouncements from Pat Robertson, Binny Hinn[17], James Dobson or the head of the Sunday School department in a local church. Simply change the religion and use the same pronouncement, then ask, "Would the person who made that statement be happy with the new outcome?"

The Morality of the Non-Theist

Now that we have established where morality comes from, what does this mean for the non-religious? If you are a non-theist, you recognize no big lawgiver in the sky. You are responsible for developing your own moral compass. Most of the time, it is not a big job. As a member of this culture, you already abide by and agree with the basic code of behavior. You didn't need a preacher to tell you not to steal, lie, cheat, rape, pillage, murder or

---

16   *New York Times,* 7 September 2007; also *European Jewish Press* 7 September 2007.

17   Binny Hinn is the leader of a major television ministry. His ministry was investigated for financial mismanagement by the U.S. Senate. Hinn along with four other ministries refused to cooperate with the investigation. Pegasus News, *Grapevine-based Benny Hinn Ministries defies U.S. Senate* [article on-line] (8 December 2007, accessed 22 November 2008); available from http://www.pegasusnews. com/news/2007/dec/08/grape-vine-based-benny-hinn-ministries-defies-us-s/; Internet.

to strive for honesty in your daily interactions and dealings with people. It comes with being a citizen of any civilized society. Your parents would have taught you this, no matter what their religion or lack of religion.

The one difference between you and those infected with the virus is that you know that you are responsible. No excuses, no "the devil made me do it." Virally infected people are not so clear on this point. Some think Satan tempts them. Others think some god has a plan and they have to figure out that plan. Still others think a god preordained it all and that they have little choice in the matter. Muslims are always saying, "Allah willing." Some Christians say it, too. It's as if they don't have any say in things; their god is going to do what he wants to do.

Being clear about responsibility is a huge advantage for the non-theist. You are not going to waste time and energy trying to read some god's tea leaves to figure out the plan. You don't worry about whether a god is looking over your shoulder when you think a bad thought. How much do you worry about disappointing the Virgin Mary? When was the last time you worried about offending Allah? In normal day-to-day life, you are saving energy and emotion for more important things.

The Tough Decisions

At times when the moral issues get big, there is no demonstrable difference between religionists and non-theists. For example, what percentage of Christians tried to protect and save Jews in Nazi Germany? Was the percentage any higher than the percentage of Atheists who tried to save Jews? You probably couldn't find a more immoral man than Oscar Schindler[18] of *Schindler's List* fame: financially shady, involved in gambling, and always with one or two mistresses besides a wife. Yet, the "moral" bishops and cardinals of Germany probably didn't come close

> "A man's ethical behavior should be based effectually on sympathy, education, and social ties; no religious basis is necessary. Man would indeed be in a poor way if he had to be restrained by fear of punishment and hope of reward after death."
>
> -Albert Einstein

---

18   Famous for saving 1,200 Jews from the death camps in WW II. He was the subject of the Steven Spielberg movie *Schindler's List* (Touchstone, 1 September 1995) and was named Righteous Among the Nations by Israel, an honor for non-Jews who saved Jews during the Holocaust.

in doing the moral actions of this one man.

Dietrich Bonhoeffer,[19] famous for his theological works, gets pretty good press for trying to assassinate Hitler, but thousands of Atheists died under Hitler's rule, including dozens who tried to assassinate Hitler as well. Those stories are not told very often. Is a Christian's heroism more heroic or important than an Atheist's? Is Albert Camus any less heroic in the French resistance because of his agnosticism?

The god virus usurps the story of the moral person who makes the hard and courageous decision. It is not interested in the millions of other religious people who made the immoral choice. It is a case of massive selective perception. For every inspirational Christian story in religious bookstores, there are a thousand stories of ministers gone bad, priests molesting children or elders and deacons lynching blacks in the 1920s.

The vast majority of Nazis were Christians; only a tiny fraction of Christians actually tried to save Jews or Communists. Christians point to those who saved Jews with pride; and they should. If their faith gave them courage to resist, all the better. However, that does not negate the bravery of Albert Camus or Oscar Schindler, or the communist resistance fighters in France, Germany and Spain. Bravery, courage and morality are not values unique to religionists. On the other hand, how did Christianity inform the morality of millions of Nazis and fascists who celebrated mass every week or attended Lutheran services while supporting Hitler's murderous regime? It is mind-boggling to see religionists hold up the tiny minority of people who behaved morally while completely ignoring the millions who did not.

Where does the non-theist get the moral compass to make the hard decisions? It comes from doing the difficult work of self-examination and definition. For me, Albert Camus and Voltaire have been far more helpful than Jesus or Moses. Albert Einstein and Viktor Frankl[20] have given me more moral guidance than any minister. From an early age, I had a sense of justice and injustice, and it often ran counter to the teachings of my church.

---

19   Dietrich Bonhoeffer, German Lutheran Pastor and Theologian, was imprisoned for his part in an assassination attempt against Hitler and executed only weeks before the fall of Germany. See Dietrich Bonhoeffer, *The Cost of Discipleship* and *Letters* (B&H Publishing Group, 1999) and *Papers from Prison* updated ed. (Touchstone, 1997).

20   Viktor Frankl (1905–1997) was a psychiatrist and Holocaust survivor. He was prominent in existential therapy and founder of logotherapy after the war. He was author of the small but extremely influential book, *Man's Search for Meaning* (Beacon Press, 2006).

Non-theists have to decide what course of action is moral. We cannot look to a make-believe god or an instruction book. We also do not have the shifting sands of religious morality to contend with. As we have seen in this chapter, morality is a moving target for the religious. The shifting nature of religious morality is hidden to those infected by a god virus.

The immoral lessons of my religious training were anything but a moral compass. Creating a sense of balance between my wants and desires and those of others has been my primary happiness in life. As long as I listened to my own moral compass, I seemed to make some good decisions.

Summary

Morality is a product of culture, not religion. The god virus is constantly changing to adjust to the culture and to survive. Moral superiority is a myth perpetuated by the virus to maintain control. Viral control is maintained through the myth of unchanging morality. Those infected have difficulty seeing the changing nature of religious morality and feel secure that they are more moral than others. This blinds religionists to real-world data needed to make hard choices. Non-theists have a huge advantage because they waste no time on fantasies, worries and fears related to the virus. While we have worries and fears, they are not complicated by the demands of a god virus.

CHAPTER 7:
JESUS MY PERSONAL SAVIOR:
THE ROOTS OF AMERICAN EVANGELISM

"There is so much in the Bible against which every instinct of my being rebels, so much so that I regret the necessity which has compelled me to read it through from beginning to end. I do not think that the knowledge I have gained of its history and sources compensates me for the unpleasant details it has forced upon my attention."

-Helen Keller, American lecturer

Overview

American evangelism is a new virus with new tools and methods for infection and propagation, including psychosocial methods such as hypnosis. Evangelical preachers are also different from the priests and ministers of the past in both style and education.

Carrie's Story

Carrie volunteered this story when she learned I was writing a book on religion. I am grateful for her willingness to share her private journey. It illustrates the nature of the new evangelical virus we will examine in this chapter.

I was raised in a chaotic, disruptive home and gravitated to ultra-conservative Baptist friends. They seemed to have all the answers. The church accepted me 'unconditionally,' provided guidance on righteous living and offered me a future in eternity. There was a trance-like joy that radiated from believers and I wanted to feel that 'good.' There's comfort in knowing the answers and knowing you are accepted because you belong.

I married a man who was raised in a very strict, deeply religious home as well. We raised our children in the Baptist church and attended five days a week. I stayed home with my children, home-schooled them and embraced my submissive wife role. I was always involved in several Bible Studies at once, taught Sunday School and led the women's groups. We lived in a large home in a wealthy neighborhood, and we 'looked' very good from the outside. My husband and I never argued. We also talked little. Internally we were both dying. My husband frequently criticized men who cheated on their wives as having a lack of morals. At the same time, he was having several affairs. I also had affairs and would repent and join another Bible Study to 'cleanse my soul.' Our faith was the band-aid that kept our marriage together. It covered the wound but didn't heal it. We just didn't have to look at the problems.

My marriage lasted for 15 years, but eventually even a magical god can't fix some problems. After the divorce, we both lost friends and few remained close. It was almost as if others thought divorce was contagious. Some even said we had "sinned" when we divorced.

In our very large conservative Southern Baptist church, I held long-standing leadership roles in women's groups. Within a short time after our divorce, I was 'encouraged' to step down. Church members often admit to being flawed and imperfect, but say they are made 'perfect through Christ.' I guess I was really flawed at this point, and not even Christ could perfect me.

I moved to another city and raised my children as a single parent. I went back to school and finished a master's degree as a therapist. I was still determined to raise my children in a Christian household. I comforted myself, knowing I had Christ beside me and I wasn't raising them alone. I became very involved in the church, taught youth and joined every Bible Study I could. I prayed daily, sometimes hourly, asking for guidance. I surrounded myself with Christian friends and spoke a language that always included god.

Over the years, I watched as my children began to parrot the words they heard in youth group and from their youth leaders, teachers and preacher. Rather than embracing a loving and forgiving 'god,' they became more rigid in their thinking, more judgmental and condescending of those who did not embrace the Baptist lifestyle. They set themselves apart as 'believers' and others as 'sinners.' Somehow, they were elite and others were 'lost.' I didn't like what I saw in my children. I felt awful. It was as if they were becoming less Christian even as we worked harder to be Christians.

About the time my children were leaving home to attend college, a friend of mine asked me to read a book with an alternative explanation for my feelings. The book explained religion in terms I had never considered. I agreed to read it with the clear purpose of showing him how wrong he was. I knew I was strong in my beliefs and would demonstrate how nonjudgmental and unbiased I could be. I even thought I could enlighten him and gently lead him back to Christ. I vehemently attacked the first few chapters. They made me angry, and the comments I wrote on the side of the pages reflected that. I was determined to not let my emotions drive my rebuttals, I would prove the book wrong by quoting from Scripture. I was certain I could make intelligent arguments that he would have to embrace.

After a few chapters, I began to notice that my arguments didn't stand up to the simple scientific facts that were methodically presented. The concepts in the book made sense to me. Slowly, then dramatically, I made a shift. When I stopped being defensive, I was able to start thinking independently about my religion and beliefs. I stopped parroting words I was taught and behaviors I mimicked.

Considering the possibility that there was no god was so very threatening to my core beliefs. As I continued to read, all of my arguments fell away. It just made sense. I always thought I was an intelligent woman. How could I embrace such mythology and teach such fantasies to my children? The same words my friends would use to comfort me, that 'God will be with you,' 'I'm praying for you', 'This is God's plan,' 'He is in control,' now sounded ridiculous. How comical. I insist on proof in everything else in my life, why did I not apply those same standards to the Master of my universe?

My world turned upside down with repercussions that I'm continuing to face. I already experienced the loss of respect and friendships through my divorce. I didn't know if I was prepared to lose more friends, business contacts and community acceptance if I admitted I was Atheist. More importantly, I knew my children would be devastated. That was the hardest adjustment.

Admitting that I am truly alone in this world and that there is no ghostly figure always listening to me or intervening on my behalf was a difficult revelation. I fought it but finally recognized that all of my struggles were not because I was punished for some 'sin' and all of my successes were because I worked hard. Although this was hard, taking responsibility for my actions freed me to live an honest life.

Let us now look at the roots of the religious movement that had such powerful control over Carrie for much of her adult life. We will revisit her at the end of this chapter.

The Roots of Evangelism

Over the centuries after the beginning of Christianity, the Catholic virus coupled with the cultures of Europe. Old European culture was changed and challenged. Catholicism adapted and adopted so completely that it appropriated many local customs. Churches were intentionally built on ancient pagan worship centers. Local holidays were adapted to reflect Catholic saints rather than pagan gods. Marriage was redefined in Catholic terms. The coupling was so strong that it was difficult to see any difference between the culture and the Catholic religion.

The first step toward uncoupling of religion from culture came when John Wycliffe (1320?–1384) and later Martin Luther (1483–1546) focused on individual accountability. This was an important departure from the Catholic communal approach. The idea of individual accountability led them to translate the Bible into the vernacular, thereby allowing common people to read and decide for themselves what to believe. For the previous one thousand years, Catholicism had controlled the Scripture.[1] Daily life, rituals, customs and all stages of life were imbued with the Catholic god virus and interpreted only by the priest. Protestantism was communal as well, but included elements of individualism in it. The tendency in both Protestant and Catholic viruses was to try to create a homogenous community where possible.

Scripture translation brought a new viral tool onto the scene. With access to the Scriptures, the Bible could now function as a vector for the new Protestant religion and become the roots of evangelism. A new approach to the priesthood allowed anyone to interpret the Scriptures. That is, each person acting as his or her own priest could interpret the Scriptures – Luther's priesthood of all believers. This new component would later allow Protestantism to survive in a highly individualistic culture and evolve into the evangelical virus we see today.

> "Pray, v. To ask that the laws of the universe be annulled in behalf of a single petitioner confessedly unworthy."
>
> -Ambrose Bierce

---

1   See our discussion of cultural coupling in Chapter 3.

Communalism in The United States

Those who left Europe to found the Colonies were highly communal in their outlook. They were NOT looking for religious freedom, as the myths of U.S. history would have us believe. They were looking for religious purity and exclusivity in a religious community. The proof is in the original charters ...."and constitutions of those pre-revolutionary colonies.

> "All civil states, with their officers of justice, in their respective constitutions and administrations, are proved essentially civil, and therefore not judges, governors, or defenders of the spiritual, or Christian, state and worship."
>
> -Roger Williams

Immediately after colonization, restrictive religious laws and customs were quickly established in the first six colonies: Plymouth (1620), Massachusetts (1630), New Haven (1638), Connecticut (1639), Maryland (1633), Pennsylvania (1682). Only Rhode Island (1635) practiced separation of church and state from its founding. Established by Roger Williams (1603-1683), who was banished from the Massachusetts Bay Colony for his insistence on religious tolerance, Rhode Island had no established religion at the time of its founding and rapidly became a haven for numerous groups who were persecuted in other colonies – especially Massachusetts – including Baptists, Quakers, Jews and others. Roger Williams was the first to use the term "wall of separation" between the church and state, later made famous by Thomas Jefferson.[2]

By 1702, all 13 colonies had some form of state support or religious requirements for office. The support came in the form of tax benefits or religious requirements for voting or serving in the legislature.

Until 1844, only Protestants were allowed to hold office in New Jersey. Thomas Jefferson, Benjamin Franklin or Abraham Lincoln would not have qualified to hold the office of governor in Massachusetts as late as 1833 since all were required to say this oath, "I ___ do declare that I believe the Christian religion ...". In the Georgia constitution of 1789, only Protestants could hold office. The Anglican Church was the state church until as late

---

2   Roger Williams was also the founder of either the first or second Baptist church in America (it is somewhat uncertain). It is ironic that today's Baptists are so adamant in rejoining religion to the state when one of their founders in the United States was so adamant about separation of church and state.

as 1875, and only Protestants had full citizenship rights. South Carolina included the following article in its constitution until 1878, "The Christian Protestant religion shall be deemed, and is hereby constituted and declared to be, the established religion of this State." In Massachusetts, Catholics could not hold public office. In New York Jews were given full political rights but not Catholics.

Thus, this country was not established on religious tolerance. The colonists were themselves victims of persecution in England and came to establish a "New Jerusalem" in America. This theme continues to haunt us today.

With the American Revolution, the 13 states came into much closer contact and alliance. With greater economic and political cooperation came the potential for religious conflicts – European style. The founding fathers, with a sense of perspective on the religious history of Europe, had the wisdom to try to tame the more virulent religious tendencies in the constitutional separation of church and state that Roger Williams had pioneered.

The New American Viral Frontier

Three conditions have merged to create individualistic protestant evangelism out of the old communal Christianity: Emergence of the protestant virus, increased literacy of the population and communities being founded on economic needs rather than religious affiliation. The American frontier was the nexus of these three trends, and they continue to evolve today.

As groups immigrated to the United States, they tended to establish religious communities wherever possible. Lutherans established Lutheran communities, Quakers established Quaker communities, Catholics created pure Catholic communities, and

> "We query whether the blood of so many hundred thousand Protestants, mingled with the blood of so many thousand papists [Roman Catholics] spilled since the Reformation be not a warning to us."
>
> **-Roger Williams**

Dutch Reformed kept to themselves. With movement west, this arrangement became less tenable. Purity became difficult to maintain.[3] With people moving west to mine or make land claims, religion was not at the top of their list. If they worked a gold claim next to a Catholic or Lutheran, so be it. The Wild West was a chaotic environment for all god viruses. In order to survive, religion had to mutate into something viable in the individualistic and isolated world of the American West. The one obvious exception to this trend were the Mormons, who were successful in creating a pure religious community in isolated Utah during the 1870s.

With increasingly mobile populations and little to hold communities together, the virus gained the capacity to infect individuals independently of their communities. This was a major change. Living on the frontier, a farmer, miner or cowboy could get Jesus just by reading the Scriptures, with no qualified minister nearby. This led to many a self-proclaimed prophet and minister. Indeed, hundreds of cults started on the new frontier in the 1800s and early 1900s. Most died out, but a few gained a foothold, Mormonism (1830) and the Church of Christ Scientists (1879), Seventh Day Adventists (1863) and Jehovah's Witnesses (1872), several different Pentecostal groups (1901-06) and The Four Square Gospel Church (1918) being among the most successful.

Super Vectors and Personality Cult

The major evolution of American evangelism came after WWI. Mutations began springing up with evangelicals like Billy Sunday and Aimee Semple McPherson in the 1920s[4] and Billy Graham in the mid-20th century. Mass media and large venues with electronic amplification made the tent meetings and revivals in the 1800s obsolete. It also allowed people to get religion no matter where they lived and to take it with them if they

---

3   A classic work by D. Elton Trueblood, *The People Called Quakers* (Friends United Press, July 1985) is a virtual case study of religious change as Quakers moved west. He traces the changes in organization and theology as Quakers adapted to the frontier environment. Many Quaker groups abandoned long-held beliefs and customs and took on elements of other frontier churches. In the quest to adapt and infect new members, some Quakers became as evangelical as many of the Baptist churches in the same community.

4   A classic novel by Sinclair Lewis, *Elmer Gantry* (Harcourt Brace, January 1, 1927), documented the new evangelical virus in its early stages. Billy Sunday publicly denounced Sinclair from the pulpit as "Satan's cohort." Another example of art documenting this phenomenon is Carlisle Floyd's opera *Susanna* (1955). The opera shows the effects of guilt, shame and self-doubt in many of the characters in a small rural community.

moved away. The highly mobile population in the United States allowed this virus to evolve from community or denomination-based to individual and charismatic-focused.

The movement to mega churches addresses the individual while bringing people back into a communal environment where infection of the next generation can be done efficiently. Mega churches are often centered on a single charismatic individual, a "super vector." In most cases, the church is organized around this person's personality. His name is always on the marquee and he controls and orchestrates the entire organization often with little accountability. Board members are frequently selected by the minister or manipulated into position by him or her.

> "Faith does not give you the answers, it just stops you asking the questions."
> -Frater Ravus

The theological training of super vectors is often abysmal, mostly from a narrowly focused Bible College. Most have little exposure to philosophy and even less to the sciences. In both their academic and practical training, these vectors study methods of infection, learning to create a sense of community around the virus. Members of the mega church find the security once felt in the village or in communal religions of the past.

A European Catholic friend of mine who lived in the United States for several years once told me about Protestant evangelical next-door neighbors. One day they asked my friends about churches in the area. They were shopping for a church home that would fit their family. My Catholic friend expressed total disbelief! "You just go to the local parish. There is no shopping as a Catholic." She could not understand how someone could shop for a church. From her perspective, it was an amazing example of how rootless American Protestantism is.

This is the nature of the new evangelical Protestant religion in America. Rooted in the Wild West's individualistic past, it seeks to bring people who are highly mobile back into a community, albeit a transient one. This flexibility allows the evangelical virus to perpetuate with few ties to community and get carried along no matter where the individual moves.

In times past, people simply went to the church their parents attended or to the only church in the village. Today people can shop around to find the church that makes them feel best. Super vectors compete to produce a product that gives people an emotionally satisfying experience. Read the Saturday Church advertisements in your local newspaper and note how many glorify the minister. This is a new phenomenon. The cult of personality has become common among evangelicals and Pentecostals. The Methodist denominational practice of moving ministers every few years was designed over 150 years ago to prevent personality cults from developing around a given minister. But Methodists are at a decided disadvantage when competing with charismatic super vectors if they continue this practice.

Like most major religions, the evangelical virus infects the mind through guilt and self-doubt. Community-based religion had the huge advantage of social sanctions for anyone who strayed. In our mobile society, people can avoid sanctions too easily just by moving or changing churches. Never before have people been able to pick and choose their religion so freely. The evangelical religion mutated to a position where it could create guilt and doubt outside of a given community by using new and more sophisticated hypnotic worship techniques that we will discuss later. This is an entirely new development and is a huge challenge to the older religions. Many have not adapted, losing many members to the evangelical movement.

> "Evangelicalism is a series of personality cults masquerading as religion."
> -Frank Shaeffer, former evangelical preacher

Today's vectors like Joel Osteen in Houston (30,000 members), Rick Warren at Saddleback Church in California (22,000 members) and Bill Hybels of Willow Creek Church, Chicago, (19,500 members) have great skill at creating the "feel good" effect paired with guilt and fear that leads to a strong viral bond. It allows for efficient exploitation of resources and infection of children. Most of these churches are non-denominational or are part of more loosely affiliated denominational groups like the Baptists. This lack of denominational affiliation is a major departure from the last four hundred years of Protestantism. The virus has taken on a new form altogether with this historic jump.

Let us now look at the specific methods super vectors use to create emotionally charged worship services that imbed a god virus deeply into individuals while creating a community for support and propagation.

Hypnotic Infection Techniques

A mega church service has fast or slow-paced music, designed to evoke specific moods and responses. It has charismatic leaders with high energy, and high levels of group participation. The evangelical virus creates a sense of belonging and transcendence through emotional group experiences. Leaders use sophisticated psychological techniques designed to evoke elation, fear and guilt all within the frame of a "praise service." A significant number of evangelical churches are also Pentecostal. The Pentecostal virus is even more emotional with heavy emphasis on group and individual trance induction. Thus, group hypnosis, trance induction and post-hypnotic suggestion are the art of the modern evangelical preacher.

These techniques tie people to the virus as they seek relief from their self-doubt and guilt through services that resemble rock concerts. Preachers employ the natural power of large-group psychology to create an experience that appears to be transcendent to the participants, using vocal rhythms, body motion, group movement and cadence.

Research in hypnosis and meditation has shown the power of these techniques to reduce pain, create euphoria, or an altered state of consciousness.[5] This well-documented effect can be produced by someone with a modest amount of training in meditation or hypnosis. It can also be created at a sporting event, a music concert or a political rally, but in a church setting, it is easily mistaken for a spiritual experience. The greatest evangelical ministers have studied these techniques for decades and perfected the art of mass emotional appeal.

Music and the Virus

In their constant struggle to propagate, biological viruses use many tools to infect. God viruses are similar. Some tools have proven remarkably effective for thousands of years. These include music, vocal rhythm in preaching, word associations that evoke specific emotions, use of parables and stories, etc. As the surrounding culture evolves, the virus must use these basic tools differently or create new tools.

Music is among the most useful of all viral tools. Independent of religion, music is capable of creating a wide range of biochemical responses. How

---

5   Journal of the National Cancer Institute Advance Access, *The Mind Prepared: Hypnosis in Surgery* [article on-line] (28 August 2007, accessed 22 November 2008); available from http://jnci. oxfordjournals.org/cgi/content/full/99/17/1280; Internet.

many times have you listened to a familiar song on the radio and had a feeling of joy, sadness, love or sexual arousal? Does a particular song bring back strong memories of a past romantic love? How does a patriotic song affect your heart rate or stomach?

Listening or singing Handel's "Hallelujah" chorus evokes strong emotion in almost anyone. Here is an interesting experiment I once tried on a friend. I played a rousing hymn sung in a foreign language and I asked him what feelings he experienced when listening. He used words like pride, aggression, solidarity and bravery. The song was a Stalinist-era military hymn performed by the Red Army Chorus! It was used to inspire soldiers going off to fight against the Nazis in WWII. While the words may add to the feeling, the music itself is exquisitely designed by the composer to evoke specific universal emotions.

Watch any number of religious videos, on-line sermons or televangelists, and you will realize that every one of them uses music to magnify and enhance the emotion of the verbal message. Subtle, quiet music at key moments in the delivery of the sermon opens up the participants to subliminal and hypnotic messages. At other times, loud, commanding music is used to create a feeling of action and purpose. The manipulation is obvious when observed from a viral viewpoint.

The American evangelicalism has fine-tuned the music of today to open the mind and prepare it to receive the virus or to support and reinforce viral responses. It is the same tool used by Stalin to prepare and inspire his armies for battle. The design of music programs gives people a strong emotional and biochemical boost each week. Sitting in the pew, the church goers feel the rush of endorphins and easily mistake the feelings and emotions for some spiritual experience or communication from a god. They would not interpret a love song on the radio that evokes similar responses as a communication from a god, but the same response in a church is easily interpreted in this way and that is the intention of the vectors.

Evangelical Hypnosis

Once the biochemical response has been created with the music, the audience experiences it in some vaguely spiritual way. Now they are ready for the message the vector wants to pour in. To a great degree, logic and critical thinking are not involved as the infected are placed in a state of receptivity that precludes critical thought. Those who go through this have no awareness of the manipulation involved, nor do they care. They come to the church to get their fix and leave feeling good about themselves and their virus.

When I was in high school, I belonged to a group called Future Physicians of America. Each month we had a different program. One month a psychiatrist came to demonstrate hypnosis. Alvin, our club president, was adamant that he could not be hypnotized. The psychiatrist asked for five volunteers, including Alvin. In the course of five minutes, all five were hypnotized at the same time. To prove they were hypnotized, the psychiatrist asked them to hold their arms out full from their body during his complete lecture. In addition, he had Alvin hold his arms AND legs out while sitting down. After another 20 minutes, he slowly released each volunteer and gave him or her a post-hypnotic command. He saved Alvin for last.

I challenge you to hold your arms out straight for 20 minutes. Two or three minutes feels impossible to most of us, but Alvin sat patiently with arms and legs outstretched until he was released and given the post-hypnotic command to scratch his nose whenever he answered a direct question from the psychiatrist. The psychiatrist asked, "Do you believe you were hypnotized?" Alvin scratched his nose and said, "Absolutely not!" A big laugh came from the group. The psychiatrist then asked, "Do you think you could hold your arms out straight from your body for 20 minutes?" Alvin scratched his nose and said, "I don't think so." The group laughed again. Alvin left that meeting convinced that he had not been, and could not be, hypnotized, but everyone else in the room knew otherwise.

It does not take a psychiatrist to hypnotize a group. Many good preachers do a credible job every Sunday. Go on line and watch any televangelist or visit a local evangelical church service. Take a pen and paper and, count the number of times he repeats himself – says the same thing twice or more in the same cadence. Repetition in cadence is a very effective hypnotic technique. Even if you are a non-believer, notice the physical effect this technique has on you when you simply listen without thinking too much. You might notice yourself going into a relaxed, altered state. Once put into an altered state of consciousness, people can receive all kinds of messages about giving money to the church, feeling guilty about sex, hating those who oppose the president of the United States or voting for anti-abortion candidates.

While our discussion has focused on American evangelical religions, all religions use hypnotic methods to facilitate infection. The Catholic and

Eastern Orthodox churches have perfected the use of ritual as well as music and the aroma of incense to create receptive states in its parishioners. Islamic preachers use techniques that incorporate Catholic, Eastern Orthodox and evangelical hypnotic approaches.

Catholic monastic orders have used hypnotic techniques for 1,400 years. Buddhists, Hindus, Native Americans and members of most other religions have discovered and used the power of altered states of consciousness to infect and maintain the god virus.

Getting the Message, Getting Action

Read each of these:

Jesus loves me this I know …
Hail Mary, mother of god …
Onward Christian Soldiers …
I believe in God, the Father Almighty, the Creator of heaven and earth …
For god so loved the world …

Reading these statements, you may have found yourself compelled to recite the entire saying in your head. It may have brought back memories or emotions. You may have learned these when you were young. You had no idea what they meant; they were just something you learned like brushing your teeth. Religious routines are an important part of religious infection, so let's learn how they work.

"Why should I apologize because God throws in crystal chandeliers, mahogany floors, and the best construction in the world?"

-Jimmy Bakker, fallen superstar American evangelist

When your alarm clock goes off in the morning, you probably go into a thoughtless routine of brushing your teeth, showering, shampooing your hair, etc. Such routines consist of a series of activities that are generally carried out in exactly the same order each time. The same is true for other activities like balancing your checkbook or driving to work. They can be complicated tasks, but the routine is so ingrained that you think little of it and complete it with relative ease.

Other routines take place throughout your day. You may have a lawn mowing routine or a laundry routine. You may have an anger routine that goes off when triggered by something your spouse says. You may have a sadness routine that runs whenever you hear a certain song on the radio. We have hundreds of these routines. We generally have enough control to decide whether to use them or not. For example, you may choose not to use your morning routine on Saturday. Other routines seem to run outside of our consciousness. Do you think about your teeth brushing technique? How much do you think about driving while on the way to the supermarket?

Your parents taught you how to wake up and get your morning routine accomplished. You don't think about these lessons every time you brush your teeth. You just do it without thinking. Once a subroutine is learned, it becomes independent of the initiating event.

Some routines are triggered by outside events. The alarm goes off, you start your morning routine. The dog whines, you start the dog walking routine. If you smoke or have smoked, you have a smoking routine that is evoked by certain triggers – after dinner, after a beer, or before an important meeting. How you learned this is long forgotten. The environment triggers the routine now.

Now let's look at how the god virus uses routines to its advantage. Routines are designed to get an emotional response. The emotion may be a feeling of love or joy; guilt or unworthiness; power or pride. No matter what the emotion, after years of repetition it is deeply tied to an environmental trigger, often outside of our awareness. The very act of walking into a church may evoke a routine. Just as you don't think about brushing your teeth, a Catholic doesn't think when making the sign of the cross after a blessing.

If you want to know some of the routines that are deeply programmed, watch a person who is unfamiliar with your religion's rituals. He will be like a fish out of water while you swim blissfully through the service. He will struggle to know what to do next. You may not look at the words in the hymnal as you sing whereas the new person struggles to find the right page and follow the music. You will know when to sit, stand and kneel, the guest will try to follow awkwardly along.

These routines appear benign and often feel good. That is exactly their purpose. God viruses long ago learned how to build and trigger simple routines that create specific emotional responses. The best vectors are masters at creating or following rituals. Rituals are key routines for a particular god virus. Catholic routines are different from Lutheran routines. And both are quite different from Muslim routines. Routines build upon one another to create a full religious experience for a particular religion.

If you were to attend a church that is very different from your own, you may find that it does not evoke your emotions or evokes negative ones. The routines are unfamiliar to you. If you are Protestant, for example, reciting the rosary probably does little for you. If you are Muslim, singing "Onward Christian Soldiers" may evoke a strong negative emotion. If you are a Christian, saying "there is but one god and Mohammed is his Prophet" may evoke an equally negative response. Religious routines are designed to evoke friendly and positive emotions within those infected with the particular religion. The religion also creates routines for strong negative emotions from other virus' routines.

Many routines were imbedded in childhood and do not change easily or often. Since these powerful programs were learned when you were largely unaware, they have emotional power that goes beyond reason and critical analysis. Just as the song on the radio or the poem from childhood can trigger a certain response, the god virus triggers a series of routines that are designed to evoke very specific responses from the infected. If you are not infected, however, you probably won't respond to the routines in the way they were designed and intended.

In your daily life, chaining one routine to another helps you accomplish many tasks without much thought. By chaining, you can get all your morning routines done while planning the day in your head. Chaining allows you to drive home from work and plan supper at the same time. Sometimes the sequence of links is important in a chain. For driving a car, there is a sequence of activities that needs to be followed. Unlock the door, adjust the seat, put key in ignition, turn key, look around, put car in gear, etc. Doing one or more of these steps out of order may make the task difficult or impossible; it can even be dangerous.

Religions also chain routines together to achieve a result. The chaining begins when you are young. You may have learned the Apostles' Creed in catechism. At the same time, you learned an emotional response. It goes like this. Say creed; feel humble; then feel secure in the church. As you grow up, you develop chains of routines that create a full religious experience. Here is a simplified example:

1. Listen to sermon
   – Feel guilt
2. Sing song
   – Feel pride

3. Listen to prayer – think of sins
    – Feel guilt
4. Sing song before offering
    – See offering plate
5. Put money in the plate. Feel satisfied.

The chain is the same each week or only slightly modified. If the chain is effective, it evokes the response that deepens the viral bond and makes you feel like you got something out of attending the service.[6]

One measure of a given chain is how much money it brings in to the church. Another is how many new people answer the altar call.[7] Skillful vectors are always looking for chain sequences that get better results. Sometimes people get satiated with parts of a chain and stop responding. For example, asking for money too often may alert some people to the manipulation of the virus. Too many song verses on the altar call may feel emotionally manipulative.

While parts of the chain may need to be adjusted on a regular basis, there are only so many ways to build a successful chain. That is why few churches start the service by asking for an offering. Altar calls don't come in the middle of services. Sequence is everything. The sequence is designed to achieve a series of emotional responses that lead to greater or renewed commitment to the virus, more resources for the virus and new members infected.

A religious service can be analyzed by looking at what emotion each of its parts is designed to evoke. Each component gets a response that leads to the next component. They build on each other to create an entire religious experience that bonds the person closer to the virus and makes him happy to give time and money to infect other people.

---

6   In applied behavioral psychology, chaining has been used with great success to teach children and adults with disabilities everything from toilet training to hand washing to homework completion. For a child, a chain is designed to achieve a certain end, such as successful toilet behavior or homework completion. For a religious vector, a chain is designed to achieve a material and emotional response – give money or time and feel good about it.

7   An altar call is a practice in many evangelical churches in which those who wish to make a new spiritual commitment to Jesus Christ are invited to come forward publicly. It is so named because the supplicants gather at the altar located at the front of the church.

Here is a simplified analysis of one fundamentalist service I attended:
1. Quiet music as you walk in
    – Sense of peace
2. Opening song about hope and triumph
    – Sense of hope
3. Song about sin and guilt
    – Sense of guilt and unworthiness
4. Song about salvation
    – Sense of guilt, ending with hope
5. Rousing song by choir about salvation
    – Sense of hope
6. Sermon on marriage and relationships
    – Sense of guilt and self-doubt
7. Song about commitment before offering plate is passed
    – Sense of resolve to give money
8. Rousing song of joy and forgiveness to end the service
    - Sense of joy and hope

What an emotional roller coaster. Most of the participants have no idea that the service was carefully designed to get exactly these emotional responses to build a complete religious experience. They just know they feel good when they leave church $100 poorer.

Mass Psychology

Master vectors tweak and modify the routines to stimulate the congregation toward more involvement and money. They are experts at group dynamics and mass psychology. They adjust the sequence and components, according to the setting and size of the group. Group size and density have a powerful impact on participants' perceptions and experiences. Just as the emotion and excitement of a football game is enhanced when the stands are full, a full church makes the individual experience far more powerful. Similarly, a prayer meeting in a small room has a more powerful feel than the same small group in a large room.

This process is extremely seductive to many people. Where else can you get an emotional high once a week without drugs? Where else can you find some relief from the guilt you were feeling about something you did? Nothing at work or at home comes close. Sports events may create a transcendent feeling, but only if your team wins. In church, your team wins every time.

People come to church for the emotional experience that a good vector can produce. They come for reassurance and validation against self-doubt. They come for the feeling of security in belonging to a group that knows the correct path in a bewildering world. They come for the absolution they feel and the endorphin high. The vector must create the proper sequence to produce an emotional experience that is satisfying and brings people back.

To effectively choreograph an entire organization, the super vector must view the church as a whole organism. Vectors teach key participants how to play their part in the religious dance. They train each of the associate ministers and key members of the church, such as choir directors, elders, and deacons. It is similar to conducting a symphony. Most of these players, once well instructed, can play their routines perfectly week after week, to achieve the emotional ends of the service.

Many humans seem to have a deep need for ritual. Creating effective rituals (routines) helps a vector capture and infect new hosts. An organization full of well-trained hosts with well-established viral routines is easily directed and controlled by a minister. Like pushing buttons on a machine, a skilled vector can work an entire organization into exactly the response he wants.

Master Controls

The routines of a religion are like individual genes in a genome.[8] Genes can be controlled and manipulated to produce certain proteins. Some genes produce higher-level results. In the genetic world, there are a set of genes called homeobox that were discovered in 1983 by Walter Jakob Gehring and his team at the University of Basel, Switzerland, and Amy Weiner and Thomas Kaufman at Indiana University in Bloomington. Homeobox genes are master genes that instigate a cascade of other genes in a certain sequence to create entire structures. Homeobox genes are involved when an organism creates an arm, a leg or other major structures in the body. Genes for creating arms and legs stay silent most of the time, if not, we all might look like centipedes! In short, a homeobox gene is required to switch on a

---

8   Definition – Genome: The total DNA present in the nucleus of every cell of an organism. It corresponds to all the organism's bases: A, T, C and G, our genome is a chain of 3.4 billion pearls.

series of leg-creating genes. When the task is complete, the homeobox gene switches the process off.

Religious vectors act like homeobox genes, creating and orchestrating entire organizations, but they can only do this if they have a library of routines and subroutines to work with. To manipulate or develop an entire organization, the vector must have a congregation that already has the routines built in, or he must build them. A vector taking over an established organization can often take advantage of routines that are already present. That is what a Catholic priest does when moving into a new parish. The routines are well established. In starting a new organization, like a mega church, the super vector may take several years to create the routines required to fully manipulate a congregation. He must teach them how to infect others – to grow the arms and legs of the organization.

Once the routines are established, the minister is in position to push all the right buttons; he can manipulate the organization effectively for years if not decades. His control can be so strong that he is essentially in place indefinitely. His ability to evoke powerful emotional routines is so addictive that people can be blinded to potential problems. He lives behind an invisibility cloak. His actions and behavior are obscured by the virus's ability to blind people. The more skillful the vector, the better he can obscure and manipulate. It is not likely that Jimmy Swaggart, Jimmy Bakker, Ted Haggard, Terry Fox or Richard Roberts,[9] or hundreds of pedophile priests and predator ministers made just one mistake and fell from grace. Every religious leader who is smart enough to run a religious organization is smart enough to avoid getting caught. The behavior that finally brought them down was very likely present for decades. In many cases, it has been clearly established that priests and ministers were involved in illicit activity for years and others knew of the behavior yet did nothing. It is easy to hide when no one is looking. The ability to create illusions of righteousness and power covers a multitude of sins in a leader.

Evangelical Meta Virus

Today's technology and techniques allow god viruses to break free of central control. The Internet, web pages, electronic publishing and the mass

---

9   Swaggart was caught with a prostitute; Bakker had both sexual and financial problems; Haggard admitted to seeing a male prostitute; Fox used church money to fund his overtly political radio show and Roberts fathered a child by his brother's wife – sounds like a story from the Bible.

media all enable preachers to operate outside of the bounds of traditional denominational and organizational structures. The evangelical virus has the ability to infect other religions and allows formerly conflicting groups to cooperate; in other words, it takes on a meta function – above, but cooperative with other viruses.

A meta virus overcomes former barriers to propagation. "Praise services" in a Nazarene church are remarkably similar to those of a Baptist, non-denominational church, and even some of the more evangelical Catholics. The songs are even the same! The virus has successfully reduced or eliminated denominationalism. That is why the likes of James Dobson can appeal equally well to a wide range of religious groups even though he is a Nazarene.

The meta virus also allows Baptists, Nazarenes and even some Catholics to carry this new mutation. Groups who started wars or persecuted one another just two or three hundred years ago are now joined through the evangelical infection.

Cursory examination of the theology preached in these various churches shows that they are saying remarkably similar things. Where huge theological differences once existed between Assembly of God, Lutherans, Presbyterians, Baptists and Methodists, they have melted away in these less denomination-ally focused evangelical churches. A plurality of mega churches are Baptist, but many of the rest are non-denominational with loose affiliations.[10] The mega churches within the Baptist denomination hold huge influence in the Southern Baptist Convention. It is a virus within a virus. The meta virus strongly influences the older Baptist virus.

Denominational mega churches (Baptist, Nazarene, Pentecostal, Assembly of God, etc.) may have more in common with other mega churches than they have with their own denomination, showing that the virus is a new and independent strain, unlike the denominational ones of old. That is not to say there are no differences, but they are downplayed in the interest of the new evangelical god virus.

To put it in genetic terms, the virus has shed many obsolete genes, keeping only those that turn off the critical areas of the brain. None of the old cultural material is necessary today. Most hymnbooks have been discarded and replaced by music that sounds remarkably like pop tunes.

10   Until his exposure in 2007, Ted Haggard was the president of the main association, the National Association of Evangelicals.

The trappings of traditional authority are deemphasized, especially in evangelical churches. Even the viral buildings are extremely simple and cheap compared to traditional church structures of only a few decades ago. Mega churches are often built out of steel with a much different feel than the stone and brick buildings of the past. They are built for mobility. When the congregation gets too large, a new and bigger building is built. Some mega churches have moved as much as three times in 20 years, so no need for elaborate trappings.

Further, doctrinal issues have been reduced to a minimum but are strongly held. It is a virus designed for the highly mobile and urban. It has paired doctrine down to a few critical items. No longer are long lists of beliefs required to enter the church. This allows for much easier infection of larger numbers of people. Confession in front of the congregation and acceptance of Jesus as a personal savior god is the primary requirement. Many require some kind of water baptism. No longer are the infected required to memorize and say creeds or profess belief in long-held doctrines like the virgin birth, or biblical inerrancy. While these may be unspoken beliefs, they are no longer required for conversion or salvation. Once converted, the newly infected soon learn that there are more beliefs than they were told. Things like original sin, creationism in some form, the trinity, opposition to abortion, the need to proselytize and much more. The evangelical approach is, "Get them in the door with a simple confession, then teach the real beliefs of the god virus."

Evangelically infected people are just as blind to reason, maybe even more so, than those infected by the viruses of a century earlier. The evangelical virus effectively creates a bubble from which the infected person views the world. This viral bubble excludes all contradictory information and opens evangelicals to amazing ideas – like the imminent end of the world, that Alaska will be the refuge for those fleeing Armageddon, the United States' special place in history as god's chosen people, the right of Christianity to dominate the world and subjugate all other religions, that the world is only 6,000 years old, that Noah floated his boat with dinosaurs aboard and that hundreds of graves opened up in Jerusalem when Jesus was crucified and dead people walked around (with no one apparently noticing, except the writer of Matthew).[11]

"Personal" As the Operative Word

The operative word in the evangelical virus is "personal," not savior. The great achievement of this new evangelism is the breaking away from communal forms to the more individualistic. Evangelicals engineer emotional and biochemical experiences that open individuals to infection independent of the culture, village or community of origin. This gives the virus unprecedented mobility. As we have seen, the focus on the personal experience means the tools of music, sermons, Bible study, etc., create elation, guilt and fear without reference to a given community. This is very different from the Episcopalians or Catholics, who depend on long-established rituals, creeds and physical motions to create trance like states that make people feel good about their infection and part of a god virus community.

Evangelical Double Message

The double message of the evangelical virus is, "God is love but has no tolerance for the uninfected or the moderate." Compromise is not a virtue. The focus is on the differences between those infected by the evangelical virus and those who are not. It is clear from most evangelical sermons that evangelicals are convinced of their righteousness and special place in god's plan. At the same time, there are certain social and political beliefs required for inclusion in the group, like opposition to gay marriage or biblical inerrancy. The evangelical virus is driving hard for viral purity. Those who disagree or exert aspects of the older viruses are suppressed or eliminated as impure.

The Baptists' purge of their theological schools in the 1990s and subsequent consolidation of power in the Southern Baptist Convention in 2001 are examples of the new virus' power to infect and purify. Where the evangelical virus has taken hold, there is no room for moderates. Nineteen churches were purged from the convention in 2006, including the second oldest Baptist church west of the Mississippi, Little Bonne Femme Baptist Church in Columbia, where the Missouri Baptist Convention was founded.

---

11   "… and the tombs were opened; and many bodies of the saints who had fallen asleep were raised; and coming out of the tombs after His resurrection they entered the holy city and appeared to many" (Matthew 27:52).

They were accused of being too moderate and having connections with groups that were too liberal.[12]

Every new mutation strives for viral purity. The evangelical virus is no exception; it has the power to cross former denominational lines and infect much wider groups.

Back to the Future

From the earliest times of Tertullian, Origen, Augustine, and Benedict, to Pat Robertson or James Hagee, the theme is always viral purity with a call to go back to an ideal past. Back to the Bible, back to the primitive church, back to the church Jesus founded – the implication is that there is some objective evidence of this ideal past. They believe there was a time when Christianity was pure. When and where is never specified except through New Testament quotes, yet even a cursory reading reveals a time of anything but love, light and purity.[13] Paul's letters as well as Timothy, Peter, John and others are full of efforts to stem heresy and ensure purity as groups were straying all over the place. From the beginning, there was little agreement on the basics. Many new mutations arose from the nascent Christian virus. Never was there a time in the first three centuries when there was a pure Christianity. Instead, there were dozens of competing viruses. Some eventually won; others went underground, died or lived on in other forms.

The focus on a past that never existed is pervasive in all fundamentaist groups – whether Christian, Hindu or Muslim. It is a most effective way to prevent critical examination of history and effectively colors perceptions of today's events as well. It is hard to look forward with clear vision when you are trying to recreate something that never existed. Today, many fundamentalist Islamic groups seek a return to the days when their religion was pure. Of course, their definitions of pure can differ quite dramatically and continues to lead to wars and conflict within Islam – Shii'a against Sunni, Al Qaeda against Sunni and Shii'a.

The Christian evangelical virus is so powerful that it sedates the infected to any inquiry about Christian beginnings. The haphazard way in which the

---

12   Associated Baptist Press, *Missouri Baptist Convention ousts 19 churches over ties to moderates* [article on-line] (31 October 2006, accessed 22 November 2008); available from http://www.abpnews. com/index.php?option=com_content&task=view&id=1582&Itemid=119; Internet.

13   I Corinthians 11:19, Galatians 1:6, I John 2:19-23

New Testament was created is of no concern. There is no need for inquiry about huge contradictions in almost every book of the New Testament. No interest in the major theological debates of the Ante-Nicene Fathers or other beliefs of the early church that were snuffed out by Catholicism. It is as if the past did not happen. One extremely well-educated physician who is quite infected once told me, "All I know is what I learn in Sunday School and church and read in my Bible. I don't need to learn anything else."

Over the years, I have talked with intelligent but infected friends who are deeply interested in history. They will debate for hours about the causes of the French Revolution, the economic consequences of WWI on Europe or the cultures of the ancient world, but when questioned about early church history in the second and third centuries, they do not know or care. They appear to have no curiosity about one of the most important times in the history of their religion.

What would make an otherwise educated and curious person totally uninterested in something so obviously important? The virus effectively blocks curiosity and questioning in any area that might be a threat. Yet, the same person, if told about the chaotic early days of Islam, will quickly see the holes in the Islamic view of the world and history. An understanding of the similar beginnings in Christianity is apparently unavailable to him.

The Culture Wars

Today's so-called culture wars are not really wars about culture. It is a conflict of religion as it attempts to couple with the culture. Western culture has been largely uncoupled from religion for some time. Unlike Islamic countries where religion is closely bound, U.S. culture develops more independently of religion. As long as culture is free to develop independently, the virus will encounter constant challenges to its existence. It does not have the cocoon of safety that a culture wholly captured provides.

A simple comparison illustrates the dilemma of an uncoupled god virus. How secure is Islam in an Afghan village? How secure is Christianity in New York City? Islam will not be dislodged from Afghanistan any time soon, but any god virus in New York City has a tenuous hold. The evangelical virus is the answer to this problem. It seeks to do what no god virus has ever done, capture the political and cultural structure of the United States.

The pressure to bind is always present. Once the virus gets one hook into the culture, it has the means to place many more. In this case a hook might be reestablishing prayer in schools, which could lead to reading Bible verses in classrooms, which quickly leads to using schools for religious instruction, and so on. A culture that is bound with religion soon becomes an oppressive and toxic place for those who are not infected with the god virus.

Carrie and Evangelism

We began this chapter with the story of Carrie and her deep evangelical infection. Carrie is but one of millions who found comfort and solace in the new evangelism. The tools we have discussed, music, prayer meetings, mass hypnosis, all played a role in keeping Carrie and her family sedated and unquestioning. While she successfully identified her infection and eliminated it, her family and friends have not. As a result, Carrie has worked to establish other relationships that are not based on the god virus. One of her children has been supportive of her, though not to the point of giving up her religion. Her other child continues to be distant and reluctant to communicate with her mother.

Carrie also reports that one of her best friends has not only been supportive but has begun reading and reflecting on her own religious infection. They now spend their Sunday mornings walking and discussing instead of going to church. She says, "It is a much better and rewarding use of my time and has drawn me closer to an incredible friend. I no longer feel the influence of the god stuff in our relationship. We just relate to one another as people without the complications of religion."

Summary

American evangelism is rooted in the Lutheran Reformation, but it is a mutation adapted to survival in the literate, urban and mobile culture of the United States today. The evangelical god virus has made a revolutionary jump from communal to individual and has become a meta virus capable of supplanting old denominational differences. The completion of this genetic transition can be seen in the last half of the twentieth century as a revolutionary decoupling of the virus and community to an individualized and highly mobile form. The new mutation spreads without the encumbrances of village or community. Sophisticated and skilled vectors use time-tested psychological techniques to attract people to mega churches where they receive an endorphin fix from well-designed services with scripted music and hypnotic vocal cadences. The infected hosts (church members) gain guilt and fear messages that bind them to the god virus and create viral purity.

In reality, today's culture wars are attempts by the god virus to bind with the culture in the interest of its own security.

CHAPTER 8:

INTELLIGENCE, PERSONALITY AND THE GOD VIRUS

"Most people would rather die than think; in fact, they do so."
                                                                    -Bertrand Russell

Overview

What are some of the differences between theists and non-theists? What is the scientific research that might shed some light on how and who religion seems to infect? In the current climate of rising fundamentalism, what can we as non-theists do to encourage rational discussion and identify the impact of religion on ourselves as well as others?

Intelligence and Curiosity

A 1999 report in *Scientific American* found that 90% of the general population believes in a personal god and a life after death. Only 40% of bachelor-level scientists had such a belief and 90% of eminent scientists had no belief in a god or an afterlife. It seems the more intelligent and educated the less belief, at least within the scientific world. Another study in *Nature*[1] found that 72% of members of the National Academy of Sciences are outright Atheists, 21% are agnostic and only 7% admit to a belief in a personal god.

But perhaps this is just a characteristic of scientists. Stepping outside of science into the general population, what relationship is there between religiosity and intelligence? In a study of religiosity and intelligence, professor Helmuth Nyborg, intelligence researcher at Aarhus University, Denmark, estimated from a sample of 7,000 subjects that Atheists' IQs, on average, were 5.8 points higher than those of religious people. His study naturally raised some controversy, but peer reviews revealed no errors in his research.[2] A review in *Free Inquiry*[3] found 31 different studies of IQ and

> "So far as I can remember, there is not one word in the Gospels in praise of intelligence."
>
> -Bertrand Russell

---

1   Ed Larson and Larry Witham, "Leading scientists still reject God," *Nature*, 394(6691) (23 July 1998):313 and Ed Larson and Larry Witham, "Scientists and Religion in America," *Scientific American* (September 1999).

2   Richard Lynn, John Harvey and Helmuth Nyborg, *Average intelligence predicts atheism rates across 137 nations* [article on-line] (4 March 2008, accessed 23 November 2008); available from http://www.sciencedirect.com/science?_ob=ArticleURL&_udi=B6W4M-4SD1KNR-1&_user=10&_rdoc=1&_fmt=&_orig=search&_sort=d&view=c&_acct=C000050221&_version=1&_urlVersion=0&_userid=10&md5=82c88cd709652a9a24d1a902d8106a8f; Internet.

3   Burnham P. Beckwith, "The Effect of Intelligence on Religious Faith," *Free Inquiry* (Spring 1986).

religiosity dating from 1927. Every study found a negative correlation between religiosity and intelligence. No peer-reviewed study to date has found anything to indicate that religiosity enhances intelligence. In fact, it seems to have the opposite effect, which leads us to the hypothesis that the intelligence of otherwise intelligent people may be suppressed or inhibited by the constrictions of religiosity.

This is treading in a sensitive area so let me be clear. Intelligent people populate the full spectrum of religiosity from theist to the non-theist. What I would argue is that intelligence is highly related to pattern recognition. People who are more intelligent tend to see patterns more easily and act on them more effectively than the less intelligent. Less intelligent people may be more easily infected by religion because they don't see the patterns as clearly – inconsistencies, contradictions and outright manipulations – and have more difficulty throwing it off once they are infected.[4] At the same time, if a person of average intelligence is given the tools of critical analysis, or is not infected early in life, she is often able to ward off infection as an adult.

In most cases, intelligence and critical thinking seem to disappear at the church door. After years of attending and teaching in church settings, I found that the basic issues are no different than they were when Thomas Aquinas wrote *Summa Theological* in 1273 or when Augustine wrote his *City of God* in the early 400s. There is nothing new under the sun (Ecclesiastes 1:9-14) where Christian dogma is concerned. Nothing seems more pitiable than otherwise intelligent people gathering every Sunday to struggle ever so hard to understand something that is unintelligible.

Intelligence is one factor that might explain the difference in religiosity in America, but there is more to be considered.

"The presence of those seeking the truth is infinitely to be preferred to the presence of those who think they've found it."

-*Terry Pratchett*

---

4   Rev. Joan Campbell, general secretary of the National Council of Churches, once asked the great astronomer Carl Sagan, "You're so smart, why don't you believe in God?" Sagan responded, "You're so smart, why do you believe in God?"

What Role Does Personality Play in Religious Infection?

Biological viruses use various strategies to open the cell wall to infection. If your body has defenses against a particular strategy, you will not get the virus. Another virus may come along that has a strategy for which you have no defenses. In that case you will get infected.

Personality may play a similar role in how one catches religious infection, but it is not a straightforward relationship. Different personality types may be more or less vulnerable to a certain god virus. One personality characteristic may leave a person open to infection by a particular type of religion but not another. Young people are the easiest to hook, since they experience insecurity and anxiety as they pass through puberty. Youth also have fewer intellectual tools with which to resist infection. If a religion calms their natural fears and anxieties, infection may follow regardless of personality.

> "You can't convince a believer of anything; for their belief is not based on evidence, it's based on a deep-seated need to believe."
>
> -Carl Sagan

Religions that promise salvation from eternal damnation may tend to more easily hook fearful or worrying types of people. People who reject fear-based tactics may find new age religions or the Quakers. Reincarnation or becoming "one with god" are attractive hooks to people who are looking for positive affirmation. Fundamentalist churches seem to attract people who have a strong need for right/wrong, good/bad, black/white approaches, with little tolerance for ambiguity.

The Hook Is Not The Personality

While some characteristics like fearfulness or need for affirmation may provide a hook for the virus, the "hook" is not the same as the personality. It is only one part of an otherwise complete person. Unlike intelligence, with a few dimensions, personality has many dimensions. With many personality characteristics, there are more and different opportunities to infect. In over 50 years of research, no clear relationship has been shown between personality and religiosity but there are interesting tendencies. Several studies found a positive correlation between religiosity and lie-scale scores. Others have found that a sense of guilt is most associated with three types of religiosity.[5]

This approach to measuring susceptibility to religiosity may be off the mark. Using our viral metaphor, religion is the infection of the mind by a religious idea. It may have less to do with personality and more with what you were exposed to as a child and what personality hooks were available to the religion.

A couple of examples might illustrate this. A child raised in a Chinese environment will become proficient in Chinese, regardless of her personality. Personality has nothing to do with language acquisition. By the same token, a child brought up in a family that plays lots of board games might have an affinity for board games for the rest of her life. A child raised in a religious family is likely to be infected with the family religion. It is less about personality and more about what kind of virus the child is exposed to in the immediate environment while maturing. That is not to say that guilt or anxiety might not contribute to religiosity, they probably do, but only tangentially. Non-religious people can be guilty and anxious as well.

> "You can choose a ready guide in some celestial voice. If you choose not to decide, you still have made a choice. You can choose from phantom fears and kindness that can kill. I will choose a path that's clear. I will choose free will."
>
> -Rush (Freewill)

A god virus may be able to penetrate and propagate in one person but not in another. It may be as simple as one person being much more intelligent and able to spot the contradictions and manipulations, or it may be that a specific god virus is best at infecting people who have been trained early in life to feel guilt. Another virus may infect people who have a high need for approval.

The question is not "what personality characteristics make a person religious?" Rather, the question is, "What types of virus are present in the environment and how do they interact with personality characteristics of the people in the environment?" In biological terms, you cannot catch a cold

5   Peter Hills, Leslie J. Francis, Michael Argyle and Chris J. Jackson, "Primary personality trait correlates of religious practice and orientation," *Personality and Individual Differences* Volume 36, Issue 1 (January 2004): 61-73.

if the cold virus is not present. You also cannot catch a cold from someone else if the virus he or she carries cannot unlock your cells and propagate efficiently.

You cannot catch the Jehovah's Witnesses virus if you are never exposed to it or if you are given the intellectual tools to resist it. In the western world, people are exposed to a wide variety of god viruses. Most catch only one in an entire lifetime – the one they were taught as a child.

So to answer the question, "What role does personality play in religious infection?" it appears that personality only plays a role when the virus has the right key to unlocking a particular person. To understand religion's power, the better question might be, "What keys does religion use to unlock a person?" Biological viruses evolved keys to unlock and infect cells. Similarly, religions use emotional keys to unlock and infect people. Just as we can learn the infection pathways of the small pox virus, viewing religion as a virus allows us to focus on religious infection pathways. Understanding small pox infection pathways allows for treatment or prevention methods. Understanding religious infection pathways does the same. It takes the focus off of personality and places it onto infection strategies.

Authority and Personality

Dogs are genetically programmed to follow the pack leader – the alpha male. That is what makes dogs such good pets: Once you establish yourself as the pack leader with your dog, it will follow and obey you. While humans are not the same as dogs, we have a strong inclination to follow the leader. This inclination has served humans well for thousands of years. It helps us organize hunting parties, develop group defenses and attack strategies and create entire corporate organizations and governments.

Part of the desire to follow the leader comes from the need for security and safety. To the degree that we cooperate under a leader, we can ensure greater security than standing alone. This tendency can be seen as the default program for a large majority of humans, as demonstrated by the experiments of Stanley Milgram in the 1960s. Milgram set about demonstrating that normal adults can and will engage in harmful, if not destructive, behaviors under the influence of an authority figure. His most famous experiment involved an authority figure in a white coat giving instructions to a subject. The instructions included administering a strong electric shock to another person. We won't recount the details of Milgram's famous experiments except to say that he found 60% of all adults tested obeyed orders from the authority figure. They were asked to do such things as administer a 450-volt shock to another person despite screams and cries from the victim to stop. His book *Obedience to Authority* gives more insight into the dynamics of leader-follower than almost any research before or since.[6] It demonstrates that many people respond to authority with little critical analysis.

Religious vectors are experts at playing the authority figure. Their pronouncements are made with strong conviction and accompanied with all the trappings of power. Whether the vector is a Catholic priest with robes, incense and symbols or an evangelical preacher in a mega church with thousands of people and rousing songs, the result is a sense of security and power against the hostile world.

Regardless of a person's personality characteristics, fear and need for security are key areas the virus uses to infect. That is why fear of damnation, hell, Satan and evil are all used to greater or lesser extents by successful vectors. If the vector can evoke a sufficient fear response in the potential host, infection is made possible. Logic and reason are suspended. The fear response and need for security pushes the person to seek the relief and protection that the preacher offers.

Most people are unaware of their response to this kind of manipulation; they only feel the insecurity, terror and fear that is evoked by the minister and the sense of relief when told that Jesus or Allah can save them. Again, watch almost any popular evangelical preacher. He evokes the authority of a god over and again as if he had a direct line. He invokes the language of fear and sometimes terror. Finally, he offers the security of salvation BUT only within his particular virus. Muslims, Mormons, Baptists, Catholics and most other successful viruses use the same formula.

A Friendly Environment

As discussed in Chapter 1, some biological viruses and parasites can modify the brain or gut of the host and direct behavior that benefits the parasite more than the host. The god virus has this power as well. Regardless of a person's personality characteristics, once he is infected, the virus sets about making his mind a friendly place for a particular religion. It systematically shuts off areas of potential threat and enhances ideas and behaviors

---

6   Stanley Milgram, *Obedience to Authority: An Experimental View* (Harpercollins, 1974).

that support the religion. Rituals, songs, repeated Scripture verses, prayers, listening to gospel music and physical positions such as kneeling in prayer or genuflecting, all create a behavioral feedback loop that makes the host feel good about his infection and creates a safe place for the virus.

To better understand this, ask a Catholic to pray on a mat, face down, Muslim fashion, or ask a Muslim to pray the "Our Father" while kneeling. Ask a Baptist to cross himself before entering her church. We could go on, the point is that these rituals are designed to reinforce a particular viral form. None of these people would be comfortable with any of these requests because their own religion does not use these rituals.

Unlocking the Victim

How does the god virus unlock a person in the first place? I have watched youth ministers, preachers, Sunday School teachers and camp counselors work on a particularly "resistant" child or teenager. The "resistant" child is often thinking quite clearly and is, therefore, able to deflect a lot of religious arguments from the infected adult. Now observe this interaction from the perspective of a virus trying to break into a cell.

The youth minister (vector) watches, listens and asks probing questions. The line of questioning is often designed to create emotional upset and turmoil about something important in the child's life. The vector probes the child here and there with questions until he finds a weakness. At that point, he drops all other lines of questioning and explores the weakness. An example might be, "I can see you are very upset about the way your mother has been treating you. Maybe we could pray about that and Jesus could help you to see what you can do next?" With enough probing, the vector will find a weak spot and offer his religion as hope. An upset child who is coaxed into calming down and praying will naturally feel much better. It is nothing more than the relaxation response any good meditative technique will create.[7] Through association, the child will interpret the new feeling of relaxation and relief as a sign that Jesus really can help him.

The virus now has an entry point. The next step is to get the child to use rituals like prayer and singing, within an infected group, to repeat this feel-good response and reinforce the notion that Jesus is the one who is making

---

7   For further reading see Herbert Benson, MD, *The Relaxation Response* (HarperTorch, 2000). Benson's insight into the mechanisms of the relaxation response can go a long way in explaining the power of prayer to create a sense of well-being and relief.

him feel better. Eventually, an otherwise clearheaded, intelligent child no longer resists. Soon, the rational and logical arguments the child initially used no longer seem relevant. Logic gives way to a feeling of transcendence and relief, but at the price of critical thinking and an infection that will impede judgment, drain resources and inhibit questioning for a lifetime.

The infection process is similar with all vectors, whether a Scientologist, Catholic priest, Pentecostal preacher or Lutheran youth leader. They all seek emotionally charged weaknesses and offer their god virus as hope. The psychological techniques generally bring relief and a change in emotional state. If these same techniques were used in a school counselor's office, without reference to religion, the child might experience the same response with no attribution to Jesus – just relief and some idea of how to proceed.

Infecting Through Pastoral Counseling

It would be unfair to characterize most ministers and priests as uncaring and manipulative. The vast majority are caring people with a strong desire to help. At one point in my career, I conducted training classes for pastors and army chaplains in pastoral counseling techniques. Most of the participants were deeply interested in helping people. They spent a good deal of their time counseling and listening to problems, but we must ask, "What does a minister bring to the table that a secular counselor, psychologist or good friend does not?" The only unique thing clergy contribute is the god virus. Everything else could be done entirely by a secular counselor. For this reason, the counsel of a minister, priest or chaplain should be scrutinized because emotional turmoil or distress are prime times for infection or strengthening the god virus. A pastor may have the skills of a secular counselor, but his paycheck comes from the god virus and he is foremost a vector.

Pastoral counselors see the hand of a god in people's lives, rather than the essential elements of a problem. Their help goes through the circus mirrors of religion, distorting reality and creating feelings and ideas that complicate emotional and interpersonal problem resolution. Pastors are the most infected and well trained to infect. They inevitably find a weakness in the person they are counseling. How can they be expected to pass up an opportunity to infect? Will they be able to separate what is best for the person vs. best for the god virus?

Imagine this scenario: A young man enters the pastor or priest's office to talk about a problem. The man's concern is that he cheated a business partner and is feeling guilty. It would not occur to most clergy that, "This is not a religious issue; it is an interpersonal problem, and a solution can be found without reference to any deity." All the training of the clergy tells him to use the guilt that the young man feels as an opportunity to involve the god virus so that any relief can be attributed to the god. While there are well-trained religious counselors who might resist this temptation, very few clergy have the training or inclination to avoid involving the god virus.

Cheating a business partner is not a religious problem; it is an ethical issue. Resolving an ethical problem can be done without reference to the god virus. We do it all the time. Only someone infected with the god virus would think to frame the problem in religious terms. Various professions have ethical codes. Doctors, accountants, psychologists, social workers, librarians, journalists and real estate professionals all have ethical codes that do not refer to religion. All human societies have ethical codes of conduct regardless of the dominant religion in the culture. Even when a culture changes religions, it continues much of the old ethical codes of conduct. Arab cultural tradition existed long before Mohammed. Many of the marriage, childrearing and ritual practices were simply adapted to his new religion. Over time, religion will change practices and influence the social contract, but only to increase the potential for viral propagation.

A common code of ethics is not grounded in religion, but in a social contract. The young man in the above example broke a trust, a social contract with his partner. Resolving his guilt is a matter of helping determine the best course of action to heal the relationship and reestablish trust and a workable business solution. Why does a god need to be invoked? Involving the god virus creates the illusion that the god is in some part responsible for the guilt, relief and problem solution. Once convinced of the god virus' involvement, the young man will be more bound to the virus – grateful and indebted to Jesus for helping him through this trial and forgiving him of his sin.

Non-Theists and God Virus?

The main thing that separates non-theists from religionists is that we are not infected with a god virus. Since many of us were exposed to religion in youth, we probably still carry residual artifacts or beliefs. We are still affected, but we have the ability to see the manipulations of religion.

Religious people tend to imagine that they see more clearly than the non-theist. Religionists see the hand of a god, miracles at work and feel the power of a god within them. They seem to see and feel lots of things we don't. While they may claim that non-theists act superior, many a sermon has been preached on the superiority of the Christian over the non-believer. They say it often enough that one begins to wonder who they are trying to convince.

Seeing the manipulations and contradictions of religion can lead to intolerance for the beliefs and behavior of the religionists around us. While not universal, it is a tendency within the non-theist community. I see it in myself at times. I have many relatives who invoke god every few sentences. A recent Christmas letter from a relative included seven references to god, Jesus, church, etc., in a seven-paragraph letter. Their god seems to infest even the most ordinary events.[8] It is a hard to keep quiet at times but arguing or pointing out the inconsistencies only creates defensiveness, and when someone is defensive, dialogue is no longer possible. **Defensive people do not learn or change because they cannot listen.** Creating defensiveness does not help the cause of rational discussion and change. Being self-aware means learning to observe not just ourselves, but the way others react to us. People mirror our impact.

The virus is designed to be defensive around people like us. If we give infected people reason to be defensive, they become more entrenched. Religion is not going away any time soon. We non-theists would do well to learn how to communicate effectively with those infected in a way that doesn't create defensiveness and entrenchment. The first and most important step in doing this is to recognize our own defensiveness. What pushes our buttons? What makes us angry or irritated? What gets our self-righteousness going?

"Atheism is more than just the knowledge that gods do not exist, and that religion is either a mistake or a fraud. Atheism is an attitude, a frame of mind that looks at the world objectively, fearlessly, always trying to understand all things as a part of nature."
-Carl Sagan

8   In animist religions, gods are seen inhabiting all kinds of objects like trees and rocks. The animist might feel the god of the tree is communicating with him, or the god in the rock is warning him. Listening to Christians talk about their personal god sounds remarkably similar. Here is a sample of things I have heard: "God sent someone to start my car." "God spoke to me through my child." "I was lost and god pointed the way when my dog pulled me into a chapel." It seems that the Christian god speaks to people in the same way as animist gods.

Pick your battles carefully and try to create an environment of trust and openness in discussion. Always keep in mind that the infected cannot see or feel their infection because the virus has rendered them blind to anything that would threaten it.

Stay calm and focused on the responses of the other person. Avoid challenges that create defensiveness. If you observe signs of defensiveness, break off the discussion or change to a less threatening subject. A little discussion can go a long way if you remain connected and accepting. Trying to convince a person of his infection in a single discussion will generally have the opposite effect.

Being Rational in a Non-Rational Culture

It is more important to stand up for rationality than it is to talk the infected out of their religion. We are not evangelists for a religion. We are rationalists who want to live our lives virus free.

Living true to ourselves is the greatest gift we can give our children and the world. Developments in recent years have given us a great opportunity to show the world what a virus-free society might look like. Current statistics say that non-theists account for as much as 9% of the U.S. population with more who consider themselves non-religious.[9] Other surveys show the "non-religious" to be 16% of the world population. If secular-non-religious-humanist-agnostic-Atheist were a religion, it would be the third largest in the world.

We are often in positions of influence and are thought leaders. Letting others know where we stand gives them the opportunity to view non-theism as a viable life choice. Simply coming out as a non-theist is challenge to god viruses of all kinds.

It took me years to fully understand the emotional and philosophical ramifications of non-theism. The same may be true for you. People go through a huge emotional struggle once they recognize their lifelong viral programming. It takes great courage to say, "I have been fooled by religion my whole life." Many ex-Catholics joke that they are "recovering Catholics." By that, they usually mean that they are learning how to deal with and eliminate a lot of the Catholic guilt they absorbed as children. In a like

---

9   Jacqueline L. Salmon, "In America, Nonbelievers Find Strength in Numbers," *Washington Post*, 14 September 2007, sec. A, p.14.

manner, a non-theist might say, "I am recovering from religion." In both cases, one is overcoming deep childhood programming.

Becoming a non-theist is an intellectual decision, but it involves dealing with strong emotions, such as the need for approval, acceptance and security. Religion has been plugged into these emotional portals for much of your life. It takes time and self-examination to recognize that these needs, once filled by the virus, now must be met in a different way.

Summary

Intelligence and personality are factors in understanding religious infection. Dependency, security and approval needs seem to drive a great deal of religious behavior and are the hooks by which the virus can infect an individual. Personality research has been looking down the wrong path for over 50 years. If we want to understand religiosity, we must better understand the virus and how it works to infect any type of personality. The need to follow a strong leader is a viral hook for many people. Even if we are virus free, we likely have residual attitudes and behaviors we need to examine. Living true to yourself can be a strong contribution to a rational world. We are not in the business of converting anyone to a religion, but we do wish to live virus free. To that end, we can let ourselves be known and stand up for a rational view of the world.

CHAPTER 9:

UNDERSTANDING AND LIVING WITH THE GOD VIRUS

"Faith is often the boast of the man who is too lazy to investigate."

-F. M. Knowles

Overview

Most of us have important relationships with people who are highly infected – brothers, in-laws, friends. In many cases these relationships suffer from tension due to the activity of the god virus. Our own behavior can exacerbate the problem. This chapter will look at what we can do to live more productively with those who are infected.

Fundamentalism, Aggression and Anger

The god virus is consumed with propagation and is concerned with challenges to its supremacy. Staying on the offensive is critical to religious survival. When a religion loses its offensive edge, it begins to lose out to other more aggressive religions. The decline of mainstream Protestantism in the United States is a result of decreased aggressiveness and increased aggressiveness in competitive religious groups. Those with the best conversion programs will thrive.

Conversion: Offense Is the Best Defense

In the current religious climate, most religions see secularism as a direct threat. Most of these groups have taken an aggressive stance against secularists, Atheists, humanists and anyone else who dares to challenge religion. Aggressiveness toward a secular worldview is a great recruiting tool for fundamentalists of all stripes. Secularism has become the new substitute for the devil. When a minister mentions "secular humanist" from the pulpit, it's almost always a spear thrown at those who would deny the god virus.

> "The beauty of religious mania is that it has the power to explain everything. Once God (or Satan) is accepted as the first cause of everything which happens in the mortal world, nothing is left to chance ... logic can be happily tossed out the window."
>
> -**Stephen King**

Go into any Christian bookstore, and you will find books about living in a secular world, living with a spouse who is not saved or how to convert friends and relatives. The god virus is always concerned with protecting and expanding its territory – that is what these books are all about.

The Fundamentalist's View of Atheists

A minister railing against Atheists from the pulpit can be entertaining if you listen for the virus. On many occasions, I have heard ministers use demeaning and sarcastic terms to refer to Atheists, attacking anyone who could possibly believe in evolution, stem cell research, the big bang, geological time and so on. Never do they attempt to discuss the scientific underpinnings of these concepts. They don't need to. Those listening have had that part of their brain infected by the virus, so no logic or science will penetrate. It is a perfect defense for the virus. In addition, it also creates an emotional window through which the vector can pour viral ideas. Here are some direct quotes from recent evangelical sermons.

> God wants you to be chaste. He doesn't want you to use a condom. People don't get AIDS from sex; they get it from sin!
>
> Satan acknowledges the divinity of Christ, not even an Atheist can deny that.
>
> Science can't save you, knowledge can't save you, medicine can't save you, only Jesus can save you![1]
>
> Satan is working to fool you; if you think you are saved, think again. There is a way to know if you are saved but most of you think it is because your Sunday School teacher said you were saved.[2]

The virally infected see and hear what the virus wants. Religionists cannot see the miracles that Muslims see and experience. They do not feel the power of the Hindu, Krishna. They do not feel the Great Spirit moving among his people that Native Americans experience. None of these are accessible to the Christian any more than the Christian's religious experiences are accessible to the Hindu, Muslim or Cheyenne. They are generally unaware of how similar their experience is to that of others belonging to different religions.

As non-theists, we can stand aside and view the virus in action across many religions with no viral lens to impede our vision. That is not to say we don't have our own blinders, but they are usually not religious. On the other hand, religionists always view the non-theist through the lens of the virus. For example, statements like:

---

1   From three fundamentalist preachers I have listened to.

2   Statements by Evangelist Paul Washer on video clips at YouTube™.

–Atheists and secular humanists are going to hell.

–Non-believers can't know the love of god.

–Agnostics are the servants of the devil, casting doubt over all believers.

Religionists have no language for talking about non-believers without reference to their own virus. They are trapped in a perceptual framework that prevents conceptualization of an alternative world.

The Angry Atheist or Angry Fundamentalist?

A number of recent news articles and commentaries by theists have cited "the angry Atheist."[3] Many have called Sam Harris, Richard Dawkins, Bill Maher and Julia Sweeney angry.[4] To me they seem level-headed or funny. Is it anger they see, or a reflection of the emotion they feel about non-believers? Non-believers don't tend to burn people at the stake, persecute, fail to hire or discriminate based on belief. The anger that believers feel about non-believers is strong and sometimes dangerous. For centuries, the anger of believers has been demonstrated in persecution, torture, discrimination, etc. Freethinkers, Atheists, agnostics have never been welcome in any society where religion is strong. Most who make the accusation that Atheists are angry fail to look in the mirror.

> "An Atheist is a man who has no invisible means of support."
>
> -John Buchan

Many a sermon seethes with anger. Few people are angrier than a righteous preacher talking about the current state of the world. If you watch a close-up shot of Pat Robertson, Paul Washer, James Hagee, Jerry Falwell, Ted Haggard or James Dobson, you will notice that their facial gestures convey anger and that their voices sound angry. Their smiles are tense. They often use sarcasm in their description of those they do not like. They use aggressive language and hand gestures. War-like words are ever present in

---

3 Rabbi Marc Gellman, "Trying to Understand Angry Atheists," *Newsweek*, 28 April 2006.

4 Sam Harris, *The End of Faith* (W. W. Norton, 2004); Richard Dawkins, *The God Delusion* (Mariner Books, 2008); Bill Maher, Comedian and narrator of the documentary *Religulous* (2008); Julia Sweeney, actress and star in the movie, *Letting Go of God* (2008).

their vocabulary. Nothing of love or tolerance comes through, except in the most superficial of gestures and only for those within their viral group.

Of course, religionists do not define righteousness as anger, but it sure looks the same. It becomes most apparent when they perceive a challenge to their authority. Infected people do not perceive this as inappropriate or pathological anger. They see it as good preaching. "Amen brother! You tell 'em." The nonverbal signs of seething anger in many ministers is simply too obvious. Their attitude is, "We should be angry about the secular world and how it treats us and our beliefs." The words are almost identical to something Osama bin Laden or the Ayatollah Khomeini might say. Anger is an underlying condition of fundamentalism.

An Experiment

Try this experiment. Watch any of the popular televangelists with the sound turned off. Pay particular attention to any close up-shots. Examine the preachers' smile, their jaw tension, neck or forehead veins; watch their hand gestures – how many aggressive, forward-pushing, knife or hatchet-type gestures do you see? Now ask: If you saw this person in a coffee shop talking like this, how would you classify his or her behavior and emotions?

"Fundamentalism isn't about religion, it's about power."

-Salman Rushdie

Now turn up the volume and listen to the words. Listen for words that evoke anger, aggression, disapproval, sarcasm and cynicism. If your experience is like mine, you will conclude, "That is a very angry person."

If you want to see how well it works in other religions, do the television experiment on a fundamentalist Muslim cleric. Even if he is speaking in Arabic, you will clearly see the non-verbal anger disguised as righteousness.

Here is a sample paragraph from a sermon written by Charles G. Finney.[5] Be warned, if it seems confusing, it is. This is the logic often found in angry preachers. It is emotional, not logical:

5   Charles Grandison Finney (August 29, 1792–August 16, 1875) was a great evangelical preacher of the 1800s. He was known for his innovations like having women pray in public meetings, development of the "anxious bench" for those who wanted to be saved, and naming sinners from the pulpit.

There are, as you know, two kinds of fear. There is that fear of
the Lord, which is the beginning of wisdom, which is founded
in love. There is also a slavish fear, which is a mere dread of evil
and is purely selfish. This is the kind of fear which was possessed
by those people spoken of in the text. They were afraid Jehovah
would send his judgments upon them, if they did not perform
certain rites, and this was the motive they had for paying him
worship. Those who have this fear are supremely selfish, and
while they profess to reverence Jehovah, have other gods whom
they love and serve.[6]

There are hundreds of sermons like this preached every Sunday. The
paragraph does not exactly inspire love, compassion or tolerance. It is designed
to elicit fear. The logic is non-existent. There is judgment and condemnation,
not only in this paragraph but in the whole sermon. Were you to read the
sermon in its entirety, you would notice the continual reference to others
who are not like us, not as holy as us, not as faithful as us, not as obedient
as us – and, by the way, don't backslide or you won't be one of us. Reading
these sermons in light of the virus offers insight into what the vector is
trying to achieve.

What would make this person perpetually angry week after week? What
would make people in the audience unaware or approving of it? Anger
has a viral function; it is designed to speak directly to the primitive limbic
system in the brain where it tends to evoke responses of fear, anger, anxiety
or other negative emotions.

Following our viral paradigm, a mosquito punches a hole in the skin and
while extracting blood also injects the West Nile virus or other pathogen.
The minister uses righteous anger and fear to punch a hole in the individual's
defenses and create a path for viral concepts into the host. The purpose is to
evoke a fight-or-flight response from the congregation. As a result, people
feel that they belong to a group under attack. If successful, the minister
will accomplish two things. First, the listeners will feel threatened; and
second, they will bond more closely to one another to feel safer and more
protected.

---

6   There are whole websites dedicated to this type of sermon. For this particular sermon see Charles
G. Finney, *False Professors* [article on-line] (accessed 22 November 2008); available from http://
www.sermonindex.net/modules/articles/index.php?view=article&aid=555; Internet.

It is a brilliant strategy that has been used in millions of sermons for almost two thousand years. For an interesting example, read Jonathan Edwards's (1703-1758) sermon, "Sinners in the Hands of an Angry God." Watch an old video of Billy Graham, one of the most seemingly benign of evangelists. There is great anger in his demeanor in every sermon I have watched. Or just look at Ted Haggard's in a close-up.[7] That is one angry face.

Not all ministers are so angry. There are exceptions like Robert Schuler of the Crystal Cathedral, who taps a different part of the limbic system. Rather than fight or flight, he pokes the hole through the need for assurance, acceptance and security. Just as there are many different ways for biological vectors to inject pathogens into the body, there is more than one way to inject the god virus into the brain.

How to Interact With the Religiously Infected

If you are involved with a deeply infected person, spouse, parent, child, neighbor or friend, recognize that they are fundamentally afraid. They are experiencing a profound and unsettling fear that they have to deal with almost daily, like a disease that can only be managed, never cured. Remember our story of Carrie in Chapter 7. She sought relief and forgiveness at Bible study, church, choir, Sunday School, prayer, reading religious books, etc., but the relief was short and often created more fear and anxiety. Relief is frequently accompanied by a subtle but effective message of unworthiness; you are never good enough.

Listen to the words of the infected. You will hear joy, praise or thanksgiving but observe their faces and body gestures. You will see fear, uncertainty, awkwardness and anger disguised as religiosity. It is not easy to satisfy a god when he never talks to you. And he he does talk, you can't be sure you are hearing correctly. He could be the devil, self-willfulness or indigestion. If Mother Theresa can't get god to talk to her, what hope does the common person in a pew on Sunday morning have?

---

7   Richard Dawkins' video, *Root of All Evil* has some very good footage of Ted Haggard preaching and being interviewed as well as other evangelical ministers. Richard Dawkins, *Root of All Evil / The God Delusion* [video on-line] (19 June 2007, accessed 23 November 2008); available from http://video.google.com/videosearch?q=Dawkins,+the+root+of+all+evil&ie=UTF-8&oe=utf-8&rls=org.mozilla:en-US:official&client=firefox-a&um=1&sa=X&oi=video_result_group&resnum=4&ct=title#; Internet.

A viral analysis gives important clues about how to interact with those who are infected. Religionists experience a constant barrage of negative messages about themselves and others. It makes them less certain of their own worthiness. It induces deep doubts and, most important, guilt. It is not surprising that the deeply infected are touchy, even angry, when their faith is questioned. They are living on the edge. There is no room for error. Their guilt can be so great that they feel they can lose salvation at any time.

The trap is profoundly exquisite and incredibly effective at capturing and controlling both the individual and the group.

Your Conversion Program

When we have a disagreement with someone, we tend to argue our point in such a way as to convert the other person to our way of thinking. When religion is the topic, the conversion program kicks in especially hard. Ironically, it kicks in as strongly for the non-believer as for the infected. We are tempted to try to convert them just as they are trying to persuade us. What is the purpose of this behavior? Will it enhance the relationship? Will it convert them? Probably not. It is ego-driven behavior probably related to power in the relationship or your own insecurity.

Be aware when your own conversion program kicks in. They cannot help it. But you can control it. No one is going to change, so define the boundaries of the discussion and the primacy of the relationship. I have a very religious friend. We discuss all manner of topics, but we are clear that our relationship is the most important thing. That distinction allows us to proceed to non-judgmentally listen to each other. As a result of this upfront agreement, we have influenced each other a lot over the years and have a deep respect for one another.

Four Principles of Interaction

First, when interacting with a religious person, be respectful. The goal is to develop or maintain the relationship, not to convert. If your goal is conversion, you will almost always be disappointed.

Second, recognize that theists are in a trap of their own making much like alcoholics. Lecturing does not help them stop drinking. Confronting just upsets or angers. Attacking the object of addiction rarely does anything but drive the addiction deeper. The worst thing you can do is to say or imply that they are infected with a god virus. You could suggest they read this book, but don't expect them to do it or even understand it.

Third, be an active listener. Let them talk to you about their religion. Listen sympathetically and openly, but don't question their faith. They cannot question their infection any more than an alcoholic can question the bottle. Also, avoid leading them on. Making them think they are converting you is inappropriate and dishonest. Respond without judgment. Be supportive and open-minded. If they punch, just bounce back. If they get angry, listen to the anger but don't get drawn in. Be calm and above all, stay positive. Sarcasm and cynicism have no place in such discussions.

Fourth, remember you have no interest in converting them to anything. They are the ones with the virus. They are the only ones who can eliminate it. This keeps the boundaries clear. Conversion behavior on your part will inevitably appear manipulative and evoke a strong viral response.

The Exorcist

I once met a woman at a social event and we began talking about children and family. Her demeanor was quite normal and engaging until I learned she traveled for her work. I asked what she did to require so much travel. In an instant her face changed, voice cadence sped up, gestures became more animated, her smile became tense and her head began bobbing in a strange way as she told me about her traveling evangelism work. She seemed to be possessed. It was an amazing transformation, like a demon took over her personality and began talking to me. She lost all interest in me, or so it seemed. When she learned I was a psychologist, she immediately started telling me what I could learn from her. She offered to share her secrets for casting out demons and became quite insistent that I could use such information in my work. I talked to her for some time just to observe the personality change. After a while, I asked her about her youngest child who was graduating from college. Within seconds, her demeanor returned to normal and stayed that way until I again asked her about her evangelism. Then she once again transformed.

I have since tried this experiment with many religious people. In most cases, the transformation is easy to observe and gives a good baseline by which to know when the person is "possessed" and when in normal communication mode. Knowing which mode they are in can help you communicate more effectively. The transformation is often most pronounced in ministers or religious professionals.

In exorcism movies, there is always a scene where the priest converses with the demon inside the possessed person. The person changes form and expression when the demon talks through her. While it is an exaggeration to say religious people go through the same transformation, there is an observable change in most religious people when they begin talking about their "faith." Voice tone, facial expressions and types of words may change. It is often a significant change from normal communication patterns. When you observe this transformation, be careful to continue to talk to the person, not the god virus. Talk to his fears, hopes, joys and doubts. Speak to the real person and ignore references to god or faith. Focus on the human part of the communication, not the supernatural.

Ignoring the supernatural parts of the conversation will prevent confronting the virus and will help you stay out of arguments and unpleasant conversation. At the same time, the person will feel you are really listening to her. Ideally, the person will find relief and comfort in your support regardless of the infection. When communicating with deeply infected people, remember that any communication with the virus only sucks you into the game. You can show care and concern without responding to the virus. Here are some examples.

If someone says:

- "God has led me to have another child." Respond to the child part, NOT the god part. "Oh, how exciting. When are you due? Do you know if it is a girl or boy?"
- "My priest asked me to chair the committee to raise funds for the pro-life drive." Respond to the committee thing, NOT the priest idea. "What kinds of fundraising will you do? Didn't you raise $2,000 for MS last year? You have a knack for fundraising."

The more you honor the person and ignore the virus, the better off both of you will be. Think of it as an unconscious game played by the virus, not the person. The game is designed to draw you into an argument so the virus can tell if you are friend or foe. If it determines that you are foe, it will escalate the conflict to try to eliminate you from the relationship.

Some viruses can talk to one another, especially if they are similar. For example, Baptists can talk to Nazarenes and even to Catholics sometimes.

This allows them to create alliances and work together occasionally as we saw in the discussion of the civil religion and meta virus in previous chapters. But god viruses do not know how to communicate with the non-infected. The very presence of the non-infected is perceived as a threat. Catholics may fear Protestants and Mormons may fear Baptists, but they fear the non-infected even more. In sermons on Sunday morning, therefore, you generally hear more vitriol against non-believers than against other religions.

A quick search of sermons on one prominent evangelical site[8] found 199 sermons that mentioned or dealt with Atheists; only 50 sermons dealt with "non-believers." Searching for the word "Mormon" found only 115 references. The evangelical virus is more concerned about Atheists than the cults of Mormonism or Scientology (only 7), or Jehovah's Witnesses (45). The term "Muslim" barely exceeded Atheists with 214 references. It appears that the evangelicals hate Muslims slightly more than they hate Atheists.

Knowing how much the infected fear non-theists is instructive about how we approach them or they approach us. Imagine a religious conversation between an evangelical and a Muslim. Chances are both will be cautious and, while polite, will perceive vast differences. Evangelicals have an extremely difficult time talking with Muslims as their god virus defines Muslims as the most dangerous enemy of Christ. This same anger, suspiciousness and outright hatred are present with respect to Atheists. Religionists, in general, and evangelicals, in particular, do not have the tools to communicate with the non-believer. Therefore, it is incumbent upon us to develop the skills and tools to communicate with them if we want to have a productive relationship or influence.

To exert influence, focus on common interests and goals. DO NOT focus on the god virus. By doing this, you will achieve something and offer a positive non-religious experience. After working with you a while, they will still believe you are going to hell, but at least you can have a productive business partnership or work on a charitable drive together without experiencing conflict or unpleasant interpersonal dynamics. You really don't care if they continue with their infection, you care that you accomplish a

---

8 SermonIndex.net, *Promoting Genuine Biblical Revival* [web site on-line] (accessed 22 November 2008); available from http://www.sermonindex.net/; Internet.

task or goal.[9] By staying focused on the goal, you minimize the power of the god virus to interrupt relationships and cause conflict.

Death and Dying

Fear of death keeps people close to religion. Most non-theists believe that death is the end. Period. When I was a young kid, my pet gerbil died. I asked my mom, "What happens to gerbils when they die?" My mother's answer was "Only people can go to heaven." I didn't believe it for a minute. I knew that god had to put pet gerbils somewhere, maybe into a gerbil heaven. It was clear my mom didn't know what she was talking about, and it put doubts in my head about other things she might not know.

The first funeral I attended as a child was for the father of my best friend, Scott. His father was a WWII veteran and died of lung cancer at an early age. My father and I attended the graveside ceremony. I was very impressed with the guns they fired at the end, but I thought the minister was stupid. He gave a short talk and told us that Scott's dad was in heaven. I knew he wasn't in heaven because my dad told me you had to go to church to get to heaven. Scott's dad hated churches and never went with Scott's mother to church on Sunday.

You probably remember the first funeral you attended. What questions did it bring for you? Death brings up the most profound questions. When you conclude that death is the end, you have made the first big step in a non-theist's journey. It is the single most important step to eliminating the virus from your life.

Now that you know how the story ends, how do you live your life? It is like opening a book full of blank pages, thumbing to the end and finding two words, "She died" or "He died." Knowing the end, how will you fill in the book? What are the rules for writing your book? What adventures do you want? Who will participate in the adventures? Who will be excluded? It is yours to write! Instead of asking, "Am I serving Jesus today?" You can ask, "Am I doing what I want to live my one life and maximize my contribution while I am here?"

Belief in an afterlife tends to pollute and deeply influence the writing of such a book. How can you concentrate on the "here and now" when your

9   For more on conflict management, read any good negotiation book. I particularly recommend Dr. Dan Dana's book, *Managing Differences: How to Build Better Relationships at Work and Home*, (MTI Press, 2005), 274 pages.

attention keeps getting drawn to something you can't experience or know? Constant focus on an afterlife creates a phobic condition – fear of death, hell or the unknown. Chronic fear of death is the condition of many people infected by the virus and can lead to neurosis, anxiety attacks, or depression. It leads to constant searching for answers that don't exist. It is a constant emotional distraction preventing clear thinking and fulfilled living.

Freely and openly acknowledging your own death as the ultimate end is the first step in virus-free living. It is kind of like getting saved, confession and giving your life to Jesus all rolled into one.

You shall know the truth and the truth shall make you free.

-John 8:32

Knowing this truth takes the virus out of the equation and a huge amount of complications melt away. Living virus-free means you can live your life without looking in the rear view mirror to see if some god or devil is coming after you. You can keep your eyes on the road and make decisions based on current reality without the interference of ever-shifting religious complications.

Helping Others Who Are Dying

Death is something religion talks about most and knows the least about. Within the Bible there are 1,610 mentions of death and 580 uses of the word "dead." The Qur'an has 695 references to death and 527 to dead. This does not count other phrases or synonyms related to death in either book. Death is a very important concept to the Christian, Jewish and Islamic god viruses. Much of the focus on death in these Scriptures relates to fear, terror, punishment, guilt and damnation. Infected persons have had the notion "death = possible damnation" drilled into their head since childhood. It is hard to treat death as a normal part of life when so much fear has been associated with it.

As a non-theist, you have a view that gives you positive power in death and dying situations. Death will inevitably lead to comments or discussion about an afterlife. You can't control that, but you may be able to mitigate its negative effect. Afterlife discussions often evoke the opposite of what is intended. Instead of consoling, they may create anxiety in the dying and in the living.

If the dying person brings up the subject of an afterlife, simply agree with whatever she says or give a consoling response. Then ask, "What can I do to make you more comfortable?" or, "Tell me more about what you are thinking," or, "I don't know what happens after you die, but I am here now to be with you and listen to you." By listening and staying away from discussing ideas like heaven and hell, you can keep your focus on the person, not the god virus.

One constructive way to be with a dying person is to help him focus on positive events in his life. If he can talk, ask him to tell you stories from his life. If he cannot talk, tell the stories yourself. For example, "Dad, tell me again about that time that you ran from away from grandpa's mule." Or "Sally, I remember the time you came to visit us when I was 12 years old. You took me to the amusement park. I can still remember the smell of the hot dogs that day and the cotton candy …".

The same principles apply to those who are grieving around you. Help them focus on what the dying person gave them, what they loved about the person. It is OK to talk about how they will miss the deceased. If they want to make statements like, "He is in heaven now," don't respond to the virus. Respond instead to their sense of relief and comfort. You might say something about how you experienced the person. It might go something like this:

Them: "He is in heaven now."

You: "I really valued his willingness to always take time to listen to me. I'll really miss that."

You don't have to endorse or respond to their viral ideas to show respect and participate in the grieving process. Stay focused on reality, the here and now, on their life and your own feelings. No one can dispute these.

The Psychology of Salvation

Death is the most powerful tool of the virus. It has taken our natural fear of the unknown and built that fear into a bonding cycle. Here is how it goes: A person experiences fear of death. He seeks comfort from the fear. A priest or minister comforts him with a fable about life after death and the idea brings relief. But relief comes at the cost of adherence to the viral conditions for the afterlife. Relief may come from reading the Bible, lighting a candle, praying to a saint or putting money in the offering plate. The recommitment gives solace until the next sin, anxiety or guilt event takes place. Then the person has to do something to assuage the guilt or fear when he is reminded of his mortality. It is a cycle that keeps people bonded to the virus by making it appear that the religion is able to relieve anxiety. Never do they suspect that it is the religion that causes it in the first place through its indoctrination about an afterlife and mortal fear of divine punishment.

Sometimes people facing death vow that if they are saved, they will give their life to the god. When they were "spared" and continued to live, they go on to build churches, start missions and witness to the world about their salvation. Of course, far more die, but we never hear about them. Many more live without making any god-bargains. I wonder what Christians and Muslims think of the man who won $330 million in the lottery in 2007. He made a deal with the gods the week before, "You let me win the lottery and I'll teach." Elwood "Bunky" Bartlett credits his winning to his Wiccan faith and the gods.[10] Looks like his gods are as powerful as the god of other winners who attribute their winning to Jesus or Allah.

> "Anyone who engages in the practice of psychotherapy confronts every day the devastation wrought by the teachings of religion."
>
> -Dr. Nathanial Branden, psychologist and author

Interestingly, the virus wins even when people try to cheat it. Many people have made bargains with a god but failed to keep their promises. They may have promised to give 10% to the church if their child recovered from a life-threatening illness. When they fail to give as they promised, they feel the guilt. This focuses attention back on the virus even if they fail to keep their bargain. If something bad happens to them or their loved one, they think it was god's punishment for not doing as they promised. If they do as they promised, they feel more bound to the god virus.

Survivor's Guilt

Imagine this scene: On a beautiful summer day, you and three friends are enjoying a blissful day boating on the lake when sud-

---

10   Virgil Dickson, "Md. Accountant Must Crunch Numbers No More," *Washington Post*, 3 September 2007, sec. B, p. 03.

denly an accident happens. Only I see the accident and I am on shore. I am standing on the shore and jump in to help. I manage to rescue only you. The other three drown. I chose you? I feel good that I saved one person but very bad that I could not help the others. How do you feel? You feel incredibly grateful but also guilty that you lived but the others died.

Six months later, I call you up to see how you are doing and ask if I can borrow $1,000 to get my car fixed. What will you do? Probably loan me the money out of your sense of gratitude or guilt.

The same is true for the god virus. When you believe the virus saved you or a loved one, you feel grateful and guilty at the same time. You may ask, "Why did he save me and not the others?" "Why did he save my child but not the other children?" Faced with these heart-wrenching questions, the virus traps you into believing the god virus was your salvation. Now the god requires dedication in return for the favor of saving you or your child. In the example of the boating accident, I only asked for $1,000; the god virus asks for a lifetime commitment. I can prove I saved your life. You can't prove the god virus had anything to do with your salvation.

If I came back in six months and said, "I saved your life and now I would like you to be my lifelong money pit. I expect 10% of your income and 10% of your time. When I need a new roof on my house, I'll call you." How would you respond? You would think I was a gold digger, yet I asked nothing more than the imaginary god.

The virus often takes advantage of survivor's guilt. Everyone on the Titanic prayed to be saved. Only a few survived. Many of those who survived were plagued by the fact that so many died and yet they lived. Their survival was often seen as a direct act of god. *"It was god's will that I survived. It was part of god's plan."* What a huge advantage the virus now has. Who can resist following god's plan when he let you survive?

You may find this pattern in yourself or someone you know. The whole notion of luck is often bound up in superstition and bargaining. While you may not bargain with the gods, you may catch yourself hoping for luck or good fortune. You may find yourself asking "why me?" like there is someone "up there" choosing to pick on you. It is an easy mistake to make. We humans are programmed to see patterns and use those patterns to protect ourselves and survive. In the case of the supernatural, the patterns are illusions that can divert energy and attention from the task at hand.

Helping Others

The key to helping someone often lies in using their worldview to communicate. This is uncomfortable for many non-theists. How do you talk with someone who believes and prays for supernatural intervention? How do you respond to someone who asks you to pray for her?

If you want to help someone, use his or her mental framework, **not** yours. If someone asks you to pray for him, say, "I will keep you in my thoughts." Keeping the person in your thoughts reminds you to call to check up or send a card. It helps both of you stay in touch during a time of crisis. The behavior is remarkably similar to that of a religionist, just don't engage in the supernatural part of the process.

One question you can use to help a person is, "What are you doing to get more of what you want?" Applied to prayer, the question might be, "Is the prayer you are saying getting you the answer you are seeking? If not, what other things might you try?" Simply asking questions like this often gets the person out of the prayer loop and into action. Many people pray because they don't know anything else to do, or because they are afraid of actually doing something. By simply using their framework, you create trust and help them move to a more positive or active role.

In no case do you have to play at believing something you don't. It is better if you use their beliefs and let your own beliefs stay out of the picture. If they ask how you pray, it is fine to say, "I don't pray, but I want to support you." Stay focused on their needs and fears, not the virus or your beliefs. They will benefit, and the relationship will be supported as well.

Giving Solace

Sooner or later, you will be in a position of wanting to give solace. Often the person you are helping knows you are a non-believer. In a crisis, it really doesn't matter. What matters is your emotional presence and loving care. Most grieving people are not thinking, "He is an Atheist; he can't know what I feel!" That is the last thing in their mind. Humans want genuine emotional connection in times of crisis, and they really don't care where it comes from as long as it is heart-felt and sincere.

Dr. Richard Selzer, a renowned humanist surgeon and author, tells of a time when a dying patient asked for a priest.[11] After several calls, it became clear that the priest would not arrive in time. Selzer turned off the lights, left the room and came back in, lowered his voice and proceeded to take the man's confession. When asked why he did that when he is a non-theist, he replied, "I just wanted to give him what he wanted as his last wish." It was not about what Dr. Selzer believed, it was what was best for the other person at that time.

Recall your own crises. Did you ask the person supporting you about his theological beliefs? That is the big mistake of professional religionists like priests and ministers. They immediately resort to theological platitudes like, "He is in heaven with his mother," or "Jesus will see her through this crisis," – when what the person really wants is a warm, loving arm and a soft voice that says, "I am here with you. I am not going anywhere and I will listen with loving, nonjudgmental care."

Eventually, they may want a minister. By all means, get them a minister. Stay focused on them, not the virus, and they will likely experience your care more powerfully.

Dealing With Viral Behavior

An Atheist woman was in her last few days of life after a long battle with cancer. Her mother asked a minister to visit her with the hope of getting a deathbed conversion. The woman's husband intercepted the minister at the door and asked to have a word with him.

"Reverend, my wife has been an Atheist for the last 20 years. If there is one thing she doesn't like, it is religion. I am happy to have you talk to her, but my most important concern is her comfort and peace of mind. If you can go in and talk to her with no mention of religion, if you can keep her mother from getting into a religious rant, then by all means visit with her. If at any time I see something that might upset her, I will ask you to leave immediately. Can you live with that?"

11   Humanist Network News, *Podcast #26: Mortal Lessons & The Art of Surgery* [interview on-line] (19 December 2007); available from http://www.humaniststudies.org/podcast/; Internet. Richard Selzer, *Confessions of a Knife* (Michigan State University Press, 2001), *The Exact Location of the Soul* (Picador, 2002) and *Down from Troy: A Doctor Comes of Age* (Michigan State University Press, 2001).

The minister agreed, went in and asked the mother to leave. He proceeded to have a low-key and uplifting conversation with the dying woman. Here are some suggestions for someone in this situation:

1. Put the dying person's comfort first and use his or her worldview. If the dying woman had been a Christian, and the minister properly trained, it may have been an equally productive visit. I have been quite impressed with the skill of Hospice and hospital chaplains in dealing with all manner of religious beliefs at death. Their training and experience is especially good in this area.

2. Protect the person from others who have their own agenda. Let the person die in whatever religious state he or she wishes. It is their life, not their father's, mother's, priest's, or child's.

3. Keep your agenda out of the picture.

4. Death brings out all sorts of irrational and emotional behavior in family, friends, parents, and children à la the mother in the vignette above). Recognize that this is often the virus speaking, not the person in front of you. Keep compassion for that person while helping to mitigate the effects of religious behavior around the dying person. The most important thing non-theism does is to buffer you from the effects of the virus. Stay above the fray while keeping compassion. You will find it extremely rewarding.

Receiving Solace

If you are the one grieving or hurting, it is your perfect right to express yourself in a way that helps you become more comfortable. Take care of yourself. Ask a friend to help buffer you from known vectors. For example, I have asked my son to ensure that religion does not come near my deathbed or my funeral. He has agreed, and I trust that he will be able to do whatever it takes to make that happen.

Now let's leave death and look at some other areas of importance in the lifecycle.

Marriage and the God Virus

Healthy marriage is an art form founded on excellent communication skills and deep concern for the needs and wants of the other. A study by the Barna Research Group in 1999 showed that Baptists were more likely to get divorced than any other Christian denomination. Evangelical groups tended to equal the divorce rate of the state in which they lived. Atheists, agnostics, and other non-believers were less likely to be divorced than evangelical groups and equal to the lowest groups. Based on interviews with 3,854 adults in the continental United States, of the currently divorced, 27% of self-described born-again Christians were divorced compared to 24% of all other adults.[12]

By religious belief (in order of decreasing divorce rate) percentage of divorce:

Non-denominational churches **	34%
Jews	30%
Baptists	29%
Born-again Christians	27%
Mainline Protestants	25%
Mormons	24%
Catholics	21%
Lutherans	21%
Atheists, Agnostics	21%

**Non-denomination refers to evangelical Christian congregations that are not affiliated with a specific denomination. The vast majority are fundamentalists in their theological beliefs.

George Barna, president and founder of Barna Research Group, commented on his research:

> While it may be alarming to discover that born again Christians are more likely than others to experience a divorce, that pattern has been in place for quite some time. Even more disturbing, perhaps, is that when those individuals experience a divorce many of them feel their community of faith provides rejection rather than support and healing. But the research also raises questions regarding the effectiveness of how churches minister to families. The ultimate responsibility for a marriage belongs to the husband and wife, but the high incidence of divorce within the Christian community challenges the idea that

12   ReligiousTolerence.org, *U.S. divorce rates for various faith groups, age groups & geographic areas* [article on-line] (accessed 22 November 2008); available from http://www.religioustolerance. org/chr_dira.htm; Internet.

churches provide truly practical and life-changing support for marriages. [13]

Other research has shown the strong correlation between fundamentalism and divorce in states like Alabama and Oklahoma. Based on studies over the last 10 years, the Bible Belt has the highest divorce rate in the nation.[14] Data from the 2000 U.S. Census show that divorce rates are highest where evangelicals are strongest: Alabama, Arkansas, Arizona, Florida, Georgia, Mississippi, North Carolina, Oklahoma, South Carolina, and Texas and lowest where they are weakest: Connecticut, Massachusetts, Maine, New Hampshire, New Jersey, New York, Pennsylvania, Rhode Island, and Vermont.[15]

Evangelicals preach that faith and belief are the foundations of a good marriage. "The family that prays together, stays together" is one example. Marital guilt is a major industry for the religion. It begins with guilt about how you are not living up to some biblical ideal from two guys named Paul and Jesus who supposedly never married; then you feel guilty about the way your sex life is going when your spouse loses interest; then guilt about raising children. There is never an end to marital guilt. It promotes religious "marriage encounters" and "marriage retreats" and keeps people looking for those elusive answers from the god virus.

Religion-based marriages focus on the god virus so much that the couple do not see or relate to one another. The relationship is colored by the god virus. It is difficult to see your partner's needs and desires when your guilt, religious ideas and expectations consume so much of your attention. There is an invisible friend in the marriage with them all the time, but they can never be sure what he is doing or thinking, except in their imagination.

Many religious people stay married a lifetime whether they are Christian, Muslim, Mormon or Hindu, but Atheists are as likely to stay married as anyone. There is no evidence that the god virus creates better and longer

---

13   The letter was unexpectedly taken off line but can still be found quoted in many other sites. See Free Christians, *Some reflections on Divorce* [article on-line] (accessed 23 November 2008); available from http://www.freechristians.com/Sex_Page/marriage.htm; Internet.

14   National Center for Policy Analysis, *Bible Belt Leads U.S. In Divorces* [article on-line] (19 November 1999, accessed 23 November 2008); available from http://www.ncpa.org/sub/dpd/index.php?Article_ID=10961; Internet.

15   "Walking the walk on family values," *Boston Globe*, 31 October 2004.

lasting marriages, but each of these religions claims their god virus is responsible for good marriages.

Summary

Religionists view non-theists through the lens of the virus. As a result, they cannot see themselves, their religion or other religions objectively. Anger is a major part of fundamentalist religion. It helps maintain control and invoke fear of retribution from the god virus. When interacting with those infected, keep the boundaries clear and do not fall into conversion behavior. Be aware of the transformation some religious people go through when talking about their faith. It will give you a good idea about how to communicate with them. The god virus makes claims about marriage and family that have no basis in fact. Non-religious people are as likely to have long marriages as are the religious.

CHAPTER 10:
THE JOURNEY: LIVING A VIRUS-FREE LIFE

"The fact that a believer is happier than a skeptic is no more to the point than the fact that a drunken man is happier than a sober one. The happiness of credulity is a cheap and dangerous quality."
-**George Bernard Shaw,** *Androcles and the Lion***, Preface (1916)**

Overview

In this chapter, we will look at some of our own issues as non-theists. Many of us were raised in the world of religion. Guilt and anxiety do not go away when we decide that religion is a manipulative tool that is largely a detriment to the human race. What does virus-free living mean and what are some of the practical issues that non-believers face?

Terrill's Story

I asked Terrill to read the manuscript for this book and provide some feedback. When she returned it, she also sent part of her own story. Here is what she had to say:

I was raised a Catholic but have been a non-believer for many years. I questioned a lot starting as a child. First, I asked, "How could something so all-loving, all-caring, cause such fear?" but I had no one to talk to about it. When I went to college, I felt guilty relief not having to go to church every Sunday.

When I read your manuscript, I found it to be so painful that I put it down only to pick it up some time later. This was a life-changing book for me! I rarely read a book twice, but this invoked such reaction that on second reading I was able to absorb more of what you were saying and put it into the context of my life.

At first, I did not understand why it was so intense; why it was evoking such strong feelings in me. I have come to realize that my intense reaction had to do with the "virus" but also my avoidance to look more in depth at my non-believing. It is almost like being gay in a heterosexual world. You deny it, or keep quiet about it, for fear someone (even liberally minded people) may reject you and/or do the conversion thing. I live in a conservative community and am surrounded by people who are deeply infected and unable to communicate or share outside of their religion. This is a "taboo" subject. There are few if any people I can talk to about this.

While I have been without religion for many years, living virus-free is new and has a feel of freedom and relief. Until I read the manuscript, I did not realize how much I still felt the effects of the virus in my life and how it has affected my family.

Understanding the god virus concept allowed me to see my behavior and those around me in a very different light. I now understand one of my infected children better and have tools to relate more constructively to her. I recognize my emotional responses and childhood programming much better. The process was painful for me, but worth the effort to get the god virus out of my life.

Virus-Free Living

Many non-theists have had experiences similar to Terrill's. The seeds of disbelief were firmly in place by their mid-teens if not earlier. Some sense the manipulation early in life, others recognize it in their teens or early adulthood but keep quiet about it for fear of rejection. You may be one of these individuals. From early on, the things you were taught did not seem to make sense. You may have made comments to parents or teachers and felt the full force of the infected come down on you.

I noticed this myself from about the time I was 13. The things I saw did not match up. The creationist view of my church, for example, made no sense. I spoke up on occasion but was tactful enough not to ruffle too many feathers. Since I was the son and grandson of elders of the church, most people just thought, "It is a teenage phase he is going through. He will come around one day."

When I was in college, I taught a course on early Christian heresies to a senior high Sunday School class. Some parents didn't approve, and my class suddenly became smaller. Some of the kids secretly found me after church to learn what we had talked about and get the handouts. At the same time I started a "bus ministry," using the church bus to pick up children from the housing projects and bring them to church. While the elders could not really criticize me for my efforts, they clearly did not want these children in our clean and orderly church. Comments and rumors soon circulated about my program and the children. The program died the week after I left for graduate school, killed by the very person I had trained to take my place. He was voted in as an elder soon after that. These experiences gave me a good sense of how the virus works, although I didn't gain that understanding until much later in life.

Another clue came when I was a 20 year-old youth leader and still in college. I intentionally brought my all-white youth group together with a black youth group from the same denomination. I was fired from the job within two weeks for reasons I was never told. The last thing any church wants is someone in its midst pointing out its own glaring inconsistencies in how they view truth, race, sex, education, etc. My big mistake was believing Jesus' words; *"Ye shall know the truth and the truth shall make you free."* [1] I didn't realize that it wasn't referring to all truth, just their version of it.

The ability to resist the god virus is built into many people, especially those with critical thinking skills, but there has to be a place to practice these skills. I was raised in a white, protestant neighborhood in Wichita, Kansas, and attended church three or more times a week. I was isolated from other religions. There was a Catholic family living on our block, but we didn't interact with them much.

The more isolated we are from other god viruses, the harder it is to see the contradictions between them and practice critical thinking skills. The Muslim child/teenager growing up in a small tribal village in Afghanistan has little opportunity to practice critical skills since he has little or no exposure to alternative ways of thinking. The home-schooled evangelical or the parochial school child in the United States can be very isolated from other religions.

In western society, we may have many different religions in our community but god viruses are remarkably good at isolating one group from another. The insular Jehovah's Witnesses function quite well within our communities. Their children are remarkably well infected and insulated. Baptists and evangelicals are not far behind in many respects. From church schools and church camps, to home schooling and frequent church activities, the goal is to keep children immersed in the god virus until the infection has taken hold. It is difficult to learn and practice critical thinking skills while immersed and isolated by the god virus. That is the purpose of immersion. When an individual is able to compare and examine the various religious claims, she soon realizes that religions are full of mythology dressed as fact. [2]

---

1   John 8:32.

2   For an excellent book on virus-free living, see Robert M. Price, *The Reason Driven Life: What Am I Here on Earth For?* (Prometheus Books, 2006.)

Self-Deception

An important part of life is learning to be honest, but religion creates many ways to fool ourselves. It is like looking into a mirror that looks at a mirror, the image recedes infinitely. As St. Paul said, *"I see through a glass darkly."*[3] Religion seems to darken the glass quite effectively.

Self-deception is the essence of religious belief. As non-theists it is important for us to identify our self-deceptions and develop the courage to face them head on. Getting the smoke and mirrors of religion out of the way is a great start, but the work is never ending. Let us explore some areas of self-deception that may affect even non-theists.

> *"An Atheist believes that a hospital should be built instead of a church. An Atheist believes that deeds must be done instead of a prayer said. An Atheist strives for involvement in life and not escape into death. He wants disease conquered, poverty vanished, war eliminated."*
>
> *-Justin Brown*

Dependency and Need for Approval

The god virus is by nature socially conservative. Change threatens its existence. Questioning within a strict religious community or family can bring strong sanctions, from family isolation to excommunication, from threats of violence to economic or social boycott. The virus has powerful ways of keeping people in line.

People with high dependency needs have difficulty standing up to this level of social sanction. The more dependent, the less able they are to use their native intelligence. They depend instead on the word of religious authority.

Dependency limits a person's ability to act as a free moral agent. Religion may sedate and undermine the courage to live life completely. People stay dependent because they are fearful of the freedom and consequences it may have. Better to stay with the religion than risk social ostracism or disapproval of others.

---

3   "For now we see through a glass, darkly; but then face to face: now I know in part; but then shall I know even as also I am known" (1 Corinthians 13:12).

Religion Through the Life Cycle

Religion takes advantage of human life stages to propagate and insulate itself, but it doesn't contribute to understanding. Understanding the adolescent stage in mental, social and sexual development can help manage and teach children, but most religions oppose this kind of study or teaching, especially when it deals with sex or values development. Similarly, understanding the marriage stage in sexuality, parenting and relationship patterns has great potential to help solve problems of divorce, but few religions want to see research that shows religiosity is correlated with divorce. In short, understanding the life cycle takes power away from religion and undermines its credibility.

The Bible is one big exploration of death and fear of death, but it wasn't until Elizabeth Kübler-Ross wrote *On Death and Dying* in 1969 that somebody undertook a non-religious exploration of death. Religious literature is full of advice on how to live your life as a youth, parent, adult or older person, but it was not until Gail Sheehy's publication of *Passages* in 1976 that a non-religious view of life stages was expounded. As in many things, religion is quick to jump on the bandwagon if it benefits the god virus, but rarely initiates the discussion.

> "Since the early days, [the church] has thrown itself violently against every effort to liberate the body and mind of man. It has been, at all times and everywhere, the habitual and incorrigible defender of bad governments, bad laws, bad social theories, bad institutions. It was, for centuries, an apologist for slavery, as it was an apologist for the divine right of kings."
>
> -H. L. Mencken

Hidden Programs

Much of guilt comes from religious training. Once you have accepted a non-theist stance in life, guilt does not magically go away. You were infected years before your consciousness had the tools to reject religion. Years after I became a non-theist, I would wake up on Sunday mornings and feel guilty about not being in church! A friend of mine felt guilt about contradicting some religious dogma his children heard from his parents. Another said she still felt guilty throwing a religious solicitation in the trash. Non-theists may notice that religious attitudes about sex, learned in early childhood, still haunt them.

Pay attention to your guilt. Let it come, let it roll over you, talk to it, feel it, listen to it, then examine it in the light of personal responsibility without any god involvement. Once the "god delusion" is exposed (to use Dawkins' term), guilt often collapses. It is liberating to know that your child-rearing, marriage or sexual practices are yours to decide in the context of the positive and negative consequences to you and those around you. Getting the god virus out of the picture connects you with yourself, others and the environment. No imaginary friend gets in the way.

The Adventure of Relationship

Awareness of your programming can enhance your marriage and other relationships, as you learn who *you* are, not what you're programmed to be. As a non-theist, you probably absorbed many ideas and assumptions of religion from family and culture that remain hidden, yet affect your life. Just because you don't believe doesn't mean the virus hasn't affected you.

My own experience has been one of learning to be who I am, not what my parents, ministers or Sunday School teachers said I should be. "Shoulds" are the tyranny of any relationship. Being in relation to another person means learning about your own hang-ups, biases and insecurities. What are your hidden shoulds? What do you expect of the other person that you never tell him? What things do you want in the relationship but are too afraid to say. How much does fear of rejection or loss play into your communication patterns?

It is difficult to communicate if you cannot recognize the "shoulds" and myths that continue to infect you. For example, many people in the United States are married in a religious ceremony with religious vows. What do those vows mean now? Is that religious pledge something you feel bound to? If not, how would you go about renegotiating it with your spouse? If you recommitted to your spouse, how would the vows be different? What unspoken assumptions or beliefs have ruled your marriage because of those vows you made years or decades ago? How does the pressure and expectations of other people influence your decisions and relationships?

Divorce is a pervasive problem in our society. How might more open and rational communication affect the quality of relationships and marriages? What if both parties were virus free and able to define the relationship in a way that ensured a safe environment for child rearing and freedom to pursue marital happiness outside of traditional, viral definitions? Many of our marital assumptions from monogamy to child rearing practices have been prescribed by religion to enhance propagation, not the best interest or happiness of the couple or family.

Child Rearing

Early in my career, I worked with children and families as a psychologist. Even though I was still ostensibly a religionist at the time, I could see the huge influence of the god virus on parental behavior. Here are some of the things I witnessed: Parents punishing children for questioning religious ideas. Children feeling great anxiety because their elders told them they would go to hell if they disobeyed, masturbated, played with children of other religions, didn't go to church every Sunday, didn't get saved at church camp, etc. I saw family members using religious scare tactics like invoking Satan if children misbehaved; couples being torn apart because one spouse became fundamentalist and insisted on raising the children by the fundamentalist dictates. My own grandmother was fond of saying that Satan was in me when I misbehaved or questioned some of her religious beliefs.

As a non-theist parent, you may experience a lot of pressure to raise your children in a religion. Other children can be cruel to children of non-believers. Just as white parents in times past taught their children to hate or mistrust black children, religionists teach their children to hate or mistrust children of non-theists or those of strongly different beliefs. Children may come under peer pressure to join school prayer groups, to join religious clubs like Crusade for Christ or Fellowship of Christian Athletes. In some schools, coaches and teachers may subtly discriminate against students that are non-theist. In team sports, coaches may put pressure on team members to pray before a game. While this seems barbaric and unconstitutional to anyone who has read the Constitution, it is common practice in many schools in places like Oklahoma, Texas and Alabama.[4] The challenge is to teach your child how to think for herself and reasonably defend herself in a world that can be hostile.

You may find yourself feeling guilty about the "extra burden" you are

---

4   For an interesting example of this kind of coercion on a school sports team and threats to an entire family with an overt attempt to run a family of Atheists out of town, read the trial of Chester Smalkowski, at Guymon, OK. American Atheists, *Smalkowski Found Not Guilty On All Counts* [article on-line] (26 June 2006, accessed 22 November 2008); available from http://www.Atheists. org/flash.line/smalko1.htm; Internet. For more information, examine the court documents also available on-line.

putting on your children for your beliefs or lack thereof. Keep things in perspective. Jehovah's Witnesses send their children to public schools where birthdays and Christmas are celebrated. Jewish parents send their children to schools where Christmas and Easter are holidays but no mention is made of Yom Kippur or Rosh Hashanah. Pagan parents have beliefs that are reviled by most Christians. Muslim parents send children to schools where pork may be the only meat on the menu on certain days.

Your task is no harder than theirs. In fact, yours may be somewhat easier because you can teach your child to defend the Jehovah's Witnesses, Pagan, Muslim or Jewish parent's child and use it as a lesson in what the god virus does to all children. Finally, raising children to think for themselves is the goal of child rearing and that is not easy in an world full of god viruses.

Meeting Emotional Needs Without Religion

There are many places where non-theists can meet their emotional needs with little or no religion. Some of these include service clubs, the Unitarian Universalists, some Quaker meetings, Habitat for Humanity, the Freedom From Religion Foundation, American Atheists, the American Red Cross, and many more. Many groups need help and don't care about your religion.

If you find the ritual of religious services comforting or gratifying, you can do at least two things. First, go to church all you want. There is no harm in it if you know how to resist the infection. For example, Daniel

> "Incurably religious, that is the best way to describe the mental condition of so many people."
>
> -Thomas Edison

Dennett, noted Atheist and author of *Breaking the Spell: Religion as Natural Phenomenon*, confesses to a particular enjoyment of religious ritual and claims to attend the Episcopal Church.

Second, you can use the feeling of needing religious involvement as a diagnostic tool to understand your emotional needs more precisely and explore alternative ways of achieving them. A friend of mine, after years of being frustrated with western religion, found a great deal of satisfaction in a Pagan group. Their irreverent and often irreligious attitudes seemed to fit her well. To her surprise, she learned that many of the members could be classified as Atheists or agnostics. They enjoyed the company of other iconoclastic people.

Religionists cannot conceive of living virus free. The terror they feel leaves them paralyzed, unable to consider other ways of living or being. To even contemplate virus-free living risks blasphemy and eternal damnation. It is similar to an alcoholic living without drinking. The very thought of it drives him to drink. The very thought of living virus free drives the infected to pray to relieve their anxiety. Their world is a fearful and dangerous world inhabited by demons, devils, gods, Satan, and angry Jehovah or Allah full of retribution and eternal consequences for not following the right virus. They can conceive of living without the Muslim virus or the Mormon virus, but not their own. The virus is like a child's warm soft teddy bear that comforts him when he goes to sleep but sends him into fits of anxiety and terror when the teddy bear is lost and can't be found before bedtime. Just as the child cannot sleep without the teddy bear, the adult religionist cannot relax and enjoy life without his virus.

Summary

Virus-free living is more a journey than a destination. We are all affected by the god virus and often carry ideas, opinions and beliefs that were programmed into us at an early age. Our continuing work to discover and change them is an important part of the journey. Natural emotional needs like the need for security and belonging are channels that the god virus exploits to infect. Gaining awareness of the ways the god virus uses them can help liberate you from the subtle effects of early religious indoctrination.

CHAPTER 11:
THE GOD VIRUS AND SCIENCE

"I have never seen the slightest scientific proof of the religious ideas of heaven and hell, of future life for individuals, or of a personal God. So far as religion of the day is concerned, it is a damned fake ... Religion is all bunk."
-Thomas Edison

Overview

In this chapter, we will look at how the god virus tries to use science for its own ends. The success of science has led to many efforts on the part of religion to associate itself with science and enhance the legitimacy of the god virus. We will also look at the fundamental difference between science and religion – error correction. Science has continuous error correction where religion has no method to correct errors. Finally, we will ask, "Why does the virus resist science?"

Is Science a Religion?

Many fundamentalists say scientific beliefs are no better than religious beliefs. In other words, religion should be given equal footing with science. The intelligent design movement is predicated on this notion. Proponents use scientific terms and arguments to push a religious view of nature. The whole enterprise was quite dramatically exposed in a Dover, Pennsylvania, case where a complaint went to trial under a conservative, Republican, G. W. Bush-appointed federal judge. The result was an unusually strong judgment from the bench that the arguments for intelligent design were nothing more than religion disguised as science.[1]

"Has science ever retreated? No! It is Catholicism which has always retreated before her, and will always be forced to retreat."

-Emile Zola

Throughout this book, I have argued that the god virus is primarily concerned with propagation. It infects a person's mind and is passed from parent to child, from vector to host, without reference to objective reality. If a religion teaches that Joseph Smith received the corrected word of god on golden tablets and read them with magical glasses, there is no objective way to establish that. It is simply a viral idea that is embedded in the minds of the infected and passed along. If the religion says that Jesus was born of a virgin, there is no gynecological or genetic method to establish that notion in objective reality. If your daughter said she was pregnant but still a virgin

---

1   Tammy Kitzmiller et al. v. Dover Area School District. The entire 139-page opinion is available online and is well worth the read. It is exceptionally informative and clearly illustrates the viral attempts to usurp science in the interest of religion. Case No. 04cv2688 Judge Jones. 20 December 2005.

and conceived by an angel, you might want some evidence beyond her word. But somehow that idea needs no verification when part of a god virus.

From these examples and hundreds more, it is clear that religion is a parasite that infects the brain of the host without regard for objective reality. The best interest of the host is not a concern, as we have shown in earlier chapters.

Scientific ideas also infect minds but with one caveat: those ideas have to create a link to objective reality in order to survive. Ideas are always moving through our heads. You may daydream about winning the lottery or marrying a movie star, but sooner or later these illusions bump against the real world and you discard them. If someone said, "I was abducted by space aliens who taught me how to live 150 years, I'll teach you what they taught me for $1,000," chances are that idea won't infect you or many other people. You have effective defenses against that kind of idea.

On the other hand, you may speculate about a new marketing plan for your company. The speculation is part of the process of creating ideas you can test against reality to see if they increase market share. If they succeed, you will retain them and may teach them to your associates at work. Few people today, outside of perhaps an Amish community, think about better ways to make buggy whips. The buggy whip idea no longer meets the test of reality.

Scientific ideas are the same. Scientists may dream up ideas about how to break down DNA to identify specific disease-causing genes, but they then have to go out and demonstrate the idea experimentally in a way that others can understand and replicate in their laboratories. Once a link is made to reality, the idea can be taught and passed on to others, who, in turn, can do the same experiments or variations on the experiment to create more and stronger links to reality. The propagation of scientific ideas requires regular and multiple links back to something that can be objectively demonstrated to the wider community of scientists.

Error Correction in Science

Science has a built-in error correction mechanism that does not exist in religion. If a scientific idea cannot be tested, or if it repeatedly fails testing, it won't last long. No one debates the four humors theory of Hippocrates today. No one argues that the night air and poisonous vapors are the cause of yellow fever. These theories did not pass the test of observation and experimentation and, therefore, were discarded.

The god virus, on the other hand, contains no reality-based error correction device. The Nicene Creed makes all sorts of wild statements, none of which can be tested against reality. To take just the first three statements, "We believe in one God, the Father, the Almighty ..." How does one test if there is one god or many? How does one test if that god is almighty? What exactly does "almighty" mean? How does one know the god is a male? While some Christians argue things like, "'God the Father' is just a metaphor, god really doesn't have a sex," the minute one starts talking in female terms, most of them get upset. The Bible thinks he is a he. Jerry Falwell, the Pope, Pat Robertson, Ayatollah Khomeini and Billy Graham, as well as Mohammed, Jesus, and Moses, all think he is male. Benny Hinn, evangelical minister and televangelist[2], wrote: "What does God the Father look like? Although I've never seen Him, I believe – as with the Holy Spirit – He looks like Jesus looked on earth."

> *"I see only with deep regret that God punishes so many of His children for their numerous stupidities, for which only He Himself can be held responsible; in my opinion, only His nonexistence could excuse Him."*
>
> **-Albert Einstein**

An Internet search using the term "god as male" resulted in 3,250,000 references. Looking through the first 25 or so revealed a hot debate among religionists, most of whom seem to think their god is a male. After 3,000 years, there is still no error correcting mechanism to determine the god gender, change it or discard it.

A little reading of religious history and theology quickly shows that the questions the god virus purports to answer are no better answered today than they were in 600 BCE. People still can't conclude which god is the right one, which pope is the real leader of the church, which book is the true holy book, which creed is the correct one, or who exactly is Satan. At the same time, most people throughout the world can affirm that the earth travels around the sun, that bacteria and viruses cause a large percentage of diseases, that a mechanic does a better job of fixing your car than praying. In

---

2   Benny Hinn, *Good Morning Holy Spirit* (Word, 1991), 87.

other words, the progress of science is demonstrable. The progress of religion is non-existent. How is the Lutheran virus better than the Catholic? Is there some way to test the value of the Scientology virus against the Baptist? Is a Coptic Christian truer than a Sunni Muslim?

Most religions make a vigorous claim that they are superior to all others, yet no objective evidence is ever produced. A reality-based, error correction function within any god virus would quickly cause its demise. Error correction in science makes it stronger. The more errors we find, the better we can create hypotheses to test new ideas.

Science can also assess at many different levels. For example, it can describe the act of throwing a ball by describing the hand motion. But it could also describe the action by characterizing it at the bone, nerve, muscle tissue or molecular level. It can also be seen from the intention level, "I threw the ball for my dog to fetch." At each level, there is the possibility of refining the description and testing our hypothesis. Do muscle cells work in a certain way? Do dogs actually fetch a ball? Do bones support throwing balls? In contrast, how does one test religion at the god, angel, Jesus or prophet Mohammed level?

> "The way to see by faith is to shut the eye of reason."
> -Benjamin Franklin

Every scientific description is false at some level. Take, for example, physics. Newtonian physics is a useful way to describe the world but does not work well at the atomic level. Quantum physics does better at understanding subatomic structures and behavior. Newtonian physics is testable. When experiments demonstrated that it performed poorly at the atomic level, people like Albert Einstein and Max Planck found new ways to describe the physical universe outside of Newtonian physics. In this fashion, science corrected errors in physics. The corrections have stood the test for over one hundred years.

Many a scientist has had to give up a pet theory when the evidence simply did not support it. You can go to scientific meetings and observe passionate debates on subjects, but 10 years from now the passion will be gone as new evidence weighs in on one theory more than another. In anthropology, the debate on the out-of-Africa vs. multi-regional theories raged for 20 years over where *Homo sapiens* originated. One school claimed the species came from several different regions, mingling and cross mating from many different populations of earlier groups. Another school claimed that *Homo sapiens* originated only in Africa and fanned out from there around 60,000 years ago, supplanting all previous populations and probably not cross breeding with them. Today with high-resolution genetic information, the debate is rapidly resolving. As a result, many who were passionate about multi-regional theory are rapidly moving to the out-of-Africa position.[3] Once resolved, a new set of questions will arise for which new theories will be developed, with more passionate debate.

When have you seen that kind of shift in any religious group? When was the last time a Baptist congregation studied the documentation, evidence and experimentation and decided that Islam is more correct than Christianity and then proceeded to become Muslims? The beauty of science is that people actually change their minds based on new evidence.

> "Lighthouses are more helpful than churches."
> **-Benjamin Franklin**

Has any study been done on why religions never seem to announce, "Amputee, through his faith, grew a new leg." In 1858, after the so-called "Apparition of Our Lady of Lourdes to Bernadette Soubirous," people started going to Lourdes, France, to get healed from diseases. Today, most of those diseases can be cured with a visit or two to the local doctor. Yet the myth of Lourdes continues, with thousands of people spending millions of dollars in the hope of healing. Oral Roberts built an entire career and university on this premise. Promise healing and thousands will come. No evidence exists that he did any better than your local doctor could with a placebo pill. No amputees grew new limbs under Oral Roberts' supervision.[4] If religion had an error correction

---

3   Science Daily, *New Research Confirms 'Out of Africa' Theory of Human Evolution* [article on-line] (10 May 2007, accessed 23 November 2008); available from http://www.sciencedaily.com/releases/2007/05/070509161829.htm; Internet.

4   For some good questions and discussion, see Why Won't God Heal Amputees, *Is God Real, or is he imaginary* [article on-line] (accessed 22 November 2008); available from http://www.whydoesgodhateamputees.com/; Internet.

method, Oral Roberts would not have been any more successful than our alien abducted fellow who wanted to teach us how to live 150 years.[5]

The Imitation of Science

At every turn in the last 500 years, religion has had to back down in the face of science. The net effect is that some viruses started trying to incorporate the idea of science (not science itself) into their self-descriptions. One of the crudest examples is the Church of Christ Scientists. There is nothing "scientific" about Mary Baker Eddy's Christian Science religion, first established in the 1870s. There is nothing testable in her assertions about how god heals and protects from disease, yet she chose to use the word "scientist" in the name of her virus. She and her followers rejected the germ theory of disease as strongly as some fundamentalists reject the theory of evolution.

A more sophisticated approach comes from Scientology and the science fiction writer L. Ron Hubbard. The notion that people are primarily spiritual beings living through many lives is not testable but has appeal for many. Intelligent design advocates are fond of using scientific language to justify their view that an invisible hand is present in guiding human evolution. How do you test that idea?

The cargo cults of the South Pacific are great examples of god viruses trying to emulate obviously

> "I don't think we're here for anything, we're just products of evolution. You can say 'Gee, your life must be pretty bleak if you don't think there's a purpose' but I'm anticipating a good lunch."
>
> -Dr. James Watson

successful concepts. U.S. cargo planes brought war materiel and supplies to the islands during WWII, things the natives had never seen. Desiring to get this wonderful cargo, the natives incorporated symbols and rituals to attract the planes to their island and bring the goods. These religions took on a life of their own despite clear evidence that building towers and airfields did not bring airplanes. Decades after the war, the cargo cults still thrived on some islands.

5   Oral Roberts downplayed the miracle healing idea toward the end of his career. His son took over as president of Oral Roberts University in 1993 and was forced out by a financial scandal in 2007.

With the successes of science in areas from medicine to physics, archaeology to psychology, many religions have tried to incorporate the façade of science in hopes of attracting the benefits to their particular virus. Many biblical archeology institutes purport to use scientific methods to prove the accuracy of the Bible. Many other organizations and individuals claim to use the tools of science to prove gods, miracles, intelligent design and much more.

These groups invoke the name of science without the critical error correction required of good science such as peer review and replicable methodology. This can be seen in the quasi-scientific approach many biblical scholars take to archeology. While religious institutions sponsor biblical archeology, you rarely see any of that research contradict their particular virus. Much is made of archeology when it confirms biblical accounts; nothing is said of the many findings that flatly contradict those accounts. The total lack of evidence for the story of Israelite slavery in Egypt and escape to Palestine is one example.

Here is the mission statement of the Bible Archaeology Search and Exploration Institute (BASE):

> BASE exists to reaffirm the Bible ... Using the Bible and other historic sources, coupled with scholarly research supported by archaeological evidence, BASE endeavors to dispel the notion that the Bible is a collection of fables and legend. [6]

No error correction in that mission statement, yet the organization purports to use scientific methods to prove the Bible. Using the scientific method would preclude the foregone conclusion that the Bible is correct and not fable or legend. We would have to examine the evidence to make that determination. Just as the cargo cults adopted the practice of making airstrips to attract cargo, religionists adopt fake science to give themselves legitimacy. What would the BASE institute do if it came across evidence that the lost tribes of Israel migrated to the Americas? Would it repent and convert to Mormonism? How would it deal with archaeological evidence that Jesus was married? Would the institute publish evidence that some Old Testament ideas came from Babylon, not from Moses? In all likelihood, such

6   BASE Institute, *Official Web Site for the Bible Archaeology Search and Exploration Institute* [web site on-line] (accessed 22 November 2008); available from http://www.baseinstitute.org/; Internet.

evidence would get hidden or destroyed as surely as the Taliban blew up the Banyan Buddhas. God viruses do a poor job of imitating science.

Challenging Quasi-Science

As non-theists, we can challenge the use of quasi-science in the service of religion. When we see religion commandeering the language of science to justify its ends, we can challenge the assumptions. When we hear a biblical archaeologist making claims about the relationship of a find to something in the Bible, we should question the scholarship and science that would make such a leap of logic. When someone wants to teach intelligent design in the classroom, we can ask if his research has been peer reviewed. In what scientific journals does the invisible hand of a god appear? We don't have to simply stand by and allow the methods of science to be used for the virus.

Religious Fear of Science

Most god viruses throughout history have opposed science to some degree. From the burning and banning of science books to the burning and banning of scientists, the church has all too often seen science as a threat. Galileo was sanctioned and put under house arrest for the later part of his life because of his claim, among others, that Jupiter had orbiting moons. Copernicus' book was banned by the church for asserting that the sun was the center of the solar system. God viruses have consistently resisted and continue to resist advancements in medical science, astronomy, biology, geology, genetics and evolution. The Catholic Church only rehabilitated Galileo in 1992 – 359 years after his condemnation. Many a protestant preacher who has never read Charles Darwin has condemned evolution from the pulpit. The Anglican Church vilified Darwin in the 1800s and didn't make an official apology until 2008.[7]

What drives the god virus to oppose science? A key strategy of most religions is fear. Throughout history, most people have believed, to some degree, that disease is a consequence of sin, Satan or some god. To avoid or cure disease, they reasoned that the gods must be appeased. People pay the priest to pray. People give money to the church when they recover from an illness. They cross themselves when entering a diseased person's home or wear a crucifix to protect them from contagion. The virus places the cause and

---

7   "Anglican clergyman: Church owes Darwin an apology," *USA Today*, 15 September 2008.

prevention of disease within the divine. Yet, there is nothing more personal than disease in your own body. The virus takes advantage of this to make the connection between your sin, the god and disease in your body.

Science interferes with this link. Science reveals the cause and prevention within biology. The god does not cause your disease as retribution for sin. Germs, viruses, parasites and environmental hazards cause the disease. Once a person learns that germs caused her particular disease, the link between a god and disease is weakened. Instead of paying the priest, she pays the doctor. Each medical discovery has the potential to weaken the critical god-fear-disease link. Instead of fearing a god, people learn to fear germs and viruses. Instead of crossing themselves, they wash their hands.

The source of fear in religion is not easily understood or manipulated. How do you get a god to heal you? How do you ward off the devil during the plague? In science, the more you know about the germ or virus, the better you can prevent or treat it. In religion, knowing about a god does nothing to prevent or treat the plague or flu. Have faith in the healing power of the god has been the mantra for centuries. Along comes science, and does more in a few decades than all the priests in history. The gods simply cannot be manipulated as easily as germs and viruses. This is a huge threat to any god virus. Today, even the most religious are likely to pray AND take the antibiotic.

Personal God and Science

Science strikes at another aspect of the virus – the god as a personal being. Most religionists believe their god is in some way personally connected to them. "Jesus, my personal savior" means I have a powerful ally in my corner. I can call upon my personal savior for help and assistance. I can ask for the laws of nature to be suspended in my favor. I can see miracles all around me. When I pray and get healthy, when my child is healed, when my spouse recovers from a deadly illness, I see the hand of the personal savior. Of course, all of this occurs in the context of modern medical treatments. Only the most infected would say that medical treatment had nothing to do with the recovery, but by claiming a role for the virus in healing, the virus can maintain the fear link. "Because you believed, and called upon the Lord, you were healed." Medicine only played a minor role. The implication is that if you had not believed and called upon the lord, you might have died.

In the face of overwhelming evidence, the virus continues to resist a strictly biological understanding of disease and health. We can see this most clearly in the way many religions treat homosexuality. The virus programs those infected with a sequence something like this: Sinful acts like homosexual behavior incur a god's wrath, the god then causes suffering because of sin, and the god punishes sin with disease. As long as the virus can maintain the god-fear-disease link, the god virus is safe. When the host recognizes that the god has nothing to do with the disease or suffering or that the so-called sin is a normal biological drive or function, the god virus is in danger. The fear factor is lost or weakened.

Here are some current preachers' writing about HIV and homosexuality.

[There is an] obvious link between AIDS and God's judgment on sodomy ... When God allows the act of sin itself to carry with it the penalty of death, the man who denies any link to divine judgment is simply a fool.[8]

The sins of the Sodomites are of the vilest nature. God's hatred of their abominations is revealed in their incurable disease that strikes with near 100% mortality – AIDS![9]

The connection between fear, disease and the god virus is clear in these quotes from three famous preachers, but what other diseases and conditions might be a result of the wrath of god? How does one stop with one disease? If the god is visiting suffering on the "sodomites," might he do the same on the gamblers, wife beaters, adulterous ministers and pedophile priests with cancer, chicken pox or the common cold? Where does godly retribution stop? With each disease science cures or treats, the view of godly retribution diminishes, and the god-fear-disease link is weakened.

With the link weakened, people may continue to pray to Jesus, but they go to their physician for real healing. To get around this weakening of the link by science, the god has become a guy that I can talk to when I am afraid and ask for special favors. The personal god part of the virus is a powerful adaptation in the face of science and reason. The person says,

---

8   Tim Bayly is pastor at Church of the Good Shephard, Bloomington, IN. David Bayly is pastor at Christ the Word Presbyterian Church, Toledo, OH. Bayly Blog, *Aids As Divine Judgment: A Personal Note...* [article on-line] (10 May 2006, accessed 22 November 2008); available from http://www.baylyblog.com/2006/05/aids_as_divine_.html; Internet.

9   BibleBelievers.com, *The Sodomites* [article on-line] (accessed 22 November 2008); available from http://www.Biblebelievers.com/Sodomites.html; Internet. editor of *The Perilous Times*, a Baptist doctrinal publication.

"I experienced the miracle, so science cannot challenge it." The god of personal experience trumps science and prevents examination, explanation and learning. If I think a god healed me, then I owe my allegiance to that god. Here is an interesting quote from a woman infected with HIV by her "unfaithful" husband.

> In the months that followed, she wondered why God had spared her. Then she came upon Psalm 118:17, which says, 'I will not die but live, and will proclaim what the Lord has done.' Then she knew God kept her alive so that she could share what God had done with others suffering from HIV/AIDS. 'If God can do this for me, and I'm nobody, than it show that He cares for us all.' [10]

In the entire article she never mentions the anti-retro-viral drugs she is taking or the insurance money she uses to pay the doctors with years of medical training and equipment, all dedicated to her survival. If there are any gods in her story, they are the missing medical practitioners who have kept her alive to propagate her god virus.

For those who are less infected, a basic knowledge of science makes it more difficult to believe that prayers give a special edge in the world. If science can heal and explain better than the god, what is the role of the god? He has become a special buddy that I talk to occasionally. Not much different from a child talking to her teddy bear as she goes to sleep. Many of the less virulent viruses have moved to this level. Unitarians, Quakers, Episcopalians and liberal Presbyterians recognize that the real player in the world is science. Their god tends to be a marginal player, more for comfort than for any healing or miraculous intervention.

Summary

The big difference between science and religion is found in the presence or absence of error correction mechanisms. Through error correction, science builds a continuing body of knowledge that can be objectively tested and relied upon. Religion has no way to correct errors or make statements about the relative truthfulness of one god virus over another. How does one test Islam against Christianity or Mormonism against Catholicism? The huge

---

10   Joan Yorba-Gray, an HIV-positive Christian from Costa Mesa, California. AFC Newsource, *HIV Devotional* [article on-line] (7 October 2002, accessed 22 November 2008); available from http://www.acfnewsource.org/religion/hiv_devotional.html; Internet.

success of science and the utter failure of religion have led many god viruses to adopt quasi-scientific ideas in the hopes of attracting some of the success of science. Unfortunately, no god virus adopts error correcting mechanisms. The result is a religious method that does nothing more than support and propagate the virus. God viruses resist science because science strikes at the core strategies of most religions. To the degree that science undermines the fear object of religion (gods, devils, demons, disease, punishment for sin), it will be seen as a threat.

CHAPTER 12:

THE FUTURE OF AN ILLUSION

"When a man is freed of religion, he has a better chance to live a normal and wholesome life."

-Sigmund Freud

Overview

Religion is not going away, but we can challenge it in the marketplace of ideas in an effort to make the future less fertile for the god virus.

Freud's Three Functions of Religion

When Freud wrote his analysis of religion in *The Future of an Illusion* (1927), he captured critical elements by suggesting that religion served three functions:

1. It provides for the child-like needs of humans – parental care and concern.
2. It explains the terrors of nature and society and promises a reward for cooperating in a civilized manner.
3. It provides explanation and solace for the ultimate individual death.

Religion served these three purposes to largely illiterate and scientifically ignorant societies of the past. Effective god viruses helped the political leadership maintain control and prevent economic rebellion. Rewards or punishments in the hereafter kept millions under the thumb of kings, popes and despots. It is in this sense that Karl Marx said that religion is the opiate of the masses.

This leaves the third function, explanation and solace for the ultimate individual death. Paul writes:

When I was a child I spoke as a child I understood as a child I thought as a child; but when I became a man I put away childish things.

-I Corinthians 13:11

As a non-theist I echo Paul in this way – it is time to put away childish things. As adults in a literate and scientifically sophisticated society, we can come to terms with our own death without recourse to a supernatural afterlife. In a childish longing to be spared the ultimate end, religionists create an illusion of eternal life that prevents fully living this life. Irrational fear freezes people and prevents clear thinking. Our natural instinct to avoid death is rational. Irrational fear of death leads millions of people to waste vast resources in pursuit of an eternal life that even their own text shows to be quite uncertain.[1]

Prophetic Virus

All of the prophetic religions – from Christianity to Islam, Mormonism to the Ghost Dance religion of 19th-century Native Americans – proclaim an end time and return of a savior god. Utter terror of a return and judgment keeps people working within the confines of the religion. Non-believers have figured out that there is no second coming, but there may be an apocalypse of viral stupidity. I am more worried that fundamentalism in all its forms will cause a holocaust than that any 12th Imam[2], Jesus or Messiah will reappear. In world history, there have been many crucified saviors. Many were born of virgins; many were of humble birth with a royal lineage. All of them claimed they will return some day. Some were resurrected; some even flew up to heaven.

This story line has been an amazingly successful ploy for many religions. In Second Peter, readers are advised to live with one eye on the second coming (II Peter 3:11-12). They are encouraged to live in a way that keeps them from taking real life seriously, because this isn't the real life anyway. In effect, trade this one biological chance as a living being for something totally uncertain. Non-theists don't have this distracting focal point, but we can see how much it affects others. It wastes their precious time on this earth, drains resources and keeps them closely bonded to the virus.

The end time focus even distracts people in high government office. James Watt, Secretary of the Interior under Ronald Reagan, made the statement, "We don't have to protect the environment. The Second Coming is at hand." [3]

The Christian Coalition, Eagle Forum and Family Resources Council all oppose environmental protection. They see environmentalism as a conspiracy

---

1   Questions like, Who goes to heaven? How many go to heaven? When do they go to heaven? are all totally obfuscated in Christian texts. Islam has a lot more clarity about this important detail and Judaism tends to sidestep it altogether.

2   Certain types of Shii'a Islam called Twelver Shii'as believe that Hujjat al-Mahdī (born in 868) has been hidden by God (referred to as the Occultation) to later emerge with Jesus to fulfill their mission of bringing justice and peace to the world.

3   James Watt, Secretary of the Interior under Ronald Reagan, *Washington Post*, 24 May 1981.

to undermine their god virus and rate legislators accordingly. In 2003, 45 senators and 186 representatives earned 80 to 100% approval ratings from the nation's three most influential Christian right advocacy groups, largely on their opposition to environmental protection, abortion and other religious issues. Many Christian fundamentalists feel that concern for the future of our planet is irrelevant, because it has no future. They believe we are living in the end time, when the son of God will return, the righteous will enter heaven, and sinners will be condemned to eternal hellfire. Here is an all too common quote from evangelical leader David Dansker,

> This emphasis on interconnecting relationships embraced by Green Evangelicals, among others, is designed to foster the world's view of communitarian equality with, and acceptance of, cultures diverse from Christianity. Young people are in these programs are acquiring a new reverence for simple life forms in order for the cult of Gaia to promote acceptance of simpler, lowered standards of living in an interconnected world community collectively fighting global warming. Shadow boxing was never so sinister; for instead of being taught to resist the arch enemy to the Church, Christian students are being trained to fight one that does not exist.[4]

There are hundreds of quotes like these on evangelical, Pentecostal, dispensationalist and dominionist web sites. It is clear that the needs of the god virus trump the reality of preserving the earth's biosphere for future generations. The earth is expendable. If the savior god is coming, he will take care of everything.

As non-theists we owe it to our children to challenge these crazy ideas and work to leave the world a more rational place than we found it. There will be more god viruses and mutations in the future. If we as non-theists offer the god virus model as an alternative explanation for religion, I believe a significant number of people may begin to recognize religious manipulation in their lives. They may be able to see when a politician is using the god virus to manipulate people into voting for him or her. They may recognize

---

4   Christian Research Network, *Climate Change: Stand Against False Gospel* [article on-line] (July 7, 2007, accessed 23 November 2008); available from http://christianresearchnetwork. com/?p=2455; Internet. David Dansker writes commentary and articles covering various topics, including ecclesiology, eschatology and theology. His focus is on those issues that deal with heresy, harlotry and the apostasy.

a viral tactic in protecting a pedophile priest or sexual predator preacher. They may see through the viral infection that sucks resources from poor people's pockets and puts them into mega church ministers' hands, allowing them to live opulent lifestyles. They may be able to see the guilt-inducing methods that create sexual dysfunction.

Once people recognize the god virus working in their lives, they gain the ability to see its manipulation in many aspects of life. Life does not suddenly become easy, but it becomes less muddled.

You may have seen the 1960 movie *The Little Shop of Horrors*. A flower breeder discovers that his new plant thrives only on human flesh and blood. As time passes and the plant grows, it demands more and more. The cry of the plant, "feed me," becomes incessant, hypnotizing the shopkeeper into murdering people to feed it. Eventually, it even consumes the flower breeder himself. Such is the god virus as it infects a person and begins recreating him to ensure its own propagation. While it rarely demands the extremes, it does have the power when the occasion calls. From church attendance to 10% of your income, from abstinence to celibacy, from Christian soldiering to suicide bombers – it demands to be fed.

The Future and the God Virus

Europe was a religious continent until WWII. Church attendance was high in almost all countries as was participation in religious organizations of all kinds. Secularism may have been present for two hundred years, but most people maintained a deep belief in the supernatural. Then came WWII. It was a watershed event in religious history. The war seemed to do what no other event could. Religious attendance dropped and never recovered. The Netherlands, where religion had been the reason for many wars and strifes, suddenly didn't care any more. Belgium, where Catholics and Protestants had been at odds for centuries, lost most of its religious fervor. Germany, where the Catholic Church celebrated Hitler's birthday through WWII, experienced a tremendous loss of religious involvement and participation.

Religious communities in Europe that kept apart for centuries now mingle and intermarry with impunity. Church attendance and giving, as a percent of disposable income, is a fraction of what it is in the United States. Italy now has the lowest birth rate in Europe – a curious fact in an officially Catholic country where the Pope preaches abstinence and the sin of contraception and abortion. Throughout Europe, the god virus that infected the minds of millions of people for centuries has seemed to almost disappear.

The people of Europe who fought so many religious wars and experienced extreme Christian fundamentalism today cannot fathom the evangelical mentality in the United States. It is like the European continent awakened from its virus-induced trance and forgot all the passion, anger and self-righteousness.

If there is hope for the environmental and political future of our civilization and planet, it will come from the uncoupling of religion from culture. Getting the holy ghosts of religion out of government will allow for rational discussion about the real challenges we face. *Those who are waiting for heaven don't focus well on the problems of today.* Their attention and energy are constantly diverted by the preachers and priests who keep them entranced in the make-believe world of gods, angels, demons and saviors and drain their pockets for propagation.

Europe has largely unbound religion from culture. The next step is for the United States to do the same. Hopefully, it will not take a major war. In other parts of the world, India may manage to uncouple Hinduism and its dangerous fundamentalism through its democratic processes. China seems to be in the act of uncoupling the Marxist virus, but who knows what the outcome might be?

Last will be the Islamic countries. Having the most advanced viral form, they are also the most infected and culturally bound. Uncoupling in the west will do more to uncouple Islam than any other force as Christian fundamentalism is a major contributor to Islamic fundamentalism. When the Christian fundamentalist virus expressed itself through the president of the United States saying, "We are on a crusade" after 9/11, there was a huge response from Islam to this inflammatory statement. Clear-headed thinking about how to deal with the virus in other countries (Iraq and the Middle East) can only come if we are clear about how the god virus is manipulating our own political system.

Threats to the God Virus

There are many powerful threats to religion today. First is the great interest in books like this one. The excesses of the religious right have awakened many to take a hard look at their beliefs. Also, the Internet has allowed people of like minds to find one another and spread information outside the influence or control of religion.

The second threat to religion is the continual march of science. While the god virus has often focused on Darwin, the advances in genetics have created a vast amount of supporting evidence for all aspects of evolution. Other branches such as geology, astronomy, psychology, neurology and anthropology have advanced in ways that continue to undermine the god virus' claims to everything from creation to human relationships.

Psychology is a third threat. Scientology and Jehovah's Witnesses both prohibit members from seeing psychologists. Fundamentalist religions are often suspicious of psychology. Many psychologists can see what religion does to people. How it destroys relationships and families, forces people into self-defeating beliefs and creates guilt and anxiety. Religion is a major contributor to mental illness. Religion is not responsible for all mental illness, but it plays a part in a great many cases. These abuses are revealed in the psychologist's office. Few others will ever hear about them. Who would they go to? The minister or priest? An elder or official of the church?

How many thousands of people have been emotionally and mentally damaged by pedophile Catholic

> "Faith may be defined briefly as an illogical belief in the occurrence of the improbable. A man full of faith is simply one who has lost (or never had) the capacity for clear and realistic thought. He is not a mere ass; he is actually ill."
>
> -H. L. Mencken

priests in the last 50 years in just North America? The scope of the problem is only recently being revealed in this country, but it continues to be well hidden in Latin America and in Catholic countries around the world. How many thousands of people have been abused by predator Protestant ministers? From 1960-1970 in seven churches of my denomination in Wichita, Kansas, eight different ministers were caught in adulterous affairs (some multiple times). What was going on in all the other Protestant churches? The Scoutmasters of the local Baptist church molested several of boys in the troop. The church board and minister ignored the complaints for years and then quietly asked them to leave. They moved on to another troop. The god virus blinds people to the truth about the behavior of their leaders and blames the victims. Families, friends and society as a whole suffer.

The www.stopbaptistpredators.org website documents dozens of churches that have protected ministers and vilified victims of many different sexual crimes. The common theme is the protection of the vector and the denigration of the victims. The Catholic Church has behaved in the same way for decades, a pattern of behavior that has been well established in the court records and settlements for the victims.

But sexual abuse is only a part of the mental health issues caused by religion. Each god virus seeks to ensure the person hosts only that particular virus. Strongly infected people tend to see those who are of a different infection or no infection as enemies or dangerous. Baptists see Jehovah's Witnesses as evil. Nazarenes tend to see Catholics as misguided. Mormons see Scientologists as an evil cult. And all of them see Muslims and Atheists as dangerous. How much hatred, suspicion, conflict, strife, even violence and death, is caused by the battle for viral supremacy? How many families are torn apart by a god virus? How many children are terrorized by the demon-haunted world – to use Carl Sagan's term[5] – they are forced to inhabit?

While respecting confidentiality, psychologists can be a voice to educate people on how the virus works to infect people. It is not the job of the mental health professional to talk someone out of religion, but we cannot deny the role religion plays in creating irrational thoughts and self-defeating behavior.

Starting the Conversation

We are in the middle of an explosion of knowledge and technology. Religion has been an impediment to science throughout history. While religionists argue that science without religion is dangerous, I would argue that religion uses the fruits of science to make the world far more dangerous. Religionists use the scientifically developed weapons of war and electronic communication to propagate their god viruses. They do not hesitate to rail against science even as they use the tools science gave them. True, we need open discussion about ethics with respect to science and its application. I cannot see where religion advances that discussion. Each god virus has its propagation strategy, and that is the primary guide to its ethical contribution.

---

5   Carl Sagan and Ann Druyan, *The Demon-Haunted World: Science as a Candle in the Dark* (Ballantine Books, 1997).

The Catholic Church ignores the spread of AIDS in Africa in favor of its prohibition on condoms, birth control and abortion. A humanist approach would look for the greater good, the most effective and humane approach to preventing the spread of AIDS. A Catholic approach looks for the greater good of the god virus. Baptists tend to focus on the evils of sex education for teenagers and promote ineffective and counterproductive abstinence programs. The Baptist virus looks for the greater good of the virus, not of teenagers. Jehovah's Witnesses see blood transfusion as immoral, preferring to see someone die rather than accept blood. The humanist perspective would be an easy decision – do the transfusion if it creates greater good and life.

By exposing the manipulations of a god virus, an opportunity for greater choice and freedom is opened. Martin Luther's reformation in the 1500s led to an exposure of the Catholic virus as an oppressor of political, economic and religious freedom. In turn, the Anabaptist movement revealed the complicity of Lutheranism in suppressing conscience and political freedom. The English Civil War and 30 Years War demonstrated the destructive power of a god virus without regard to human suffering and led the framers of the U.S. Constitution to ensure separation of church and state.

Local god viruses have justified slavery throughout the world. The Southern Baptist church was born to justify slavery. Abraham Lincoln, a non-Christian and probably a deist, was able to play the virus against itself in a way that allowed him to guide the country through a civil war and out of slavery. Nevertheless, as soon as the war was over and Lincoln had died, god viruses went to work to repress those who were once slaves. The virus was just as active in the North in maintaining discrimination and withholding full citizenship to blacks.

The Christian god virus provided all the justification necessary to commit genocide on virtually every native group in the western hemisphere. Every major church in Germany supported Hitler. No effective opposition to genocide came from the churches. The perpetrators of genocide in Rwanda and Bosnia were all too often clergy preaching ethnic hatred. From Catholic priests in Rwanda to Orthodox priests in Serbia, there were pitifully few religious leaders putting their lives on the line to stop the murder. Several religious officials were actually involved in the persecution.[6]

---

6   BBC News, *Rwanda priest tried for genocide* [article on-line] (20 September 2004, accessed 23 November 2008); available from http://news.bbc.co.uk/2/hi/africa/3671464.stm; Internet. For an unblinking account see Carol Rittner, John K. Roth and Wendy Whitworth, *Genocide in Rwanda: Complicity of the Churches?* (Paragon House Publishers, 2004).

Where is the religious moral leadership? Our viral metaphor explains the lack of powerful and effective moral leadership, the god virus is most concerned with survival, not with leadership. Leadership requires risk and creates opposition; neither is good for propagation. One does not need a god to oppose such atrocities. Those who have a god all too often are a part of the problem. Jim Crow was supported and preached from thousands of pulpits in the South as recently as the 1970s. Where was the religious opposition? Pointing to the few religious leaders who did oppose Jim Crow or genocide ignores the thousands who did not.

The ethics discussions in theology schools are designed to ensure the propagation of the virus, but add little or nothing to addressing poverty, racism, discrimination, militarism, etc. Those who claim that religion has brought about great change often point to people like Martin Luther King, Jr. I would suggest that Dr. King was a pragmatist who used religion as his method of communication. His ethics were more informed by Mohandas Gandhi (a Hindu in India) than by Jesus. His reading of the Bible was extremely selective and in strong opposition to many other Christian experts. White supremacists have many more scriptures to quote than Dr. King. His genius was his ability to play the virus against itself. Through speeches and actions, he illuminated how religion maintained oppression. His followers were from many different churches, and a surprising number were non-religious or Atheist.[7]

The poor ethical and moral record of religion does not bode well for religious leadership in today's world. Science is moving forward. Fundamentalist resistance in Missouri will not stop stem cell research in Korea, China or even California and Massachusetts. Nuclear proliferation will not be controlled by prayer in a church. The question is beyond religion's ability to stop or even influence on a global scale. Religion provides little or no guidance that a rational person could not determine without religion. There is still a need for moral and ethical debate, and non-theists are in a position to influence that debate.

Religion had little or nothing to do with preventing nuclear war during the cold war. Cold, hard geopolitical analysis on both sides allowed the world

---

7   Atheist and white postal worker William L. Moore marched many times for civil rights in the south. On April 23, 1963, he was murdered on his last march. The murder weapon was identified and its owner, Floyd Simpson, was charged. Witnesses said he had argued earlier that day with Moore. See Mary Stanton, *Freedom Walk: Mississippi Or Bust* (University Press of Mississippi, 2003).

to prevent such a holocaust. Religion had nothing to do with the major discoveries in physics, medicine, biology, genetics and other fields, but it has tried to impede or prohibit their use at times. From early opposition to in-vitro fertilization to opposition to birth control, from the Scopes Monkey Trial to the Dover, Pennsylvania, intelligent design trial, religion has been an impediment to science, and it shows no signs of stopping. In almost every case, religion has lost, but as long as children are deeply exposed to the god virus and science education is curtailed, ignorance will continue.

The Influence of Non-Theists

As non-theists in the United States, we probably have more influence on the ethical use of science and technology than religionists. Surveys beginning in 1914, show that scientists are losing their belief in the supernatural.

Comparison of survey answers among leading scientists[8]

Belief in personal God	1914	1933	1998
Personal belief	27.7	15	7.0
Personal disbelief	52.7	68	72.2
Doubt or agnosticism	20.9	17	20.8

Belief in human immortality	1914	1933	1998
Personal belief	35.2	18	7.9
Personal disbelief	25.4	53	76.7
Doubt or agnosticism	43.7	29	23.3

The vast majority of the Nobel Prize science winners of the last 20 years have expressed some form of non-belief. We need to use our influence wisely and ensure the dialogue is based on rational analysis of humanistic goals. We must become proficient at identifying the goals of god viruses and challenge them. God viruses seek to use the means at hand – whether scientific, social or political – to propagate, not to serve the best interest of humanity.

Other countries are not handicapped by anti-science god viruses. China, India, Japan, Taiwan and many others are producing scientists and engineers in record numbers. No society is free of god viruses, but some are not as

8   Edward J. Larson and Larry Witham, "Leading scientists still reject God," *Nature* 394, no. 6691, (1998): 313 .

burdened with the politically strong anti-science ones of the United States. The health of U.S. science and technology is influenced by how much god viruses inhibit funding or research. When religions get involved in funding decisions, rational choice is less likely. Religionists in Texas, Florida, Pennsylvania, Kansas and many other states have worked hard to directly fund non-scientific intelligent design and abstinence programs, and direct funds away from stem cell research, evolutionary biology and scientifically validated sex education programs. As non-theists we need to let our voices be heard on these issues if we are to help keep the United States economically viable and at the forefront of science and technology.

Government Policy

Informed policy requires open discussion and clear cost-benefit analysis. When religion gets in the mix, imaginary costs and benefits influence the calculations. Our liberal democracy works despite religion, not because of it. When religion has been subdued in the debate, this nation has made great strides. Beginning with the deistic founders and presidents of the early United States to the deistic leadership of Abraham Lincoln to the liberal, non-religious leadership of FDR, progress comes when the nation makes decisions in the best interest of the people, not religion. The decades-long fight over abortion has given the god virus the means to infect the central nervous system as never before. With five Catholic Supreme Court justices, religion is rapidly becoming a key factor in judicial decisions.

Despite the U.S. Constitution's prohibition against religion as a test for office, presidential candidates have been made to wear their religion on their sleeve since at least 1976. The non-religious Ronald Reagan suddenly became interested in attending church when he ran for governor of California. The religious right questioned George H. W. Bush's religious credentials because his wife, Barbara Bush, was pro-choice in 1988. During the 2008 presidential debates, candidates advertised their religion in ways that would have been seen as shameful in the 1800s.

As non-theists, we can support rational discussion in the public square and help discourage the drive to inject religion into every aspect of electoral politics. We can ask the question, "How does religion qualify a person for good governance?" Most school board members made little of their religion in the past. Why has religious affiliation suddenly become so important in school board elections if not to drive religion into the classroom? When candidates advertise their religion or make blatant statements to pander to the god viruses, we must be prepared to call them on it.

The god virus will happily take a culture back to the Iron Age, or even Stone Age, if it enhances propagation. Look at the stagnation of Islamic culture for the last 800 years. Islam was once the cradle of science and math. Christian fundamentalists would do the same. Evangelical vectors preach every Sunday about going back to the Iron Age in terms of education, science, marriage, politics, etc.

Here are their visions for our future:

This is our land. This is our world. This is our heritage, and with God's help, we shall reclaim this nation for Jesus Christ. An no power on earth can stop us.
-D. James Kennedy, A Nation in Search of Its Soul

If you don't want a Christian nation, then go to one of the many nations that are heathen already, rather than perverting ours.
-Jeff Fugate, Pastor of Clays Mill Road Baptist Church

Those who study jihad will understand why Islam wants to conquer the whole world. All the countries conquered by Islam or to be conquered in the future will be marked for everlasting salvation. For they shall live under God's law.
-Ayatollah Ruhaollah Khomeini, Islam is Not a Nation of Pacifists

Nobody has the right to worship on this planet any other God than Jehovah. And therefore the state does not have the responsibility to defend anybody's pseudo-right to worship an idol.
-Rev. Joseph Morecraft, Chaldedon Presbyterian Church. Speech

Religions will be with us as long as humans seek easy answers; as long as skilled vectors sedate people to avoid life's difficult questions; as long as the infected let their preachers, popes and imams do their thinking for them, we will have religion.

As non-theists, we can work to make this religious environment less toxic to our culture and to ourselves. Identify and challenge viral behavior in yourself and learn to live virus free. You can support science education and challenge the encroachment of fundamentalism in our public systems. Support university professors under fire from god viruses. Talk and teach "religion-free ethics" and how to make rational, ethical choices without reference to Allah, god or Satan.

Being alive today is the only thing you or I know. We are the product of an amazing biological process in which one sperm out of millions met one egg. This event will never happen again. Make the most of it.

INDEX